perspectives

Educating Diverse Populations

perspectives

Educating Diverse Populations

Academic Editor
Linda Orozco
Coastline College and
University of California, Irvine

coursewise
publishing
inc.

Boulder • Bellevue • Dubuque • Madison

Our mission at **coursewise** is to help students make connections—linking theory to practice and the classroom to the outside world. Learners are motivated to synthesize ideas when course materials are placed in a context they recognize. By providing gateways to contemporary and enduring issues, **coursewise** publications will expand students' awareness of and context for the course subject.

For more information on **coursewise** visit us at our web site: http://www.coursewise.com

coursewise publishing editorial staff

Thomas Doran, ceo/publisher: Journalism/Marketing/Speech
Edgar Laube, publisher: Geography/Political Science/Psychology/Sociology
Linda Meehan Avenarius, publisher: courselinks
Sue Pulvermacher-Alt, publisher: Education/Health/Gender Studies
Victoria Putman, publisher: Anthropology/Philosophy/Religion
Tom Romaniak, publisher: Business/Criminal Justice/Economics

coursewise publishing production staff

Lori A. Blosch, permissions coordinator
Mary M. Monner, production coordinator, print/online
Victoria Putman, production manager

Library of Congress Catalog Card Number: 98–072187
ISBN 0-395-92153-8

Printed in the United States of America by **coursewise publishing, Inc.**
1379 Lodge Lane, Boulder, CO 80303

10 9 8 7 6 5 4 3 2

from the
Publisher

Sue Pulvermacher-Alt

coursewise publishing

Just Like Me?

Right after college, I taught high school English in a small rural community. Every student I had looked basically the same, and they all looked a lot like me. We were all white and all living in or near a small town in the upper Midwest.

But we were not all the same. John, perhaps the most intelligent student I ever taught, happened to be blind and took notes on his braille writer. Stephanie came from a home where she was abused—physically and I suspect sexually (she was eventually removed from her parents and put in foster care). Darrell was a devout Mormon who wrote nearly every open-ended assignment on some aspect of his faith. Andrea was the youngest child in a family known for their wealth and political power in the community. George spoke German fluently and said his grandparents still spoke German more often than English. We had our race in common but differed in many other ways.

We've put together *Perspectives: Educating Diverse Populations* and the accompanying **courselinks** site to help you prepare for the diverse students you'll meet in your classrooms. In this volume and at the **courselinks** site, we've covered many kinds of diversity—gender, exceptionality, culture, linguistics, economics, and race. Through the articles and the web sites, we want to help you explore many facets of diversity.

In our efforts to cover different kinds of diversity, we've tried to offer different kinds of materials. You'll find a variety of article sources—some from academic journals (such as "Bilingual Education Program Models: A Framework for Understanding" from the *Bilingual Research Journal* in Section 4) and others from the popular press (for example, "A Room of Their Own: Single-Sex Classrooms" in Section 1 from *Newsweek* magazine). Both in this volume and at the **courselinks** site, we've integrated a variety of web sites—commercial sites such as a *Washington Post* site (Amazing Grace: The Lives of Children and the Conscience of a Nation), professional sites such as the Council for Exceptional Children, and governmental sites such as the National Clearinghouse of Bilingual Education.

In developing this volume, I worked with Linda Orozco as the Academic Editor. Linda's knowledge of the content, magnified by her professional passion, is capped by her diligence in meeting deadlines and getting the job done right. As you'll read in her "From the Academic Editor" note, she brings a variety of experiences to this project.

Linda and I were helped by a top-notch Editorial Board. At **coursewise,** we're working hard to publish **R**elevant, **E**xciting, **A**pproved, and **L**inked (what we call R.E.A.L.) learning tools. Articles and web sites were selected with these criteria in mind. The Editorial Board offered critical feedback and posed some interesting challenges. They know their content and are a web-savvy bunch. The result is a R.E.A.L. learning tool. My thanks to Linda and the entire Editorial Board.

Before I close, I want to invite your comments because whoever you are and wherever you are, I know you aren't just like me. What did *you* think? How did we do in representing the subject of diversity? What worked and what didn't work in this *Perspectives* volume and the accompanying **courselinks** site? Do you feel better prepared to teach the diverse students you'll meet in your classrooms? I'd love to hear from someone just like you.

Dr. Linda Orozco is Dean of Instruction at Coastline College in Southern California, and is also an adjunct professor at the University of California, Irvine. She received her Ph.D. from the University of Minnesota in educational administration. For over 20 years, she has served as an educational leader in a variety of organizations, including K-12 school districts, regional educational agencies, private schools, and institutions of higher education.

from the
Academic Editor

Linda Orozco
Coastline College and University of California, Irvine

As we approach the new millennium, educators are increasingly focused on the needs of all learners, particularly those who bring diverse needs to the classroom. The "global village" is now our reality. Few individuals need to be convinced of the interdependence of diversity in our world. Economics, environment, community, and simple human communications necessitate improved services in learning for diverse populations.

Born and raised in Los Angeles, I grew up in an era and neighborhood filled with the diverse cultures of Southern California. I appreciated the sounds of other languages and music, and the flavors of ethnic cooking. Years later, I began my teaching career in the same school I had attended as a child. When I later pursued a doctorate in Minnesota, I became a transplanted Californian introduced to the diversity now experienced in America's heartland. And now, as a college administrator and professor, I strive professionally to bridge the "quality" gap that exists in schools today and to assure educational success for all of our learners. This volume is my effort in that regard.

This reader focuses on six types of diversity prevalent in schools today. These are gender, special education/gifted, culture, linguistics, economics, and race. Each of these was selected because of its impact on the lives and learning of children. As educators search for answers to assure success for each learner, this reader can illuminate the learning styles, needs, and commonalities among diverse populations. In addition to the readings, the R.E.A.L. sites mentioned in the book and at the **courselinks** site for Educating Diverse Populations expand on the topics surrounding these six types of diversity. The R.E.A.L. sites offer the latest information and some additional resources we can call upon in our quest to understand our diverse learners.

As educators, we are charged with affirming and educating our diverse learners. This challenge can only be undertaken when policies and practices are grounded in the research and goals of student capacity building toward academic success. By assuring success for each student, we and our students contribute to the quality of the community, the country, and the world in which we live.

Editorial Board

WiseGuide Introduction

Critical Thinking and Bumper Stickers

The bumper sticker said: Question Authority. This is a simple directive that goes straight to the heart of critical thinking. The issue is not whether the authority is right or wrong; it's the questioning process that's important. Questioning helps you develop awareness and a clearer sense of what you think. That's critical thinking.

Critical thinking is a new label for an old approach to learning—that of challenging all ideas, hypotheses, and assumptions. In the physical and life sciences, systematic questioning and testing methods (known as the scientific method) help verify information, and objectivity is the benchmark on which all knowledge is pursued. In the social sciences, however, where the goal is to study people and their behavior, things get fuzzy. It's one thing for the chemistry experiment to work out as predicted, or for the petri dish to yield a certain result. It's quite another matter, however, in the social sciences, where the subject is ourselves. Objectivity is harder to achieve.

Although you'll hear critical thinking defined in many different ways, it really boils down to analyzing the ideas and messages that you receive. What are you being asked to think or believe? Does it make sense, objectively? Using the same facts and considerations, could you reasonably come up with a different conclusion? And, why does this matter in the first place? As the bumper sticker urged, question authority. Authority can be a textbook, a politician, a boss, a big sister, or an ad on television. Whatever the message, learning to question it appropriately is a habit that will serve you well for a lifetime. And in the meantime, thinking critically will certainly help you be course wise.

Question Authority

Getting R.E.A.L.

This reader is a R.E.A.L. learning tool.™ This means that the readings and other learning aids explained here are **R**elevant, **E**xciting, **A**pproved, and **L**inked. They will help you think critically about the important issues of the course. Feedback from both instructors and students has helped us to develop some suggestions on how you can wisely use this R.E.A.L. learning tool.™

WiseGuide Pedagogy

A wise reader is better able to be a critical reader. Therefore, we want to help you get wise about the articles in this reader. Each section of *Perspectives* has three tools to help you: the WiseGuide Intro, the WiseGuide Wrap-Up, and the Putting It in *Perspectives* review form.

WiseGuide Intro

In the WiseGuide Intro, the Academic Editor introduces the section, gives you an overview of the topics covered, and explains why particular articles were selected and what's important about them.

Also in the WiseGuide Intro, you'll find several key points or learning objectives that highlight the most important things to remember from this section. These will help you focus your study of section topics.

At the end of the WiseGuide Intro, you'll find questions designed to stimulate critical thinking. Wise students will keep these questions in mind as they read an article (we repeat the questions at the start of the articles as a reminder). When you finish each article, check your understanding. Can you answer the questions? If not, go back and reread the article. The Academic Editor has written sample responses for many of the questions, and you'll find these online at the **courselinks**™ site for this course. More about **courselinks**™ in a minute. . . .

WiseGuide Wrap-Up

Be course wise and develop a thorough understanding of the topics covered in this course. The WiseGuide Wrap-Up at the end of each section will help you do just that with concluding comments or summary points that repeat what's most important to understand from the section you just read.

In addition, we try to get you wired up by providing a list of select Internet resources—what we call R.E.A.L. web sites. The information at these web sites will enhance your understanding of a topic. (Remember to use your Passport and start at http://www.courselinks.com so that if any of these sites have changed, you'll have the latest link.)

Putting It in *Perspectives* Review Form

At the end of the book is the Putting It in *Perspectives* review form. Your instructor may ask you to complete this form as an assignment or for extra credit. If nothing else, consider doing it on your own to help you critically think about the reading.

Prompts at the end of each article encourage you to complete this review form. Feel free to copy the form and use it as needed.

The courselinks™ Site

The **courselinks**™ Passport is your ticket to a wonderful world of integrated web resources designed to help you with your course work. These resources are found at the **courselinks**™ site for your course area. This is where the readings in this book and the key topics of your course are linked to an exciting array of online learning tools. Here you will find carefully selected readings, web links, quizzes, worksheets, and more, tailored to your course and approved as R.E.A.L. learning tools.™ The ever-changing, always interesting **courselinks**™ site features a number of carefully integrated resources designed to help you be course wise. These include:

- **R.E.A.L. Sites** At the core of a **courselinks**™ site is the list of R.E.A.L. sites. This is a select group of web sites for studying, not surfing. Like the readings in this book, these sites have been selected, reviewed, and approved by the Academic Editor and the Editorial Board. The R.E.A.L. sites are arranged by topic and are annotated with short descriptions and key words to make them easier for you to use for reference or research. With R.E.A.L. sites, you're studying approved resources within seconds—and not wasting precious time surfing unproven sites.

- **Editor's Choice** Here you'll find updates on news related to your course, with links to the actual online sources. This is also where we'll tell you about changes to the site and about online events.

- **Course Overview** This is a general description of the typical course in this area of study. While your instructor will provide specific course objectives, this overview helps you place the course in a generic context and offers you an additional reference point.

- **www.orksheet** Focus your trip to a R.E.A.L. site with the www.orksheet. Each of the 10 to 15 questions will prompt you to take in the best that site has to offer. Use this tool for self-study, or if required, email it to your instructor.

- **Course Quiz** The questions on this self-scoring quiz are related to articles in the reader, information at R.E.A.L. sites, and other course topics, and will help you pinpoint areas you need to study. Only you will know your score—it's an easy, risk-free way to keep pace!

- **Topic Key** The Topic Key is a listing of the main topics in your course, and it correlates with the Topic Key that appears in this reader. This handy reference tool also links directly to those R.E.A.L. sites that are especially appropriate to each topic, bringing you integrated online resources within seconds!

- **Web Savvy Student Site** If you're new to the Internet or want to brush up, stop by the Web Savvy Student site. This unique supplement is a complete **courselinks**™ site unto itself. Here, you'll find basic information on using the Internet, creating a web page, communicating on the web, and more. Quizzes and Web Savvy Worksheets test your web knowledge, and the R.E.A.L. sites listed here will further enhance your understanding of the web.

- **Student Lounge** Drop by the Student Lounge to chat with other students taking the same course or to learn more about careers in your major. You'll find links to resources for scholarships, financial aid, internships, professional associations, and jobs. Take a look around the Student Lounge and give us your feedback. We're open to remodeling the Lounge per your suggestions.

Building Better Perspectives!

Please tell us what you think of this *Perspectives* volume so we can improve the next one. Here's how you can help:

1. Visit our **coursewise** site at: http://www.coursewise.com

2. Click on *Perspectives*. Then select the Building Better *Perspectives* Form for your course.

3. Forms and instructions for submission are available online.

Basically, we want to know whether you agree or disagree that a particular reading is R.E.A.L. (**R**elevant, **E**xciting, **A**pproved, and

Linked). You do this by indicating which articles, in your opinion, have the R.E.A.L. attributes and which ones don't. That's all there is to it. Thanks in advance for helping us build better *Perspectives*.

Student Internships

If you enjoy evaluating these articles or would like to help us evaluate the **courselinks**™ site for this course, check out the **coursewise** Student Internship Program. For more information, visit:

http://www.coursewise.com/intern.html

Brief Contents

Contents

section

Spicing It Up: Cultural Diversity and Schooling

section 4

Speaking the Lingo: Diverse Language Learners

section 5

Rich Man, Poor Man, Knocking on Heaven's Door: Educating the Poor and Homeless

section 6

Blending Colors: Multiracial and Bicultural Learners

section
7

Future Perspectives: Society's Conscience

Topic Key

This Topic Key is an important tool for learning. It will help you integrate this reader into your course studies. Listed below, in alphabetical order, are important topics covered in this volume. Below each topic you'll find the article or articles and, for most topics, one or more web sites relating to that topic. Note that the Topic Key might not include every topic your instructor chooses to emphasize. If you don't find the topic you're looking for in the Topic Key, check the index or the OnLine Topic Key at the **courselinks**™ site.

Bilingual Education

WebSites
National Clearinghouse of Bilingual Education
http://www.ncbe.gwu.edu/

Summing up the Lau decision
http://ourworld.compuserve.com/homepages/JWCRAWFORD/summing.htm

Biracial/Multiracial

WebSites
Interracial Voice
http://www.webcom.com/~intvoice/

Association of MultiEthnic Americans
http://www.ameasite.org/index.html

The Multiracial Activist
http://www.geocities.com/CapitolHill/Lobby/5006/

Culture

WebSites
ERIC Clearinghouse on Urban Education
http://eric-web.tc.columbia.edu/

Multicultural Pavilion
http://curry.edschool.virginia.EDU/go/multicultural/

Intercultural E-mail Classroom Connections
http://www.stolaf.edu/network/iecc/

National Clearinghouse of Bilingual Education
http://www.ncbe.gwu.edu/

Summing up the Lau decision
http://ourworld.compuserve.com/homepages/JWCRAWFORD/summing.htm

Teaching Tolerance
http://www.splcenter.org/teachingtolerance.html

Curriculum

Discrimination

WebSite
Teaching Tolerance
http://www.splcenter.org/teachingtolerance.html

Diversity

WebSites
Gifted and Talented Education
http://www.edweek.org/context/topics/gat.htm

Global Schoolhouse
http://www.gsh.org/

Educational Policy

Section 1

Pink and Blue: Learning About Gender Differences

Learning Objectives

- Identify genetic, physical attributes and social messages that form one's gender identity.
- Identify teaching strategies, student opportunities, and classroom environments that assure effective education for both boys and girls.
- Define and describe attributes of gender equity in education.
- Describe the effects of gender equity and gender-bias in single-sex and coeducational classrooms.

? Questions ?

Reading 1. What messages do young children use to define gender roles? What true genetic and physical differences exist between the sexes?

Reading 2. What is cultural literacy? What kinds of activities assist students in identifying messages of cultural expectations and accepting and/or denying these messages?

Reading 3. What is gender-equitable education? What can be done to eliminate barriers to gender-equitable education?

Reading 4. What are the major criticisms of single-sex classrooms? What evidence exists to support single-sex classrooms?

Reading 5. What teaching strategies enhance learning for girls in math/science?

WiseGuide Intro

Throughout their lives, children receive messages that they use to define gender roles. Those messages influence how they see themselves, their place in the world, and even their potential. Yet stereotypes and gender bias continue to prevail, limiting students' vision of their future. Girls as well as boys are diminished by restricted gender roles at school, at home, in their community, and in the workplace.

Yet teaching and learning about issues of gender provide a foundation for students to create and change their future, as well as change the world in which they live. Gender equity is a complex challenge, and gender issues will be defined and debated in schools, families, churches, communities, and other social institutions. But education holds the greatest promise for changing a society's views and expectations of gender, and it is the best source of hope for reaching true gender equity and enhancing the potential of both girls and boys.

Section 1 includes selected readings that address issues of gender and its broader impact on education. Even very young children interpret messages in their world to form gender definitions, as detailed in "The Gender Gap: Why Sexism Flourishes in Kindergarten." Messages from family and peers are combined with genetic and physical gender differences to form our earliest impressions of ourselves and our potential. Later, as students grow older, their gender definitions are influenced by various media, including print, television, and advertising. "Reading the Subtext on Gender" highlights influences and educational strategies to provide students with realistic and positive alternatives to gender stereotyping and bias. Focusing on gender-equitable education, "Shortchanging Girls and Boys" reviews the need to eliminate barriers and stereotypes that limit the educational options of both sexes. The final two articles in this section, "A Room of Their Own" and "Closing the Gender Gap," look at the debate over single-sex vs. coeducational classrooms, and their advantages and disadvantages.

What messages do young children use to define gender roles? What true genetic and physical differences exist between the sexes?

The Gender Gap
Why sexism flourishes in kindergarten

Nancy Seid

Nancy Seid is a writer in Saratoga Springs, New York.

In the fall of his kindergarten year, my son, Zack, surprised me one day by refusing a cupcake. The reason? There were pink sprinkles on top. Then he turned up his nose at *Pocahontas*, calling it a "girl movie." Worst of all, for a short time he even rejected *me*, explaining, "Boys don't like to play with girls, and you're a girl, Mom."

What bothered my husband and me most of all about this sudden surge of male chauvinism was that it directly contradicted everything we were trying to teach Zack at home about male and female roles. Without being too rigid or didactic, Matthew and I have always stressed to Zack that we're equal partners—that we both share dishwashing as well as money-making, and enjoy classical music concerts as well as ball games. Even our society is working to break down rigid gender definitions: Look at how many more women have become senators, astronauts, and construction workers in the last 20 years, and how many more men these days have chosen to be stay-at-home dads.

However, anyone who is the parent of a 5- or 6-year-old, boy or girl, is aware that young children's perceptions of gender roles are firmly rooted in the old days. Part of the explanation has to do with the way children develop. "Kids this age are the worst chauvinists, because they're trying to define the really rather fuzzy categories of male and female," says Paul Jose, Ph.D., associate professor of psychology at Loyola University, in Chicago. "They have just learned that the categories of boy and girl are exclusive. So they think that if you're a boy, you do boy things and *not* girl things. The same goes for girls. In trying to make sense out of these categories, they make them much more separate than they need to be."

Add in the often subtle—and not so subtle—messages children receive from the media, their peers, and adults, including their parents, and it should come as no surprise that even in households that pride themselves on being egalitarian, kids can suddenly embrace the very stereotypes their parents are attempting to dispel. The parents are left wondering how seriously to take this sudden outburst of sexism, and how to respond to it.

The first step is to accept that it's a perfectly natural and typical phenomenon for this age group. According to Jose, children as young as 2 can recognize differences between genders, but the concept of gender constancy—that boys stay boys and girls stay girls, no matter how they behave or what they wear—doesn't hit kids until roughly age 4. Once they make that realization, their daunting task becomes to figure what being a boy or a girl means.

At about the same time that they're facing this question,

Sexism: watching our words
Parents can say things that unwittingly reinforce gender stereotypes. If any of the following sounds familiar, consider what impression you really want to give your children about sex roles.
To boys
"Big boys don't cry."
"Why don't you fight him back?"
"Other boys will make fun of you."
To girls
"That's too heavy. Let your brother carry it upstairs for you."
Don't be upset, sweetheart. Math can be pretty hard for girls."
"Are you sure you want to play baseball with the boys? They're kind of rough."

---

kindergarten begins, and kids become keenly aware of the power of peers. Often, kids are hit with time-honored "rules," such as "Boys don't play house" or "Girls don't play with boys because they're dirty."

These edicts, delivered with utter certainty by their peers, carry ultimate authority, even when they contradict the child's experience. My friend Jane, who is a licensed pilot, was startled one day to hear her 5-year-old nephew declare, "Only men can fly airplanes, you know!" He remembered flying with her on several occasions previously, but didn't think that fact was relevant to his new rule.

During this stage, children also begin to form ideas about basic male and female personality traits. Long-term studies have been conducted by Deborah Best, Ph.D., chairperson of the department of psychology, and John Williams, Ph.D., professor of psychology emeritus, both of Wake Forest University, in Winston-Salem, North Carolina. According to these studies, children of 5 and 6 see women as being emotional, nurturing, and prone to crying, while men are perceived as being strong, aggressive, and dominant.

They also found that "boy behavior" is considered more acceptable for girls than "girl behavior" is for boys. "Girls can play baseball, but boys can't do ballet," Best notes. "Our society seems to do somewhat better opening up new opportunities for females. Socially acceptable options close fast for little boys."

Why do these stereotypes persist? To a degree it's due to the very real genetic and physical differences between boys and girls. According to an extensive body of research, from birth boys are generally taller and weigh more than

girls, and from toddlerhood are more physically aggressive. Girls tend to be more verbal, begin smiling at an earlier age, and have slightly better physical coordination than boys.

In addition, recent research suggests that boys and girls have markedly different approaches to learning styles and conflict resolution as well. Girls tend to learn well in teams, prefer to achieve solutions through compromise, and avoid confrontations. Boys tend to be more competitive and prefer to resolve problems by getting their own ideas accepted rather than by finding a compromise.

In the long run, though, when it comes to ideas about gender roles, the major formative influence on children is what they see in their own families. "Girls want to be just like their mothers, and boys like their fathers—so if roles and behaviors within the house are stereotypical, the children will imitate that," says Jose. Carmen Bassin-Beumer, of Saratoga Springs, New York, notes that her 6-year-old son, Mischa, "used to love to cook and bake. Now he just stands back and watches my daughter and me. 'Cooking is for mothers,' he says. But when his father makes pancakes on Sunday mornings, Mischa is right there with him."

Family, however, isn't the only source of kids' information about gender roles. The messages contained in books, movies, and television can be enormously powerful. "Take a look at advertising," says Julie Dobrow, Ph.D., coordinator of the Children and Media Initiative at Tufts University, in Medford, Massachusetts. "Toys are consistently designated as 'boy toys' or 'girl toys.' Boy ads are accompanied by loud, rhythmic, rap-like music and colors that are either dark or bold. Girl

ads have soft, melodious music, a slower pace, and lots of pastel shades. Kids pick up on these things." Which means that parents need to give their children a larger perspective on both masculinity and femininity.

Monitor the Media's Gender Messages

If you're concerned about the influence that TV and movies might be having on your child, make a point of being around to watch along with him. If you're not comfortable with what your child is viewing and you can't be there, you might say, "I don't want you to watch that program when I'm not with you, because we need a chance to talk about some of the things it says."

At the same time, realize that television also offers a number of positive gender role models for school-age kids. "Even though kids this age have grown out of *Barney & Friends* and *Sesame Street,* they can still find characters to emulate on shows such as *The Magic School Bus,* with the female science teacher Ms. Frizzle and a class of boys and girls who don't necessarily fall into typical gender roles," says Dobrow.

When you do watch TV together, discuss the messages he's getting in ways that encourage him to make his own discoveries, rather than dictating to him what he's seeing. The best way to do this is by asking appropriate questions. You might ask him, for example, how he feels about Fred Flintstone always yelling at Wilma—which is something he probably wouldn't notice on his own. Or ask why the girls on many superhero adventure shows can't save themselves, and whether the superhero might have figured out a way to save the day without using violence.

In addition, realize that this is one area in which what we do is just as important as what we say. If the chores in a household fall along traditional lines—if the husband balks at cooking or cleaning, while the wife reflexively hands her spouse the tool kit for household repairs—then you can hardly expect a child to believe that gender stereotypes are unrealistic.

Try to keep your behavior consistent with your beliefs when it comes to gender roles. Encourage your daughter to compete as energetically on the soccer field as your son. When you see your son engaged in a nurturing act— gently petting the family cat, for example, or holding a baby—say to him, "It's great the way you're showing how you care. I'll bet you're going to be a really loving father when you grow up." There's no need to make sweeping declarations about sex roles if you pay attention to the specifics.

Finally, if you're being driven crazy by your child's insistence that only boys like tractors and only girls have tea parties, take heart in the knowledge that, "to a large degree, children grow out of this by late grade school," says Jose. "That's when they become more comfortable with their gender identity and no longer need the security of black-and-white thinking."

I'm starting to see a change in Zack already. He is finally relaxing his guard enough to be affectionate again. "Kisses are for girls," he still grumbles, "but you can give me a bear hug if you want. And remember, don't call me beautiful," he warns. "Call me handsome instead."

 Article Review Form at end of book.

What is cultural literacy? What kinds of activities assist students in identifying messages of cultural expectations, and accepting and/or denying these messages?

Reading the Subtext on Gender

Merryn Rutledge

In the Vermont Equity Project, educators are helping children of all ages to recognize and interpret the cultural messages that may shape the way they see themselves as boys, girls, and people of color.

Melody Daigle encourages her 6th graders to view popular culture as a powerful teacher. As one of her students wrote during a unit on social studies and literature:

Think about the last time you watched television and saw commercials for kids' toys. Think about all those ads for "girl" products. Did you see much besides dolls and fashion-oriented stuff?

If you are a girl, you hear these ads saying that you should just worry about raising a family and looking good. If you aren't as thin as a beanpole, you should go on a major diet.

Diagle created her unit on popular culture when she received training, along with dozens of her colleagues, in the Vermont Equity Project, a state- and grant-supported program. Our aim is cultural literacy—the ability to read, interpret, and bring a critical perspective to the way our culture shapes our identity and expecta-

tions. Our guiding principle is that only by learning to read their world can children grow into citizens able to shape their own lives.

Cultural literacy extends and gives depth to multicultural education. Students not only celebrate diverse cultures but also recognize their society's pressures to fit the dominant cultural milieu—in terms of ethnicity, gender, family, and education. We see culture as Julian Weissglass (1994) defined it: "the attitudes, beliefs, values, and practices shared by a community of people which they often do not state or question and which they may not be consciously aware of."

Since 1994, when I launched the Vermont Equity Project in co-operation with middle school parent (now school board member) Kathy Olwell and Hunt Middle School Principal Linda Carroll, I have been leading 15 weekly seminars each autumn. James Loewen, author of Lies My Teacher Told Me, was one of our speakers (1995). Forty-two Burlington, Vermont, teachers have participated.

The Media's Messages

Ann Park, another of our participants, begins her cultural geogra-

phy unit by asking students to describe their family culture and then, working in groups, their school culture. The students choose language and symbols that distinguish each. They then identify cultural expectations for boys and girls as reflected in newspaper cartoons and television shows from the 1950s and 1990s. Comparing the television shows from these two decades helps them to see that current depictions of gender roles do not reflect the way boys and girls have to be. Finally, the students compare these depictions with the real people in their lives. They thereby gain new perspectives on how popular culture images purvey stereotypes and fail to reflect the diversity that students know.

Melody Daigle begins one unit by having her students read The True Confessions of Charlotte Doyle (Avi 1992). The class discusses how perceptions of gender roles led to the dilemma of this 19th century heroine, who was persecuted because she learned boys' work as a sailor. Working in small groups, students talk about the behavior now expected of boys and girls. In full-group discussion, they eagerly talk about

Merryn Rutledge, Director of the Vermont Equity Project, gives workshops throughout the U.S. and Canada on creating inclusive curriculum. Her consulting firm, ReVisions, helps people integrate vision and skill in organizations experiencing change. 233 Van Pattern Pky., Burlington, VT 05401-1135.

the pressures they feel to fit preset gender roles.

When Diagle and the Equity Project teachers watched a videotape of this class, they sensed that the students not only welcomed such a discussion, but were relieved to be able to unburden themselves of their feelings. Thus we are finding that children are experts on the pressures they feel from their cultural surroundings. But they may need teachers to create a safe place for discussing limiting gender roles and stereotypes based on race, class, and other characteristics of themselves and to help them name these stereotypes.

For example, after Patty Kissell shared with her 2nd graders ways in which her awareness is heightened in Equity Project seminars, she noticed children volunteering their own insights. "A book I read said 'Pilgrims and their wives,'" one 7-year-old related, emphasizing the word wives. "Sounds like only men were Pilgrims, doesn't it, Mrs. Kissell?" When such moments occur, teachers and students become partners in exploring how our culture shapes us.

Adding Up Disparities

Molly Snow integrated her math unit on bar graphs with cultural investigation. She asked her 6th graders to count the number of female and male athletes featured in the sports section of the local newspaper. Students kept records for a month, and then made graphs comparing the numbers. This exercise led to discussions about why male sports predominated.

Pauline Mallory challenged her 7th and 8th graders to carry out similar research in a Vermont Math Portfolio project—part of the state's pilot program in using qualitative as well as quantitative assessment methods. Mallory read aloud a news story about a 10-year-old who surveyed her classmates about the amount of their allowances. The survey showed that girls received less than boys even when they did more chores. Mallory invited her students to develop, administer, and report on a survey of their own classmates to see whether such a gender gap existed. Their results varied considerably, but the students did find that, overall, girls received less money for doing more chores.

These math projects exemplify curriculums that connect students' cultural milieu and the math skills and critical perspectives they need to decipher their world. Students want to learn skills that help them see through and into their world, as an X-ray lets us see into an otherwise opaque body. Like cultural X-rays, the projects reveal pressures to act in certain ways. They also help children answer key questions of identity: Who am I? Where do I stand compared to others? Where am I headed?

What Is Normal?

When my predominantly white college students survey articles and ads in the magazines they read, they find that most of the people depicted are white, affluent, slender, heterosexual, sighted, and able to walk unassisted—except for athletes, who often are African-American men. That this profile reinforces stereotypes is obvious.

I encourage my students to see how such images may harm them by asking them: Who are you when you compare yourself with these images? Where do you stand compared to these people? Very few students see themselves mirrored here. But they often say that these images represent what is normal, and therefore they and others who don't match the profiles are abnormal. They also agree that because they've grown up watching these recurrent images, their aspirations have been influenced by them.

Our students also join us in asking hard questions of textbooks and course units: Who are we and where are we in this curriculum? A class at Burlington's Hunt Middle School, for example, reviewed several textbooks to determine how many and what types of women and men were depicted. "Did you see your own life or that of your parents in these illustrations?" their teacher asked. "If not, what messages did you get about your own worth and place in history?"

This assignment, in which students found far more men than women represented, came shortly after teachers in the Equity Project discovered that even in a new history text, The American Nation (Davidson and Stoff 1995), white men predominated, while the contributions of white women, people of color, and people with disabilities seemed to be tacked on as an afterthought. Students may counter such findings by arguing that few white women and people of color made history. But this claim depends on whether the focus in the study of history, literature, or any other subject is primarily on the public achievements of people who became famous (Mcintosh 1983).

Recasting History

For an 8th grade unit on the U.S. Constitution, Equity Project teachers realized that asking all students to research and role-play the events at the Constitutional Convention would tell only part of the story. Accordingly, they invited half their students to assume the roles of wives like Abigail Adams, whose insightful voice we know, and the roles of anonymous shopkeepers, cooks, laborers, and children of all ethnic groups and classes.

As the authors of How Schools Short-change Girls observe, history that includes those responsible for "the cyclical nature of daily life, the making and mending of the social fabric," reflects most of our lives and in so doing reinforces our self-worth (Wellesley Center for Research on Women 1992). Conversely, students' identities are assaulted by invisibility, underrepresentation, and stereotyping, as well as by an emphasis on individual achievement that overshadows collective and collaborative achievement.

In short, our project seeks to do what Paulo Freire (1970) has advocated: To teach children "to perceive critically the way they exist in the world," so that they can grow up to be truly literate, able to name their world, and be free.

References

Avi. (1992). *The True Confessions of Charlotte Doyle.* New York: Avon Books.

Davidson, J. W., and M. B. Stoff. (1995). *The American Nation.* Englewood Cliffs, N.J.: Prentice Hall.

Freire, P. (1970, 1993, 1996). *Pedagogy of the Oppressed.* New York: The Continuum Publishing Co., p. 64.

Loewen, J. (1995). *Lies My Teacher Told Me: Everything Your American History Textbook Got Wrong.* New York: W.W. Norton & Co., Inc.

Mcintosh, P. (1983). "Interactive Phases of Curricular Re-Vision: A Feminist Perspective." Working Paper No. 124. Wellesley: Wellesley Center for Research on Women.

Weissglass, J. (1994). *Changing Mathematics Teaching Means Changing Ourselves: Implications for Professional Development.* Santa Barbara,Calif.: Center for Educational Change in Mathematics and Science, p. 1.

Wellesley Center for Research on Women. (1992). *How Schools Short-change Girls.* Washington, D.C.: American Association of University Women Educational Foundation: National Education Association, p. 65.

 Article Review Form at end of book.

What is gender-equitable education? What can be done to eliminate barriers to a gender-equitable education?

Shortchanging Girls and Boys

Susan McGee Bailey

Susan McGee Bailey is Director, The Wellesley Center for Research on Women, Wellesley College, 106 Central St., Wellesley, MA 02181.

Gender equity in education is more than putting girls on equal footing with boys—it's eliminating the barriers and stereotypes that limit the opportunities and choices of both sexes.

Recently gender equity in education has become a hot, or at least a "reasonably warm," topic in education. Higher education institutions across the country are under renewed pressure to provide equal athletic opportunities for female students. The U.S. Supreme Court is considering cases involving the admission of women to all-male, state-supported military institutions. And the continued under-representation of women in tenured faculty positions is prompting many donors to withhold contributions to Harvard University's fundraising campaign.

But it is at the elementary and secondary school levels that the shortchanging of girls has been most extensively documented (Wellesley College Center for Research on Women 1992, AAUW 1995, Orenstein 1994, Sadker and Sadker 1994, Thorne 1993, Stein et al. 1993). Twenty-four years after the passage of Title IX—which prohibits discrimination on the basis of sex in any educational programs receiving federal funds—girls and boys are still not on equal footing in our nation's classrooms. Reviews of curricular materials, data on achievement and persistence in science, and research on teacher-to-student and student-to-student interaction patterns all point to school experiences that create significant barriers to girls' education. These factors have fostered widespread discussion and action among parents, educators, and policymakers.

Barriers to Gender Equitable Education

As the principal author of the 1992 study, How Schools Shortchange Girls, I have followed the discussion with considerable interest and mounting concern. The central problem posed in the opening pages of this report continues to be ignored in our discussions of public K–12 education.

[There are] critical aspects of social development that our culture has traditionally assigned to women that are equally important for men. Schools must help girls and boys acquire both the relational and the competitive skills needed for full participation in the workforce, family, and community (Wellesley College Center for Research on Women 1992, p. 2).

Too much of the discussion and too many of the proposed remedies rely on simplistic formulations that obscure, rather than address, the complex realities confronting our society.

First among these are the assumptions that (1) gender equity is something "for girls only" and (2) if the situation improves for girls, boys will inevitably lose. These constructions are dangerously narrow and limit boys as well as girls. Gender equity is about enriching classrooms, widening opportunities, and expanding choices for all students.

The notion that helping girls means hurting boys amounts to a defense of a status quo that we all know is serving too few of our students well. Surely it is as important for boys to learn about the contributions of women to our nation as it is for girls to study this information. Surely adolescent pregnancy and parenting are issues for young men as well as young women. And surely boys as well as girls benefit from instructional techniques that encourage cooperation in learning.

From Susan McGee Bailey, "Shortchanging Girls and Boys" in *Educational Leadership*, Vol. 53(8). May 1996, pp. 75–79 by permission from Susan McGee Bailey.

A second set of assumptions concern the single-sex versus coed dichotomy. During discussions of gender equity, rarely does anyone stop to consider that coeducation, as the term is generally used, implies more than merely attending the same institution. It is usually assumed to mean a balanced experience as compared to an exclusive, one-sided, single-sex, all-female or all-male one. Thus the term itself undercuts our ability to achieve genuine coeducation by implying that it already exists.

We would do better to describe U.S. public elementary and secondary education as mixed-sex education rather than as coeducation. Girls and boys are mixed together in our schools, but they are not receiving the same quality or quantity of education—nor are they genuinely learning from and about each other. Our task is to find ways to provide the gender equitable education the term coeducation promises, but does not yet deliver.

Lessons from All-Girl Schools

It may indeed be easier in an all-girl setting both to value skills, career fields, and avocations generally considered feminine and to encourage girls in nontraditional pursuits. Pressures on students from peers, from popular culture, and even from many adults around them all define gender stereotypic behavior as normal, expected, and successful. Particularly for young adolescents, the clarity of these stereotypes can be reassuring; questioning them can be uncomfortable and risky. In a world where being labeled a "girl" is the classic insult for boys,

single-sex environments for girls can provide a refuge from put-downs and stereotypes.

But these environments may also send messages that can perpetuate rather than eliminate negative gender stereotyping. Removing girls from classes in order to provide better learning opportunities for them can imply that girls and boys are so different that they must be taught in radically different ways. When all-girl classes are set up specifically in science or math, an underlying, if unintended, message can be that girls are less capable in these subjects. Separating boys from girls in order to better control boys' behavior can indicate that boys are "too wild" to control.

Rather than assuming that we must isolate girls in order to protect them from boys' boisterous, competitive behavior—or that boys will be unduly feminized in settings where girls are valued and comfortable—we must look carefully at why some students and teachers prefer single-sex settings for girls. We must understand the positive aspects of these classrooms in order to begin the difficult task of bringing these positive factors into mixed-sex classes.

In U.S. public schools, this is not only a matter of good sense, but it is a matter of law. Title IX permits single-sex instruction only in very specific situations.[1] In doing so, we will be moving toward genuinely coeducational environments where the achievements, perspectives, and experiences of both girls and boys, women and men, are equally recognized and rewarded whether or not they fall into traditional categories.

How to Eliminate Barriers

As long as the measures and models of success presented to students follow traditional gender stereotypes and remain grounded in a hierarchy that says paid work is always and absolutely more important and rewarding than unpaid work, that the higher the pay the more valuable the work and the worker who does it, we will be unfairly limiting the development of, and the opportunities available to, all our students. Gender equitable education is about eliminating the barriers and stereotypes that limit the options of both sexes. To move in this direction, we need to take three major steps.

1. We must acknowledge the gendered nature of schooling. Schools are a part of society. Educators cannot single-handedly change the value structure we ourselves embody, but we can acknowledge and begin to question the ways in which gender influences our schooling. How Schools Shortchange Girls points out that the emotions and the power dynamics of sex, race, and social class are all present, but evaded, aspects of our classrooms. We can begin to change this by fostering classroom discussions that explicitly include these issues and that value expressions of feelings as well as recitations of facts.

2. We must take a careful look at our own practices. Years ago as a first-year teacher, I was proud of my sensitivity to the needs of my 6th graders. I carefully provided opportunities for

---

[1]Under Title IX, portions of elementary and secondary school classes dealing with human sexuality and instruction in sports that involve bodily contact may, but do not have to be, separated by sex. (Title IX Rules and Regulations of the Educational Amendments of 1972, section 86.34)

boys to take part in class discussions and lead group projects in order to channel their energies in positive ways. I was equally careful to ensure that two very shy, soft-spoken girls never had to be embarrassed by giving book reports in front of the class.

Only much later did I realize that rather than helping the boys learn cooperative skills, I may merely have reinforced their sense that boys act while girls observe, and that I may have protected the girls from exactly the experiences they needed in order to overcome their initial uncertainties. Further, in protecting the girls, I also deprived the boys of opportunities to learn that both girls and boys can take the risks and garner the rewards of speaking up in class and speaking out on issues.

One technique that teachers can use to gain a picture of their classes is to develop class projects in which students serve as data collectors. Students are keen observers of the world around them. Having them keep a record of who is taking part in class can serve as a springboard for important discussions. These discussions can raise everyone's awareness of classroom dynamics, dynamics sometimes so ingrained that they have become invisible.

3. We must learn from all-girl environments about teaching techniques and curricular perspectives that have particular appeal to girls and determine how to use these approaches successfully in mixed-sex classes. In talking with teachers working in all-girl environments, I hear three

frequent suggestions: (1) place less emphasis on competition and speed and more emphasis on working together to ensure that everyone completes and understands the problem or project; (2) place more emphasis on curricular materials that feature girls and women; and (3) increase the focus on practical, real-life applications of mathematics and the sciences.

Three Practical Suggestions

Teachers can apply these three suggestions in mixed-sex settings. The first is the most difficult. What appears to happen naturally in all-girl settings—for example, girls' working together in an environment where they feel empowered to set the pace—must be deliberately fostered in settings where a different style has been the norm. Girls and their teachers speak of all-girl classes as places where fewer students shout out answers and interrupt one another. Teachers indicate that they deliberately work to ensure that all girls take some active part in class activities. If teachers can directly address these factors in an all-girl setting, surely we can begin to address them in mixed-sex settings.

Further, teachers must experiment with instructions and with reward systems that will encourage students to value a thorough understanding of a task as well as a quick answer, and of group success as well as individual performance. In doing so, we will be encouraging strengths many girls have developed and helping boys acquire skills that they need.

The second suggestion is also not without difficulties when

transported to mixed-sex settings. As television producers have discovered, girls may watch programs with male characters, but programs featuring girls are less likely to attract or hold boys' interests. But schools are places where students come to learn. Boys and girls need to learn to appreciate and value the accomplishments of women and women's groups who have succeeded in traditionally male fields: Shirley Chisholm, Indira Ghandi, Sally Ride, the Women's Campaign Fund, as well as those whose success has been in traditionally female areas of employment and avocation: Jane Addams, Mary McLeod Bethune, the Visiting Nurses Association.

In Natural Allies, Women's Associations in American History, Anne Firor Scott notes that "by the 1930s the landscape was covered with libraries, schools, colleges, kindergartens, museums, health clinics, houses of refuge, school lunch programs, parks, playgrounds, all of which owed their existence to one or several women's societies" (1991, p.3). Our students—male and female—need to learn more of this work if they are to grow into adults who can carry on activities vital to our survival as a viable, humane society.

The third factor is perhaps the least problematic. Although girls may be most enthusiastic about pursuing science when they see it as relevant to daily life, boys will surely not be less interested when presented with more relevance! For teachers to develop new lesson plans and materials in the sciences, however, will require increased support from school administrators and school boards for professional development, new materials and equipment, and perhaps a reorganization of class time.

Operation Smart, an after-school informal science program for girls developed by Girls, Inc., is just one example of new relevant science programs. A unit on water pollution, for example, offers middle school and junior high school girls an opportunity to study the effects of pollution in their own communities and to gain an understanding of the value of scientific knowledge and procedures in improving living conditions (Palmer 1994).

Mixed-sex classes can easily adapt such projects, and many have. Last year my nieces, both middle school students in mixed-sex classes in Mystic, Connecticut, eagerly showed me their science projects. Sarah's, done with her close friend Caitlin, contained several different pieces of cloth, each of which had been put through a series of trials: burned, washed, stretched, and frozen. "We thought the synthetic pieces of cloth would be stronger, but they weren't! Now we know natural material is very tough."

Aidan, a year older, collected samples of river water at points varying in distance from the mouth of the Mystic River where it joins the salt water of Fisher's Island Sound. Expecting that the water would be less salty the farther away it was from the Sound, she was surprised to find that her graph was not a straight line: a very salty sample appeared at a point quite far up river. Trying to figure out what might account for this became the most interesting aspect of the project. For both Sarah and Aidan, science is about their own questions, not out of a book or in a laboratory and it is certainly not a boys-only activity!

Moving Beyond Stereotypes

As we move into a new century, we must leave behind our boys-only and girls-only assumptions and stereotypes. On any given measure of achievement or skill, we can find greater similarity between the average score of girls as a group and the average score of boys as a group than we can find when comparing among individual girls or among individual boys. We must no longer allow stereotypic assumptions to guide our expectations or obscure the reality that empathy, cooperation, and competition are all important skills—and are important for all our students.

References

Orenstein, P. (1994). *SchoolGirls: Young Women, Self-Esteem, and the Confidence Gap.* New York: Doubleday.

Palmer, L. (1994). *The World of Water: Environmental Science for Teens.* New York: Girls Incorporated.

Sadker, D., and M. Sadker. (1994). *Failing at Fairness: How America's Schools Cheat Girls.* New York: C. Scribner's Sons.

Scott, A. F. (1991). *Natural Allies: Women's Associations in American History.* Urbana, Ill.: University of Illinois Press.

Stein, N., N. Marshall, and L. Tropp. (1993). *Secrets in Public: Sexual Harassment in Our Schools.* Wellesley, Mass.: The Wellesley College Center for Research on Women.

Thorne, B. (1993). *Gender Play: Girls and Boys in School.* New Brunswick, N.J.: Rutgers University Press.

Wellesley College Center for Research on Women. (1992). *The AAUW Report: How Schools Shortchange Girls.* Washington, D.C.: American Association of University Women Educational Foundation; reprint ed., (1995), New York: Marlowe and Company.

 Article Review Form at end of book.

What are the major criticisms of single-sex classrooms? What evidence exists to support single-sex classrooms?

A Room of Their Own

Single-sex classrooms

LynNell Hancock and Claudia Kalb

Who can forget the pubescent pain of junior high? Boys sprout pimples, girls sprout attitude and both genders goad each other into a state of sexual confusion. Teachers in Manassas, Va., figured that all these colliding hormones were distracting students from their academic tasks. So officials at Marsteller Middle School decided to try something old: dividing girls and boys into separate academic classes. Eighth-grade girls say they prefer doing physics experiments without boys around to hog the equipment. Boys say they'd rather recite Shakespeare without girls around to make them feel "like geeks." An eerie return to the turn of the century, when boys and girls marched into public schools through separate doors? Yes, say education researchers. But will it work—and is it legal?

In districts across the country, public schools are experimenting with sexual segregation, in the name of school reform. There is no precise tally, in part because schools are wary of drawing attention to classes that may violate gender-bias laws. But, researchers say, in more than a dozen states—including Texas, Colorado, Michigan and Georgia—coed schools are creating single-sex classes. Some, like Marsteller, believe that separating the sexes will eliminate distractions. Others, like Robert Coleman Elementary in Baltimore, made the move primarily to get boys to work harder and tighten up discipline.

The great majority of the experiments are designed to boost girls' math and science scores. The stimulus for these efforts was a report four years ago from the American Association of University Women, which argued that girls were being shortchanged in public-school classrooms—particularly in math and science. The single-sex classroom, however, is not what the gender-equity researchers involved with AAUW had in mind as a remedy. Their report was meant to help improve coeducation, not dismantle it. Research shows single-sex schools tend to produce girls with more confidence and higher grades. But single-sex classrooms within coed schools? There are no long-term studies of that approach, only a smattering of skeptics and true believers. "It's a plan that misses two boats," charges David Sadker, coauthor of "Failing at Fairness"—the education of boys, and the reality that children need to learn how to cope in a coed world. In short, says University of Michigan researcher Valerie Lee, "these classes are a bogus answer to a complex problem."

Critics worry that segregated classes will set back the cause of gender equity just when girls are finally being integrated into all-male academies. Half a century ago, boys in advanced science classes learned, for example, that mold is used for penicillin while girls in home economics learned that mold is the gunk on the shower curtain. "It's not an era we're eager to return to," says Norma Cantu of the U.S. Office of Civil Rights.

Miracles happen: As a general principle, federal law doesn't permit segregation by sex in the public schools. (Exceptions can be made for singing groups, contact sports and human-sexuality and remedial classes.) Some schools have survived legal challenges by claiming that their all-girl classes fill remedial needs. A middle school in Ventura, Calif., faced down a challenge by changing the name of its all-girl math class to Math PLUS (Power Learning for Underrepresented Students). Enrollment is open to boys, though none has registered yet.

Despite the skeptics, single-sex experiments continue to spread. Teachers and students believe they work. At the high school in Presque Isle, Maine, members of the popular all-girl algebra class go on to tackle the sciences. University of Maine professor Bonnie Wood found that girls who take the algebra course are twice as likely to enroll in advanced chemistry and college physics than their coed counterparts. Michigan's Rochester High School turns away 70 students every year from its girls-only science and engineering class. Marsteller boys raised their collective average in language arts by one grade after a single term. Girls boosted their science average by .4 of a point.

For the teachers involved, the progress is no mystery. Sheryl Quinlan, who teaches science at Marsteller, knows single-sex classes let her kids think with something besides their hormones. Impressing the opposite sex is a 14-year-old's reason for being. Take away that pressure, and miracles happen. Quinlan recalls the girl who took a "zero" on her oral report rather than deliver it in front of her boyfriend. Those days are over. Now, says Amanda Drobney, 14, "you can mess up in front of girls, and it's OK." We've come a long way, babies—or have we?

 Article Review Form at end of book.

What teaching strategies enhance learning for girls in math/science? What differences exist between the way boys and girls approach technology, and what teaching strategies can enhance learning?

Closing the Gender Gap

Innovative teaching techniques that help girls excel in science and math

Ann Pollina

Ann Pollina is a dean of faculty and head of the Mathematics Department at Westover School in Middlebury, Connecticut.

For the last 20 years, I've been immersed in one of the most interesting laboratories in the world—an all-girls' classroom. In that time, my students have taught me an enormous amount about how girls learn, what attracts them to science and mathematics, and why some lessons work better than others. Whether or not you feel girls take a backseat to boys in your classroom, all your students will benefit from these ideas.

Connect mathematics and science to art, to the lives of real people, and to the good of the world. Bring to life the people who do mathematics and science. Ask your students to reflect on the kind of mathematics and science you would need to live as a Plains Indian; in Colonial America; in 14th-century China; or as a prehistoric hunter-gatherer. You may push your students to wonder for the first time: What is mathematics? What is science? How do math and science work together?

Examine your assessment strategies: Do you focus on process as well as product? Do you reward reflection over speed? Many girls do not typically think in terms of right or wrong, but look at both sides of a dilemma and try to develop strategies in which everyone wins. Mix questions that require written explanations with multiple-choice questions. Students should be amply rewarded for thoughtful insights. Writing portfolios are as viable a tool in math and science as they are in language arts.

Foster an atmosphere of true collaboration. Having students work in groups of threes and fours does not ensure a collaborative experience. The group members should need one another; the group task should be too big for anyone to do alone. Even in small groups, girls may question their first reaction to questions and need time for reflection if they are to contribute fully. It can help to assign the question for homework so all students will have ideas to contribute.

Encourage girls to act as experts. Keep expectations high and give frequent feedback. Girls demonstrate great practical intelligence in real-world situations, but they are often reluctant to use information gained because it hasn't been imparted by an expert. Life experience should be celebrated as a strong source of conjectures. Having girls present topics to the class, using girls to staff the technology room, having a science lab for extra help staffed by girls—all of these strategies help girls gain confidence.

Help girls become comfortable with technology by emphasizing both purpose and opportunity for its use. When researchers Cornelia Brunner and Margaret

Honey at the Center for Children and Technology ask children to create their dream machine, boys build vehicles and weapons; girls design helpers and friends. The computer industry tends to develop games filled with weaponry and vehicles, which fuels girls' perception that computers are boys' domain. Encourage girls to recognize the networking and communications capability of the computer along with its link to writing and research and its use as a tool in mathematics and science.

If we stop trying to change girls, and instead let a feminine approach to math and science inform our pedagogy, we will benefit boys, girls, and scientific inquiry.

 Article Review Form at end of book.

WiseGuide Wrap-Up

- Students use family, peer, and media messages to create their own gender definitions.

- Cultural literacy assists students in recognizing and critically analyzing the way our culture shapes identity and expectations.

- Designing gender-equitable classrooms enhances the learning of both girls and boys.

- All-girl classrooms enhance female learning by providing an environment that values cooperative learning, reduces negative stereotypes, and removes competitive influences.

- Specific advantages of single-sex schools/classrooms may be replicated in coeducational classrooms.

- Segregating boys and girls in education eliminates opportunities for the sexes to learn, adjust, and succeed in a coeducational world.

- Specific teaching strategies can enhance learning opportunities for girls.

R.E.A.L. Sites

This list provides a print preview of typical **coursewise** R.E.A.L. sites. (There are over 100 such sites at the **courselinks**™ site.) The danger in printing URLs is that Web sites can change overnight. As we went to press, these sites were functional using the URLs provided. If you come across one that isn't, please let us know via email to: webmaster@coursewise.com. Use your Passport to access the most current list of R.E.A.L. sites at the **courselinks**™ site.

Site name: Closing the Equity Gap in Technology Access and Use

URL: http://www.netc.org/equity/

Why is it R.E.A.L.? This resource presents an overview of equity issues in three areas—access, type of use, and curriculum—and presents this information in the form of a self-assessment that can be completed online. Strategies to combat inequities in the three areas are provided, as well as planning steps and forms, and pointers to other Internet resources.

Key topics: gender equity, technology

Activity: Visit the website and list barriers to gender equity currently experienced by girls in schools.

Site name: Women in World History Curriculum

URL: http://home.earthlink.net/~womenwhist/index.html

Why is it R.E.A.L.? Interactive site full of information and resources about women's experiences in world history. Includes female heroes, instructional lessons, and review of resources featuring women in history. For teachers, parents, and history buffs.

Key topics: gender equity, Title XI

Activities: Review the offerings of lessons in the website and select one for development in a classroom activity. Or use the section titled "Female Heroes" to highlight a women's contribution in a classroom lesson.

Site name: A Celebration of Women Writers

URL:
http://www.cs.cmu.edu/afs/cs.cmu.edu/user/mmbt/www/women/writers.html

Why is it R.E.A.L.? A comprehensive site focused on the contributions of women writers throughout history. Includes texts of novels, poems, letters, biographies, travel books, religious commentaries, histories, economic, and scientific works.

Key topics: gender equity, girls in math/science

Activity: Review some of the many writers and their contributions on the site. Select one to include in a term paper, report, or presentation.

section 2

Unique Learners: Special Needs of Special Learners, and Unwrapping the Mysteries of the Gifted

Learning Objectives

- Describe responsible inclusion practices in educating special education students.

- Identify promising programs for inclusion, and identify classroom and school methods for implementation.

- Outline prevention and early intervention strategies effective in meeting the needs of diverse learners.

- Identify teaching strategies that address the needs of gifted students and factors that hinder effective program implementation.

- Outline the current disproportionate ethnic/cultural distribution in gifted programs, and describe modifications in assessment criteria.

 **WiseGuide Intro**

Educational systems, reforms, and practices are often designed with a generalized concept of "student." This generalization facilitates broad-based and sweeping attempts at solutions. But these solutions address a generalized perception and average expectation of public school students, and clearly we cannot define the total school population as average.

Experienced educators will confirm that although "average students" do exist, all classrooms are also composed of diverse learners who bring with them a variety of strengths, weaknesses, and learning styles. And part of this diverse population are very special learners who challenge instructional delivery systems in unique ways.

Two distinct populations are at opposite ends of the education spectrum. These two segments of the school population are students in special education and gifted programs. Although these two groups are initially distinguished by their capacity as learners, they have significant similarities for educators to consider.

This collection of articles contains information, research, and practices for educators to consider in the delivery of instruction to these two groups of learners. "Responsible Inclusion: Celebrating Diversity and Academic Excellence" and "Inclusion: 12 Secrets to Make It Work in Your Classroom" describe the special challenges teachers face in providing quality education in classrooms that include special education learners. Diversity in inclusive classrooms is further discussed in "A Change in Focus: Teaching Diverse Learners Within an Inclusive Classroom." Presenting an alternative to special education is "Neverstreaming: Preventing Learning Disabilities," which promotes early intervention programs to ensure student success before remedial needs develop. Also addressing the needs of unique learners is "Educating the Very Brightest," which details how to build effective programs for the gifted. Examining the causes of underrepresentation by minorities in gifted programs, "Meeting the Needs of Gifted and Talented Minority Language Students" suggests assessment and delivery strategies for this increasing population.

Questions

Reading 6. What kinds of school practices should be explored for responsible inclusion? How does responsible inclusion relate to student diversity?

Reading 7. Teachers should engage in what kinds of collaboration activities to assist special education students? What kinds of activities should a teacher consider in order to prepare for success in an inclusive classroom?

Reading 8. What are some of the reasons for lack of interaction between regular and special education teachers? What are some of the modifications recommended to improve learning for all students in an inclusive classroom?

Reading 9. What are the advantages of implementing early intervention programs to ensure that students are successful and *not* in need of special education services? What is "neverstreaming," for which students is it most appropriate, and what are the key concepts for student success?

Reading 10. If gifted students are not challenged educationally, what are some of the consequences? Why do parents of gifted students believe their children should have individualized learning plans similar to those of special education?

Reading 11. Gifted programs for language minority students should consider what factors? What types of assessment criteria should be used in identifying language minority students as gifted?

What kinds of school practices should be explored for responsible inclusion? How does responsible inclusion relate to student diversity?

Responsible Inclusion

Celebrating diversity and academic excellence

William Malloy

William Malloy is assistant professor of educational leadership and special education, University of North Carolina at Chapel Hill.

School reform strategies created to increase standards of academic excellence are on a collision course with strategies designed to increase the inclusion of exceptional students in general education classes. Responsible inclusionary practices, focused on all students, will eliminate this potential clash by providing an educational atmosphere that encourages heterogeneity in all classroom settings and school activities.

As a result of America 2000, many school districts are confronted with school reform strategies created to increase standards of academic excellence that perpetuate the "sorting role" society has defined for public education (Winfield and Woodard, 1992). This situation has been disquieting for many school districts that are in the midst of addressing challenges presented by strategies to expand the inclusion of the disabled in general education classes.

School reform focuses on improving academic achievement rather than the diverse needs of students; special education inclusion strategies address the equity issue. This clash between these two objectives can derail the general direction of school reform because in traditional schools children who do not achieve in general education are "handed off" to specialists rather than remaining in the general education milieu (Skritic, 1991).

How can this fundamental assumption of the way the traditional school operates be refocused in a manner that accommodates both initiatives? Schools must adopt inclusionary practices that enable them to responsibly include students in general education according to the similarity of their educational needs rather than excluding them based on their dissimilarities.

The Degree of Inclusion

The acceptable degree of inclusion has been the source of much debate among scholars (Singer, 1988;

Fuchs and Fuchs, 1991; Kauffman, 1993; Stainback, Stainback, and East, 1994). Full inclusion as a special education strategy for equity promotes the total integration of special education students within the general education domain regardless of the severity of the disability.

According to Fuchs and Fuchs (1991), two distinct positions have emerged, which they define as abolitionists and conservationists. Abolitionists contend that the special education program should no longer be a separate entity and support services should be provided within the orbit of general education. Conservationists hold that such a move is too drastic, is unwarranted, and tends to emphasize the social integration of students above their other needs.

This polarization may be circumvented if the degree of inclusion is introduced in a responsible manner that reduces the apprehension of general educators while maintaining the integrity of the initiative. Responsible inclusion may be the best model for eliminating the debate because it addresses the individual needs of students within the context of permeable boundaries between general and special education.

What are the parameters of responsible inclusion? First, all students, not just special education students, benefit from most inclusionary practices. Second, the continuum of special education administrative arrangements, i.e., consultation, resource rooms, and self-contained classes provide immeasurable assistance with individualized strategies for integrating regular and special education.

The North Carolina Partnership Training System, a federally funded special education technical assistance project, convened a Principals Task Force to examine the concept of inclusionary practices more closely. This group was assigned the task of identifying responsible inclusionary practices that would be beneficial to all students throughout the elementary, middle level, and high school years. In addition, the group was to highlight the facilitators and barriers to responsible inclusion. Finally, the task force was responsible for developing a method for assessing school readiness for inclusionary practices.

Responsible Inclusionary Practices

Responsible inclusionary practices that might be explored include: block scheduling, collaborative teaching, cooperative learning, interdisciplinary planning, heterogeneous grouping, alternative assessments such as portfolios, active learning projects, and coaching techniques. These practices provide an ample array of techniques with which to explore responsible inclusionary initiatives.

Block scheduling eliminates the traditional six to seven-period day with each period being 45 minutes, a serious impediment to efforts to provide inclusive educational experiences for students in a responsible manner. Another shortcoming of the traditional schedules, Lee and Smith (1994) assert, is that it tends to separate the student body into high and low tracks, with the less-advantaged student overrepresented in the lower track.

A more flexible schedule offers teachers opportunities to embark upon interdisciplinary initiatives, explore collaborative teaching ventures, engage students in learner-centered action projects, and increase the variety of learning experiences needed for portfolio assessments.

Without an increase in time for planning and teaching, the effort to explore responsible inclusionary practices becomes more difficult but not impossible. Within the constraints of the traditional schedule, individual teachers still have many degrees of freedom within which to explore the use of coaching techniques, cooperative learning, alternative assessments, and seminar-style instruction.

The way the topic is introduced is the most important aspect of the exploration of responsible inclusionary practice. The emphasis must be on the need to identify methods of engaging in heterogeneous group instruction to meet the challenges presented by diversity. This approach sends a clear message that diversity is welcome and not used as a basis for sorting children.

The Principals Task Force recommends systematic methods of introducing inclusionary practices. The child study team and the multidisciplinary team are the processes used to provide special-

ized services to children. At the prereferral stage, the child study team is the vehicle for initiating responsible inclusionary practices for at-risk students and students with mild exceptionalities who are in transition from special education resource rooms.

Generally, students who are experiencing learning or adjustment problems are referred to the team for exploration of alternative educational strategies at the building level. A host of inclusionary practices could be offered to modify or restructure their educational programs. Exceptional students who are leaving special education also would be considered a part of this group.

At the referral stage, the multidisciplinary team would be the other vehicle for introducing inclusionary practices. Students identified as exceptional students should be the beneficiaries of these practices based on the degree of severity of their disabilities and general education needs.

Facilitators

To bring about inclusionary schools, Leonard Burello and Carl Lashley (1992) state:

The primary task of the leadership team in an inclusive school organization is to build a joint model for the school, a way of believing and seeing the patterns, relationships, and linkages between one another and their shared values and purposes. When leaders articulate this vision, they are inductively setting a direction for the school organization. The second key leadership role is building policy that supports a shared culture of inclusiveness. Developing teamwork is the third key leadership role necessary to develop an integrated delivery system. The final leadership task is encouraging a culture of critical inquiry which asks about the unequal access of children to the resources of society and encourages constant reflection about the practice of education (pp. 80–84).

Collaborative efforts between special education and general education personnel are particularly important in creating inclusionary schools, as are cooperative learning experiences for the students. The flexibility that is built into the IEP should be used to facilitate these primary inclusionary practices. Other enhancements to these central practices are reduced class size and increased seminar-style instruction. Additional financial resources would be beneficial but not imperative. A spirit of cooperation among classroom teachers who demonstrate a willingness to participate in organizational patterns that facilitate inclusionary practices, such as the middle school plan and its emphasis on teaming, will increase the potential for such plans to succeed.

Barriers

There are barriers that must be removed before inclusionary practices can become a reality. Schools' curricular and organizational designs must complement one another if the diverse needs of students are to be met. Student diversity is normal; unfortunately, a hierarchical organization often forces removal of those who do not fit the uniform operating procedures. There is no real incentive for change until the emphasis is placed on the school's changing to serve the student's needs rather than the student's changing to fit the school's organizational structure.

Teacher preparation has not emphasized the need for educators to be more adept at addressing the needs displayed by heterogeneously grouped classes. Other

barriers to implementing inclusionary practices may be funding and the expectation that each student must be seen every day by the special education teacher.

Assessing School Readiness

When is a school ready to engage in dialogue related to responsible inclusion? The culture of each school is different, thereby negating the development of a systematic procedure for determining a certain stage of readiness to explore the inclusion initiative. With this thought in mind, the task force developed a set of questions that each school should address before embarking upon a school-wide adaptation of selected responsible inclusionary practices, practices that go beyond superficial efforts that eventually die for lack of faculty support. Responses to these questions will assist the school in deciding to what degree should responsible inclusion be developed. This process of inquiry is extremely important because it also facilitates greater ownership in the adoption process.

A method of assessing school readiness for consideration of inclusionary practices should rely on expectations of and support from site-based management teams and local boards of education. Questions to be raised include:

1. What are the beliefs about collaboration between general and special education?

2. Is there a need to change beliefs? Why or why not?

3. What is inclusion?

4. Do the classroom teachers have appropriate planning time?

5. Is the typical teacher-student ratio in the school low enough to support inclusion?

6. What inclusionary practices should the school adopt?

7. Are the teachers trained in providing appropriate modifications and accommodations?

8. How will the effectiveness of the practices be evaluated?

Conclusion

The initiation of responsible inclusion strategies will provide an inclusive school atmosphere that welcomes and celebrates diversity. This initiative, while beneficial for all students, will require some extensive paradigm shifts for administrators and teachers or the transformation from a traditional to an inclusive school will only involve cosmetic changes.

The focus is on improving statistical reports related to the number of students who are minority, poor, language different, and/or disabled that remain in general education that are driven by the standard operating procedures. These procedures, such as uniform curriculum, standardized testing, and traditional 10-minute learning periods, will require drastic changes, changes in the educational program that benefit children. If these changes are to truly benefit our students, they will focus on the education program rather than identifying youngsters who do not fit within the parameters of this program.

References

Burello, L., and Lashley, C. "On Organizing for the Future: The Destiny of Special Education." In *Special Education: The Challenge of the Future*, edited by K. Waldron, A.

Riestel, and J. Moore. San Francisco, Calif.: EM Text, 1992.

Fuchs, D., and Fuchs, L. S. "Framing the REI Debate: Abolitionists Versus Conservationists." In *The Regular Education Initiative: Alternative Perspectives on Concepts, Issues, and Models,* edited by J. W. Lloyd, N. N. Singh, and A. C. Repp. Sycamore, Ill.: Sycamore, 1991.

Kauffman, J. M. "How We Might Achieve the Radical Reform of Special Education." *Exceptional Children* #1 (1993): 6–16.

Lee, V., and Smith, I. "High School Restructuring and Student Achievement." *Issues in Restructuring School,* Fall 1994.

Singer, J. D. "Should Special Education Merge with Regular Education?" *Educational Policy* 2(1988): 409–24.

Skritic, T. "Students with Special Educational Needs: Artifacts of the Traditional Curriculum." In *Effective Schools for All,* edited by M. Ainscow. London, England: Fulton Publishing, 1991.

Stainback, S., Stainback, W., and East, K. "A Commentary on Inclusion and the Development of a Positive Self-Identity by People with Disabilities." *Exceptional Children* 6(1994): 486–90.

Winfield, G., and Woodard, M. "Where Are Equity and Diversity in Bush's Proposal 2000?" *Education Week,* January 31, 1992.

 Article Review Form at end of book.

Teachers should engage in what kinds of collaboration activities to assist special education students? What kinds of activities should a teacher consider in order to prepare for success in an inclusive classroom?

Inclusion
12 secrets to make it work in your classroom

Mary Pearce

Mary Pearce, a former teacher, is an educational writer and editor based in New York City.

Some of the new faces you see in your classroom this fall may belong to students with special needs. The law mandates that special-education students be schooled in the least restrictive environment, so more of them are being included full time in regular classrooms. How do you manage to meet their needs along with those of the rest of your students'? We visited 13 schools where inclusion is a reality. Here's what teachers in those schools suggest.

Set Up for Success

1. Develop Classroom Rules

Clear rules with consistent consequences are crucial. Marsha Kessler, head of the Churchill Center for Learning Disabled Children in New York City, advises, "Keep it simple. Respecting others and keeping safe are global rules."

Kim Meininger at Gardner Elementary in Gardner, Kansas, helps her third graders brainstorm what following each rule would look and sound like, then posts a chart (see below*) so kids can monitor themselves.

2. Focus on Structure

Students with special needs should know exactly what classroom routine to expect—and what is expected of them. Mary Ellen Burke, director of special education in District 45, Villa Park, Illinois, looks for ways to convey that information visually. For example, she suggests giving kids a photo or diagram of a neat desk to make it clear what neat means.

3. Teach Students How to Learn

By explicitly teaching study skills such as skimming subheads, you can help special-ed kids unlock the secrets of classroom success. Mary Ellen suggests taping directions for important study procedures ("Before turning in a paper, check the following . . .") to students'.

*Not included in this publications.

Collaborate!

4. Work with Specialists to Adapt Your Curriculum

A big concern teachers have in taking on an inclusive classroom is how to adapt their curriculum. At Barrington Elementary, in upper Arlington, Ohio, the learning-disabilities teacher helps grades 3/4 teacher Betsy O'Brochta by doing a task analysis of each classroom activity. Together, they list the steps kids have to follow—then, with a particular child in mind, they star the steps they'll have to adapt. For example, if a child has trouble with the physical act of writing, Betsy can plan to have him or her give dictation or use the tape recorder.

In the beginning of the year, K–2 learning support teacher Donna Nebistinsky meets with each regular teacher in Northern Elementary in Dillsburg, Pennsylvania. They go through the curriculum to identify what Donna will concentrate on with the special-needs kids. Then she plans her activities to what the class is doing; for example, if the class is learning to tell time to within five minutes, her students might work on telling time to the hour.

5. Use Special-ed Teachers to Help All Your Students

In most inclusive schools, special-ed teachers work with kids in the regular classroom. While having another teacher in your room may take some getting used to, Kim Meininger points out, "you can get twice the work done."

Kay Williams works with regular teachers to plan activities that they couldn't do alone. In a third-grade class, for example, she and the classroom teacher created a unit that required each student to write and illustrate a "baby book" for an animal. Kay was there to help all the kids—not just the ones with special needs.

When Linda Goode, a special-ed teacher at Stanford Elementary in Las Vegas, Nevada, visits a class for reading, the group she works with usually includes one or two learning-disabled (LD) kids and three or four "gray-area kids," regular students who are struggling but don't qualify for special services. The LD kids get the help they need without being made to feel different—and the gray-area kids get extra help, too.

6. Ask for Help!

Donna Nebistinsky advises, "When you have a kid who is driving you nuts, don't be afraid to ask the special-ed teacher for help." The specialist may offer to work with the child in or out of the classroom or just be a sounding board for your frustrations.

Get the Whole Class Involved

7. Tell Students What to Expect from Their Inclusive Classroom

"Kids know other kids are different," says Betsy O'Brochta. She talks to her students about special needs, explaining that some kids' disabilities require them to need to use tape recorders or to draw instead of write—and that all students may be able to use these options when possible.

At the Janet Berry School in Appleton, Wisconsin, special-ed teachers Jane Zwickey and Diane Zwierz say that when a special student enrolls, they talk with the class about the student's needs and goals. So if a goal is to walk independently, classmates will know not to take the student by the arm; instead, they'll offer emotional support. "That way everybody is working to help," Jane says.

8. Use Cooperative Learning, Peer Tutoring, and Other Group Work

All the teachers we talked to stressed the value of grouping to meet students' needs.

Kim Meininger says cooperative learning is key to making her class work. She offers the following tips:

- Start with simple cooperative-learning techniques. For example, in a basic pairs structure, one child reads a math problem to a partner.

Once they agree on the answer, the other child writes it down.

- Help children use their strengths. Let a poor handwriter draw the answer to a problem.

- Make each child accountable for assignments and have children practice handling a situation in which one partner isn't working.

Linda Goode trains peer tutors in her class. After they practice with each other, she matches tutors with kids who need help.

Donna Nebistinsky established "study buddies" for special-needs kids. She provides an activity box with flash cards, folder games, and so on.

9. Help Kids Develop Friendships

Many teachers find that connecting special and regular kids helps inclusion run more smoothly.

On the playground, Betsy O'Brochta helps her special students find ways to play—for example, a kid with cerebral palsy could hold the jump rope. "The others see that this child has to work hard, and they respect that," she says.

Putting special ed children in groups with others helps at Kay Williams's school. She recalled one emotionally disturbed fifth-grade boy who was grouped with "two very nice girls. If the boy did something inappropriate, they told him, 'That's not what we do in fifth grade.' Soon, peer acceptance became very important to him, and his behavior improved."

When Problems Flare Up in Class

10. When a Child is Disruptive, Look for Patterns

As Mary Ellen Burke points out, "Kids who act out are communicating. It's up to you to figure out what they're saying." Marsha Kessler suggests you ask yourself the following questions about a flare-up: At what time of day did the incident happen? What was going on around the child? What was I doing before and during?

"Once you figure out why a behavior is happening," says Marsha, "then you can head it off before it happens again."

11. Make Use of "Time-out"

Many teachers have a place where disruptive kids can go for time-out. For Kristina Mowles, a fourth-grade teacher in North Sacramento, California, this is a nook in her classroom where she can conference privately. Kim Meininger has a buddy teacher who takes time-out kids into her classroom until they're ready to return.

12. Know When to Change Course

Flexibility is key. Gretchen Goodman, an instructional support teacher at the Derry Township School in Hershey, Pennsylvania, had a child who just wouldn't stay in his chair—so she changed the rule to require that one part of his body had to touch the chair.

When a child is having a problem in Donna Nebistinsky's school, the instructional support team brainstorms strategies and the teacher selects three to implement.

But when no strategy seems to work, it may be time to reevaluate the child's placement. Kim Meininger recalls one LD boy who was fully included in her classroom. Gradually Kim saw that the child couldn't handle the demands of the regular classroom. All involved, including the boy's mother, agreed that a partial day pullout would be a better approach.

"We did not consider this a failure," Kim says. "To be successful in meeting the needs of students, you must consider each case individually. It relieves some of the stress about inclusion if you know that if it is truly not working, each case can be reconsidered."

Books/Digests

Adapting Curriculum and Instruction in Inclusive Classrooms: A Teachers' Desk Reference, Institute for the Study of Developmental Disabilities, 2853 E. 10th St., Bloomington, IN 47408-2601; (812) 855-6508

Creating Schools for All Our Students: What 12 Schools Have to Say (publication #P5064), Council for Exceptional Children, Dept. K50170, 1920 Association Dr., Reston, VA 20191; (800) CEC-READ

Children with Exceptional Needs in Regular Classrooms (ED 341 213) by Libby G. Cohen and Strategies for Full Inclusion (ED 338 638) by Jennifer York are available in libraries that have ERIC microfiche collections. Call ACCESS ERIC at (800) 538-3742 for the collection nearest you, or order from the ERIC Document Reproduction Service at (800) 443-ERIC

Educational Care: A System for Understanding and Helping Children with Learning Problems at Home and in School by Dr. Mel Levine and Educational Prescriptions for the Classroom for Students with Learning Problems by Lynn Meltzer and Bethany Solomon, Educators Publishing Service, 31 Smith Place, Cambridge, MA 02138; (800) 225-5750

Inclusive Classrooms from A to Z and I Can Learn! Strategies and Activities for Gray-Area Children by Gretchen Goodman, Crystal Springs Books, 10 Sharon Rd., P.O. Box 500, Peterborough, NH 03458-0500; (800) 321-0401

Integrating Students with Special Needs: Policies and Practices that Work, National Education Association, NEA Professional Library, P.O. Box 509, West Haven, CT 06516; (800) 229-4200

Taming the Dragons: Real Help for Real School Problems by Susan Setley, Starfish Publishing Company, 5621 Delmar Blvd., Suite 110, St. Louis, MO 63112-2660; (314) 367-9611

Teaching Kids with Learning Difficulties in the Regular Classroom by Susan Winebrenner, Free Spirit Publishing, 400 1st Avenue North, Suite 616, Minneapolis, MN 55401; (800) 735-7323

"Including Students with Disabilities in General Education Classrooms" (ERIC Digest #E521), ERIC Clearinghouse on Disabilities and Gifted Education, 1920 Association Dr., Reston, VA 20191; (800) 328-0272 or e-mail:erice@ inet.ed.gov

"Winners All: A Call for Inclusive Schools," the Report of the National Association of State Boards of Education (NASBE) Study Group on Special Education, NASBE, 1012 Cameron St., Alexandria, VA 22314; (703) 684-4000

Organizations

The Churchill Center: curriculum materials for use in teaching students with learning disabilities. Contact Marsha Kessler, Churchill Center, 22 E. 95th St., New York, NY 10128; (212) 722-7226.

Council for Exceptional Children (CEC): comprehensive information and publications on students with disabilities; access to the ERIC Clearinghouse on Disabilities and Gifted Education, CEC's own database, and the National Clearinghouse for Professions in Special Education; national and local conferences. Write CEC, 1920 Association Dr., Reston, VA 20191; (800) 641-7824.

The National Center on Educational Restructuring and Inclusion (NCERI): information and training in inclusion; network of inclusion districts. Write the NCERI, City University of New York, 33 W. 42nd St., New York, NY 10036; (212) 642-2656.

Online Resources

Focus on Education is an on-line chat moderated by Louise Elkind every Thursday at 11 P.M. ET in the CNN open studio area on America Online. Keyword: CNN; then click on the icon: live chats in the lower right hand corner; then click on open studio.

Special Education Through Technology, Media, and Materials (http://www.edu.org/FSC/NCIP/), developed and maintained by the National Center to Improve Practice (NCIP), integrates resources on technology as it relates to students with disabilities, and includes eight discussion forums.

Article Review
Form at end of book.

What are some of the reasons for lack of interaction between regular and special education teachers? What are some of the modifications recommended to improve learning for all students in an inclusive classroom?

A Change in Focus

Teaching diverse learners within an inclusive elementary school classroom

Mary C. McMackin and Elaine M. Bukowiecki

Mary C. McMackin and Elaine M. Bukowiecki are both Assistant Professors in the School of Education at Lesley College, Cambridge, Massachusetts.

Elementary school teachers today are confronted with the challenge of educating an increasingly diverse population of children within their classrooms. A report from the National Center for Education Statistics (1993) stated that African Americans, Latinos, Amerindians, and Asians made up more than 30 percent of the total public school enrollment in the nation. Furthermore, 33 of the largest school districts had an enrollment of over 50 percent ethnic- and language-minority students. Additionally, many school districts are now implementing full or partial inclusion models in which students with various disabilities (physical, visual, emotional, cognitive, speech/language, and learning) are being included in general

education settings. According to the National Center for Education Statistics (1993), at least 11 percent of school age children, or approximately 4.9 million students, are classified as disabled.

The National Joint Committee on Learning Disabilities (1993) reported that "more than 90 percent of students with learning disabilities are [currently] taught in regular education classrooms for some part of their school day" (p. 330). Thus, classroom teachers are now working with students with special needs who would have previously received instruction in a resource room or in an alternative setting. This placement of more and more students with diverse needs into general education classroom settings has raised questions for administrators and teachers as to the optimal instructional methods and materials to use with these students. The Joint Committee on Teacher Planning for Students with Disabilities (1995) recently stated that, "While

teachers report having a great deal of confidence in their planning for general education students, they note that they do not have the necessary competencies to plan for and teach students with disabilities" (p. 42).

As instructors in a multi-sectioned, graduate level language arts course at Lesley College School of Education, Cambridge, Massachusetts, we became increasingly aware of the diverse student needs that elementary school classroom teachers are confronted with today. The K–12 practitioners we worked with taught children who were homeless, children of alcoholics and substance abusers, children from foster homes, children with a wide range of physical, emotional, and social concerns, and children who spoke little or no English. For example, in one upper elementary class of 22 students, there were seven students with Individual Education Plans (IEPs), including one who found it difficult because of physical limitations to interact socially and who often perseverated. Another student, a non-reader, had yet to master basic letter/sound relationships, while other students were reading two or three years above grade level. Over 30 different languages were spoken in this school. In this particular classroom, Icelandic, Vietnamese, and Hindu languages were spoken alongside more frequently heard Portuguese, Spanish, Haitian Creole, and English. This teacher's greatest challenge was meeting the needs of two new students who spoke no English and for whom no bilingual program was available.

The following exchange illustrates this point. While interviewing the principal of the Harry L. Johnson Elementary School, Salisbury and colleagues (1994) asked about student enrollment. The principal replied that there were 650 students in grades K through 4. When asked how many children with special needs were serviced in this same school, the principal replied, "650" (p. 311*). This principal further explained that some of the students were homeless, some witnessed violence in the home, and others spent many of their waking hours with babysitters while parents worked the late shifts. With all this information in mind, we knew that we had to redesign and revise our literacy course in order to better prepare our students for the many challenges they will face as new teachers or are currently facing as in-service professionals.

We initiated this course revision as a result of over two years of informal data collection, based on our own observations in various elementary school classrooms; conversations with teachers and administrators working in school

*Not included in this publication

systems throughout Massachusetts; comments from our students, both stated in class discussions and written on course evaluations; and interactions with colleagues who teach special education courses at Lesley College. From these sources, the point was clearly made that teachers today need to be thoroughly prepared to teach the diverse learners found in current elementary school classrooms. Although we hesitate to over generalize about the preparedness of educators to effectively plan for and teach students with diverse needs, it appears from our observations that there is a growing desire by many teachers and administrators to find ways to modify curriculum, instruction, and assessment to meet these and other challenges.

In this article, we define *diversity* to include students with special needs, second language learners, and learners who come from cultures outside the dominant culture of the schools. We will discuss the changes we made in our graduate level literacy course in order to prepare all teachers, novice and veteran, for the wider diversity of learners found in today's elementary school classrooms. We will share impressions of inclusive classes from the perspective of general education and special education teachers. Finally, we will recommend specific classroom modifications which may hold promise for improving instructional practices. It has been our intent to explore avenues that will increase our own awareness of issues surrounding equity for all learners in today's heterogeneous classrooms and to raise the awareness of our students who will be meeting the challenges and rewards of working directly with children of diverse learning styles and needs.

Our Changing Focus

To help prepare preservice and in-service teachers for the demands of diverse elementary school classrooms, we made the following changes to course EEDUC 5121, *Literacy: The Integration of the Language Arts.* First, we refocused our course objectives to include class lectures, activities, and course projects which would increase our students' awareness of the diversity found in today's heterogeneous classrooms. Second, we expanded our own knowledge-base through literature on second language learners, strategies for teaching students with learning and behavior difficulties, and curriculum considerations for the range of needs (learning, behavioral, physical, cultural, and linguistic) found in today's general education elementary classrooms. We incorporated this new information into our class lectures and included these text titles in our course syllabi. Third, we instructed our students to read several additional articles and texts that provide information about including students with special needs in whole language and literature-based learning environments (see Appendix*). Fourth, in our class lectures we directly discussed and presented various modifications for teaching diverse students. In turn, our students included modifications for student diversity in the various lesson plans they wrote throughout the course; and for the final course project they created a literature-based learning sequence.

Finally, we added three elementary school classroom observations to our course assignments. Each graduate student visited an inclusive elementary school classroom and interviewed both the general education and the special education teachers regarding the work each was doing. Then, each graduate student visited another elementary school classroom to observe a language arts lesson and to focus on a child about whom the classroom teacher had a concern. Following these observations and interviews, each graduate student presented a case study of the observed pupil to our literacy class. Finally, each graduate student was asked to visit an urban or suburban school to evaluate how cultural pluralism was being fostered (or in some cases, could have been fostered).

From these school visits, the 50 graduate students who participated in the first semester of this revised course gained valuable information concerning the diversity of learners found in general education classrooms. In turn, our graduate students informed us about their various impressions of the 50 inclusive elementary school classrooms they visited in Eastern Massachusetts. Through the interviews that our graduate students conducted with these teams of inclusive teachers, we were able to appreciate the myriad models that exist under the rubric of inclusion, discern some of the needs and concerns of general education classroom teachers who work in inclusive classes, and better understand our role as college faculty in preparing our students to be effective teachers.

These strategies for increased understanding all call out for further research and deeper knowledge. This article only presents a narrative of a change process—for us and for our students—in which we sought to address immediate realities and needs for effective literacy instruction in inclusive elementary classrooms.

Field-Based Impressions of Inclusion

The results of our students' field-based observations appear to indicate that inclusion models often span a wide spectrum. For example, one graduate student visited a classroom where "inclusion" was defined as two teachers co-teaching throughout the entire day. Each teacher worked with all children, but the special education teacher monitored the lower-achieving students more closely. The teachers planned together every day for forty-five minutes and had a four-hour planning block each week. They jointly accepted responsibility for providing instructional and assessment practices that focused on dignity and equity for all learners. At the other extreme was a classroom where "inclusion" referred to a pull out program within the regular classroom. The special education teacher worked specifically with the lower-achieving students at a table at the back of the classroom while the classroom teacher worked with the other students. The teachers spent about one hour each week planning lessons together.

In many cases, classroom teachers reported that, although there may be several students in their classes who have IEPs, the special needs teacher is able to provide support for only a few minutes each day. For example: "The SPED teacher generally spends her day visiting various grades and classrooms for one hour at a time." "Currently there is one aide in the classroom for two periods of the day and only one full time specialist for the 250 sixth grade students." In these and similar classrooms, the re-

sponsibility to modify the curricula for students is left to the general education classroom teacher for the majority of each day.

Unfortunately, there is often very little interaction between the general education classroom teacher and the special needs teacher. One reason for this may be a lack of common planning time. Another reason for this lack of interaction may be the classroom role that each teacher assumes. The roles of the teachers in the team may not be clearly defined, or there may be conflicts regarding these roles. In many instances, the special needs teacher in the inclusive model works solely with students who have IEPs, and thus is relegated to a role similar to an assistant teacher for the general education classroom teacher. For example, our students reported that:

- "The classroom teacher instructed the class, while the SPED teacher quietly instructed the SPED students. If the teachers had discussed the lesson, the SPED teacher could have modified the lesson by pre-cutting some of the shapes."

- "T. C. [the special needs teacher] works in one corner of the room with her group, while Mrs. C.[the classroom teacher] works with the other children."

Unfortunately, regardless of the reasons for these situations (lack of personnel, budget constraints, inadequate staff development, etc.), it seems that issues of equal access to educational opportunities for children continue to plague our educational system.

Adapting a Language Arts Curriculum

Our students reported that, while many general education teachers are very interested in meeting the diverse needs of students, they are unsure of how to make appropriate modifications. Gaps sometimes exist between the social, educational, and cultural experiences of teachers and those of their students. We continue to meet with teachers in both urban and suburban schools who are anxious about working with students from diverse backgrounds. Many are not sure how to bridge these gaps. It appears that without planning time, general education teachers are often left on their own to design and implement modifications to meet the needs of all learners. As part of our course assignments, we asked students to list modifications that they observed during their field visits to the schools.

For some starting points and models, we provided our students with modifications suggested by Choate (1993); Lombana (1992); McShane & Jones (1990); Tompkins & Hoskisson (1995); and Salisbury, et al. (1994). The list in Figure 1 represents a compilation of modifications provided by our students and derived from the literature cited above. Although these suggestions may enhance the specific learning needs of individual students within a class, they also represent effective teaching practices from which all students in a single classroom could benefit.

Adapting curriculum and instruction to meet the needs of all students is a formidable task. Yet, many of the activities that are commonly found in elementary school classrooms can easily be modified to meet a wider range of abilities, learning styles, and spe-

cial needs. Figure 1 lists some general classroom modifications that can be used to shape the curriculum to better meet the needs of students with various learning differences. We realize this is a broad list which may need to be modified further to meet specific students' special needs. To illustrate this point, we will describe specific modifications for the practice of story retelling, which is often used in elementary classrooms to recall and understand specific story elements (setting, characters, problem, events, and resolution). As an oral or written exercise to focus awareness on the structure of narrative, story retelling can be a very effective strategy to enhance comprehension. Story retelling strategies can provide students with a framework for recognizing key points of narrative texts. These strategies combine well with story maps to provide the students with a visual guide to understanding and retelling stories.

Suppose, however, that you have a particular fifth grade student whose learning differences are impeding her literal and inferential comprehension success. This learning difference may be a result of a difficulty with language processing, limited vocabulary knowledge, or gaps in skill application. For this child, additional modifications to oral or written story retellings may be appropriate. For example, Idol (cited in Bos & Vaughn, 1994) described a Model-Lead-Text Approach when teaching story mapping to intermediate grade students with learning disabilities. In the *model* phase, the instructor reads the text aloud, stops at specific points where various story grammar elements are presented, and demonstrates to the students how to write this information onto a story

map. The students in turn write this information on their own maps. During the *lead* phase, the students read the story independently and complete their own maps, with teacher prompting where necessary. Finally, during the *text* phase, the students read a story, generate a story map and then answer teacher-directed questions such as: "Who were the characters? Where did the story take place? What was the main character trying to accomplish?" (p. 189). This teacher-directed story mapping procedure, as described by Idol, should help guide a learning disabled student to recall specific elements of a story and thus aid that student in comprehending the text.

A second example of how story retelling may be modified is illustrated through the work of Bos (cited in Bos & Vaughn, 1994), who developed a specific story retelling strategy to recall specific elements of a story. Bos' procedure fits in well with Idol's guided story mapping technique. To begin Bos' retelling strategy, the teacher motivates the students by demonstrating for them how this strategy will help them remember what they have just read. Second, the instructor explains the components of any story and describes how to employ the "SPOT the Story" technique (p. 190*):

Setting—Who, What, Where, When

Problem—What is the problem to be solved?

Order—What happened to solve the problem? (correct/logical order)

Tail End—What happened in the end?

Third, the teacher models the procedure by orally reading the story,

*Not included in this publication

Figure I

General Education Classroom Modifications

Modifications: The Context for Learning

____ Be alert for signs of fatigue.

____ Create a non-distracting learning environment (e.g., limit the amount of visual displays around the room).

____ Allow preferential seating.

____ Provide clear transitions.

____ Post daily agenda on board.

____ Offer clear explanation of what is changing and what will stay the same.

____ Use cooperative learning groups, paired reading, and small groups.

____ Model effective collaboration (e.g., reader and recorder).

____ Make available special stands, clip boards, line tracker devices.

____ Send home duplicate set of books to eliminate carrying between home/school.

____ Keep the activity the same for all students but substitute more appropriate objectives and materials for students with special needs.

____ Provide additional time for student to process language.

Modifications: Instructional Strategies/Instructional Materials

____ Establish clear goals.

____ Limit the number of steps in process.

____ Allow students to respond orally to questions.

____ Have less accomplished student begin the process and more accomplished student take over when less accomplished needs help (saying a.b.c.'s, etc.).

____ Plan a variety of multisensory lessons/activities to teach/reinforce the same concept.

____ Allow the child to dictate ideas.

____ Model clear, uncomplicated directions, procedures, and processes.

____ Continuously review new information, using visual props when possible.

____ Provide clear, uncluttered copies of worksheets and materials.

____ Modify amount of in-class and homework assignments.

____ Encourage the use of the computer with large keyboards to record ideas and to check spelling and grammar.

____ Provide tape recordings of literature and content area texts.

____ Use overhead projectors to enlarge images that may be too small on a chalkboard.

____ Allow opportunities to participate in role-playing, drama, sing-alongs, games, formal and informal discussion groups.

____ Engage students in story retelling as a technique to foster comprehension.

____ Provide specific, positive, immediate feedback on process and product.

____ Directly teach purposes and uses of strategies for each task.

____ Arrange for one-to-one assistance with motor tasks such as cutting, pasting, and coloring.

____ Create open-ended lessons to encourage children to work at their own levels.

____ Use pictures to teach new words and concepts.

____ Focus on student's individual strengths.

____ Plan lessons that involve Gardner's 7 Intelligences: Linguistic, Logical, Interpersonal, Intrapersonal, Kinesthetic, Musical, Spatial.

____ Provide individual replicas of charts, maps, etc.

____ Use tape recorder for students to respond.

____ Stand behind the student with special needs when giving directions so that you can point to the student's work while explaining the assignment to the other students.

Continued on next page

Figure I *Continued*

Modifications: Organizational and Study Skills

____ Adapt length of work and time on task.

____ Limit choices.

____ Prepare discussion questions and give them to students ahead of time.

____ Have texts available on tape or video.

____ Use paired reading and writing.

____ Increase the use of graphic organizers or semantic maps.

____ Hang visual aids on the walls.

____ Use colored highlighters to emphasize important information.

____ Give more time to complete assignments.

____ Provide envelopes to organize information and papers (may attach to side of desk for younger students).

____ Have students stop at designated checkpoints for peer or teacher feedback.

____ Tape checklist of student's behavioral or organizational goals to student's desk.

____ Have papers with headings and margins prepared ahead of time.

____ Introduce students to reading guides, marginal glossing, word banks.

____ Use contracts.

---

labeling each component as the story is read, and retelling the story with the "SPOT the Story" chart as a guide. Fourth, the teacher and students practice this procedure as they read and retell several stories together. Finally, the students independently read stories and retell them using the "SPOT the Story" technique.

Both Idol and Bos have discovered through their research that, with teacher modeling and guidance of a story mapping and retelling procedure, "students were able to recall substantially more relevant information and were able to answer more implicit and implicit comprehension questions about the stories" (p. 191). Both of these strategies represent appropriate modifications to a more traditional retelling procedure where students would simply recall the story orally or in writing.

Salisbury et al. (1994) offers the following general suggestions for teachers to consider when planning learning opportunities for their classrooms:

1. Students need not all be working on the same activity at the same time.

2. It is appropriate and necessary to vary the type and degree of involvement in activities.

3. Curriculum and tasks should be adjusted to meet the needs of the learner, not the reverse.

Fortunately, designing activities for students with diverse needs does not necessarily require major revisions to the existing curriculum. Through the general examples provided in Figure 2, we illustrate how many tasks that are prepared for the entire class can easily be modified in specific ways so that all students can participate, be successful, and be respected. However, sometimes in specific cases, these modifications must be more finely adjusted. As a final caveat, it is important to mention that, because many of the characteristics of second language learners may resemble those of students with special needs (e.g.,

difficulties in processing language), one must carefully discern whether or not these characteristics are indigenous to the newly acquired language or are inherent in both the student's primary language and second language. If students are having no learning difficulties within their primary language, the problems they are experiencing may be indicative of weak skills in the acquisition of a second language, and not indicative of a learning disability as such. In either case, however, classroom teachers may be left with questions that focus on ways to improve educational opportunities for second language learners, students with special learning needs, and second language learners who may have special learning needs.

With careful planning and thoughtful reflection, teachers can provide successful learning experiences for all learners, making classrooms more rewarding for all students (and teachers).

Figure 2

Representative Inclusion Language Arts Activities	Suggested Modifications for Classrooms
READING **Buddy Reading** Two students take turns reading portions of a text to each other.	• Have text on tape and have less accomplished reader play taped section during his/her buddy reading section, using a shared reading approach. • Preview the text with the less accomplished reader ahead of buddy reading. • Have text on tape for student to listen to before engaging in buddy reading (in class or at home). • Highlight the section(s) that the less accomplished reader will read. Make selections based on student's ability.
Readers' Theater Students read lines of a script aloud. Students may write own script or read prepared script.	• Highlight the sections that the less accomplished reader will read. • Give less accomplished readers vital roles that require less reading.
Expository Reading Students read content area texts and other informational print materials.	• Provide advanced organizers and other graph organizers. • Leave plenty of white space on handouts. • Highlight important vocabulary, key points, major concepts. • Encourage frequent summarization and other comprehension monitoring strategies. • Teach strategies for remembering (mnemonic devices, charts). • Encourage use of computers. • Have study buddies and peer note takers.
WRITING **Word Wall** A wall is sectioned off with one block for each letter of the alphabet. Interesting and important words are listed on the word wall.	• For visually impaired students or students who have difficulty tracking, have individual word walls taped to desks. • Add pictures to aid recall of definition. • Color code important words.
Journals Individual notebooks for recording own thoughts and reactions.	• Have students dictate their ideas for another student or adult to record. • Have students use a word processor instead of a notebook. • Have students use a computer with a voice synthesizer. • Have students draw a picture to convey thoughts. • Provide extended time.
Writer's Workshop Status-of-the-Class; Mini-lesson; Writing; Group Share.	• Keep structure of the workshop consistent (e.g., always write immediately after lunch; always begin with Status-of-the-Class).
LISTENING **Directed Listening-Thinking Approach** Story is broken into sections. For each section, students predict, listen, and reflect on the accuracy of the prediction.	• Give students a specific purpose for listening. • Think aloud the process you use as you predict, listen, and reflect on the accuracy of your prediction. • Start with small selections and easily predictable texts. *Continued on next page*

Figure 2 *Continued*

Meaningful Listening

Three classifications:
Aesthetic Listening (pleasure)
Efferent Listening (take away information)
Critical Listening (interpretations, judgments,
evaluation).

- Use visual aids (e.g., homework written on blackboard, diagrams, etc.) to supplement listening.
- Have student sit with a peer partner.
- Establish peer support system (e.g., note taker).
- Activate prior knowledge before beginning the activity (e.g., brainstorm, semantic webs).
- Provide direct instruction for word, sentence, paragraph levels of understanding.

SPEAKING
Show and Tell

Students bring items from home to present
to peers.

- Allow students to talk in small comfortable group settings.
- Use of a computer with a speech synthesizer to express and receive speech.

"Grand Conversations"

Oral exchange of ideas, information.

- Demonstrate how several short sentences can be combined into one longer sentence.
- Have students include who, what, where, when, why information into conversations.
- Use pictures to stimulate oral language.
- Focus on the content of the message and ignore speech problems.

Conclusion

The preparation that many of us received in our early childhood or elementary teacher certificate programs may not have adequately prepared us for our changing roles in today's classrooms. Cultural, social, and economic gaps may exist between classroom teachers and their students. Changes in both demographics and instructional practices have transformed the roles and responsibilities of educators. Teacher preparation programs and inservice staff development initiatives can no longer afford to overlook these changes. By increasing our awareness and modifying our curriculum, instruction, and assessment for students with varying needs, we can help ensure that all students will be provided with equitable educational opportunities and will find success in an environment that promotes diversity.

References

Bos, C. S., & Vaughn, S. (1994). *Strategies for teaching students with learning and behavior problems.* Boston: Allyn and Bacon.

Choate, J. S. (1993). *Successful mainstreaming: Proven ways to detect and correct special needs.* Boston: Allyn and Bacon.

Joint Committee on Teacher Planning for Students with Disabilities. (1995). *Planning for academic diversity in America's classroom: Windows on reality, research, change and practice.* Lawrence: University of Kansas Center for Research on Learning.

Lombana, J. H. (1992). *Guidance for students with disabilities* (2nd ed.). Springfield, IL: Charles C. Thomas, Publishers.

McShane, E. A., & Jones, E. L. (1990). Modifying the environment for children with poor listening skills. *Academic Therapy, 25*(4), 439–446.

National Center for Education Statistics. (1993). *The condition of education.* Washington, DC: U.S. Department of Education, Office of Educational Research and Improvement.

National Joint Committee on Learning Disabilities. (1993). Providing appropriate education for students with learning disabilities in regular classrooms. *Journal of Learning Disabilities, 26,* 330–332.

Salisbury, C. L., Mangino, M. Petrigala, M., Rainforth, B., Syryca, S., & Palombaro, M. M. (1994). Innovative practices: Promoting the instructional inclusion of young children with disabilities in the primary grades. *Journal of Early Intervention, 18*(3), 311–322.

Tompkins, G. E., & Hoskisson, K. (1995). *Language arts: Content and teaching strategies.* Englewood Cliffs, NJ: Prentice-Hall, Inc.

Appendix: References Used by Students and Instructors in *EEDUC 5121, Literacy: The Integration of the Language Arts*

Block, C. C., & Zinke, J. (1995). *Creating a culturally enriched curriculum for grades K–6.* Boston: Allyn and Bacon.

Bos, C. S., & Vaughn, S. (1994). *Strategies for teaching students with learning and behavior problems.* Boston: Allyn and Bacon.

Choate, J. S. (1993). *Successful mainstreaming: Proven ways to detect and correct special needs.* Boston: Allyn and Bacon.

Crawford, L. W. (1993). *Language and literacy learning in multicultural classrooms.* Boston: Allyn and Bacon.

D'Alessandro, M. (1990). Accommodating emotionally handicapped children through a literature-based reading program. *The Reading Teacher, 44*(4), 288–293.

Freeman, Y. S., & Freeman, D. E. (1992). *Whole language for second language learners.* Portsmouth, NH: Heinemann.

Hardman, M. L., Drew, C. J., & Egan, M. W. (1996). *Human exceptionality: Society, school and family* (5th ed.). Boston: Allyn and Bacon.

Hill, L. B., & Hale, M. G. (1991). Reading recovery: Questions classroom teachers ask. *The Reading Teacher, 44*(7), 480–483.

Nieto, S. (1992). *Affirming diversity.* New York: Longman.

Paratore, J. R., Brisk, M., Fountas, I., Homza, A., Jenkins, C., Lin, Y., Quellette, J., & Pho, L. (1995). *Teaching literacy to bilingual children: Effective practices for use by monolingual and bilingual teachers.* Boston: Massachusetts Reading Association Primer.

Pinnell, G. S., Fried, M. S., & Estice, R. M. (1990). Reading recovery: Learning how to make a difference. *The Reading Teacher, 43*(4), 282–295.

Piper, T. (1993). *And then there were two: Children and second language learning.* Markham, Ontario: Pippen Publishing, Limited.

Roser, N. L., Hoffman, J. V., & Farest, C. (1990). Language, literature, and at-risk children. *The Reading Teacher, 43*(8), 554–559.

Scala, M. A. (1993). What whole language in the mainstream means for children with learning disabilities. *The Reading Teacher, 47*(3), 222–229.

Stainback, S., & Stainback, W. (1992). *Curriculum considerations in inclusive classrooms.* Baltimore, MD: Paul H. Brookes Publishing Co.

Vacca, J. L., Vacca, R. T., & Gove, M. K. (1995). *Reading and learning to read* (3rd Edition). New York: HarperCollins College Publishers.

Zucker, C. (1993). Using whole language with students who have language and learning disabilities. *The Reading Teacher, 46*(8), 660–670.

 Article Review Form at end of book.

What are the advantages of implementing early intervention programs to ensure that students are successful and *not* in need of special education services? What is neverstreaming, for which students is it most appropriate, and what are the key concepts for student success?

Neverstreaming
Preventing learning disabilities

Robert E. Slavin

Robert E. Slavin is Co-Director, Center for Research on the Education of Students Placed at Risk (CRESPAR), Johns Hopkins University, 3505 N. Charles St., Baltimore, MD 21218-2498.

Once upon a time, there was a town whose playground was at the edge of a cliff. Every so often a child would fall off the cliff. Finally, the town council decided that something should be done about the serious injuries to children. After much discussion, however, the council was deadlocked. Some council members wanted to put a fence at the top of the cliff, but others wanted to put an ambulance at the bottom.

In this parable, the idea of putting an ambulance at the bottom of the cliff clearly is foolish on many levels. Waiting for children to be injured and only then providing them with help is cruel and inhuman if the damage can

Author's note: I wrote this article under funding from the Office of Educational Research and Improvement, U.S. Department of Education (Grant No. R117D-40005). Any opinions expressed are mine and do not necessarily represent the OERI positions or policies.

be prevented. Further, it is needlessly expensive; an ambulance costs far more than a fence.

Yet longstanding policies in special education, especially for children with learning disabilities, are very much like this ill-considered idea. Schools generally provide pretty good programs in kindergarten, 1st grade, and beyond, but they know with certainty that a number of children will fall by the wayside. In particular, a certain number of children of normal intelligence will fail to learn to read. After a while, these children are very likely to be retained, assigned to long-term remedial services, or labeled as having specific learning disabilities and provided with special education services.

By the time these services are rendered, most of the children will already have realized that they have failed at their most important task—learning to read. Accordingly, they likely will have lost much of their earlier motivation, enthusiasm, and positive expectations. Schools will be paying for years—in special education and in remedial instruction costs—for

failing to ensure that students succeed in the early grades.

Neverstreaming: Does It Work?

Today, most children with learning disabilities are mainstreamed for much of their school day. Mainstreaming is better than self-contained placement, but it is far from ideal. Mainstreamed students with academic deficiencies often are poorly accepted by their peers, struggle with academic content, and develop low self-esteem (Bear et al. 1991).

Obviously, students fare better when they succeed the first time they are taught, thereby avoiding both special education and mainstreaming. We call this never-streaming: implementing prevention and early intervention programs powerful enough to ensure that virtually every child is successful in the first place (Slavin et al. 1991).

Few people would deny that this is a nice policy in concept. The question is, would it be practical with real kids in real schools? Evidence is accumulating that it is in fact possible to ensure the success of almost all children in the early elementary grades—at least in reading. And this has profound implications for special education for children with reading disabilities. Let's look at that evidence.

Exhibit 1: Success for All

Perhaps the strongest evidence for the feasibility of neverstreaming comes from research in our own Success for All program (Slavin et al. 1996), a comprehensive approach to restructuring elementary schools. The Johns Hopkins University's Center for Research on the Education of Students Placed at Risk (CRESPAR) is implementing the program in more than 300 schools in 70 districts in 24 states. The focus is prevention and intensive early intervention for children in preschool through 6th grade.

As preventive measures, we provide research-based instruction in reading, writing, and language arts. The programs emphasize cooperative learning and maintain a balance among phonics, children's literature, creative writing, and home reading. We back up these programs by offering (1) intensive professional development, (2) a full-time building facilitator to help teachers continue to improve their instructional strategies, (3) a curriculum-based assessment program to monitor student progress and identify children in need of additional help, and (4) a strong parent involvement program.

Even the best instructional programs cannot ensure success for every child. For this reason, Success for All schools also provide one-to-one tutoring for 1st graders who are struggling in reading. The tutors typically are certified teachers. Their goal is to see that the students never become remedial readers. To do this, they provide students with instruction that is closely tied to classroom reading instruction and teach them metacognitive skills—for example, how to ask themselves whether what they read makes sense and relates to what they've been taught.

A family support team in each school also provides intensive early intervention. Team members get parents involved and give them strategies for helping their own children. They also develop programs to improve attendance, resolve behavior problems, and work with local agencies to see that children have eyeglasses, hearing aids, health services, or other needed assistance.

Research on Success for All (Slavin et al. 1992, 1994, 1996; Madden et al. 1993) has shown that the program has consistently improved children's reading skills, as measured by both individually administered reading tests and standardized assessments. Students in nine school districts across the United States have average scores three months ahead of those of matched control students by the end of 1st grade, and more than a year ahead by the end of 5th grade. The effects are particularly dramatic for students who are most at risk, those in the lowest quarter of their grades.

These findings have direct relevance to special education. A longitudinal study in very high-poverty Baltimore schools found that of 3rd graders participating in the program, including those in special education, only 2 percent were performing two years below grade level, the usual criterion for identifying reading disabilities. In the control groups, by contrast, 9 percent of 3rd graders were performing this poorly (Slavin et al. 1992). Overall, special education placements were cut in half.

In a study conducted in Ft. Wayne, Indiana, Smith and colleagues found that special education referrals in grades K–3 were more than three times higher in control schools than in Success for All schools. In another study, across four districts, Smith and colleagues also found that 1st grade special education students in Success for All schools had substantially higher achievement than 1st graders in control schools (Smith et al. 1994).

Success for All is usually funded by reallocation of Title I funds, supplemented on occasion by special education funds. Very few schools have funding beyond what they would have had without the program. This means that even without extra resources, schools can substantially reduce reading failure. With additional resources to pay for more tutors, they can further reduce the number of children failing to meet adequate reading standards (see Slavin et al. 1992).

Exhibit 2: Reading Recovery

Reading Recovery is a 1st grade tutoring program being used successfully in thousands of U.S. schools. It was developed in New Zealand by Marie Clay (1985), and researched and disseminated in the United States by Gay Su Pinnell and her colleagues at Ohio State University (1988).

The program provides 30 minutes of daily, one-to-one tutoring to 1st graders who score poorly on a battery of diagnostic tests. Tutors are certified teachers who complete an extensive professional development program.

As with Success for All, research on Reading Recovery shows that the vast majority of children can be well on the way to reading effectively by the end of 1st grade (Pinnell et al. 1994). Further, Reading Recovery students are more likely than matched comparison students to stay out of special education (Lyons 1989).

Exhibit 3: Prevention of Learning Disabilities

As the name suggests, Prevention of Learning Disabilities is designed to keep children from ever needing special education services for learning disabilities (Silver and Hagin 1990). Like Reading Recovery, this program provides one-to-one tutoring to at-risk 1st graders. The tutoring, however, focuses on general perceptual skills as well as reading. Studies of the program have found that 1st graders have substantially higher achievement than do similar control groups (Silver and Hagin 1990).

Exhibit 4: Early Childhood Interventions

The Carolina Abecedarian Project (Campbell and Ramey 1994) is the best example of an intensive early intervention program. Research on this program has found that following children through the critical first five years of their lives has strong and lasting effects.

Reading Recovery and Prevention of Learning Disabilities start with children in 1st grade, and Success for All starts with 4- and 5-year-olds. Yet much of children's cognitive development has already taken place by age 4 (Carnegie Corporation 1994). This project offers further evidence that if young children growing up

in poverty are effectively stimulated and their parents are helped to create a healthy home environment, they are more likely to perform well in school and to stay out of special education.

Exhibit 5: Family Support and Integrated Services

Two national programs designed to improve school-home collaboration and services for children in the early grades are Comer's (1988) School Development Program and Zigler's Schools of the 21st Century (Zigler et al. 1992). These programs aim to head off the causes of school failure that have nothing to do with children's cognitive capabilities: conflicts between parents' and schools' values and expectations; erratic attendance; or the need for eyeglasses, hearing aids, or more adequate nutrition, for example. Family support and integrated service programs can solve many of these problems.

The Verdict Is In

Up to now, no one program has been able to ensure that all children are reading well enough to stay out of special education. However, the programs described here have come close, and with additional research and experience are sure to come even closer.

Moreover, imagine what would happen if all children in need of early intervention participated in multiple programs as intensive and comprehensive as these, from preschool through the elementary grades. The number of children still having reading problems would almost certainly be a fraction of what it is today.

A useful and appropriate debate is going on about special education versus inclusion for children with more serious, low-incidence disabilities. For children at risk of learning disabilities, however, neither of these alternatives is the answer. Instead, we need to focus on prevention and early intervention. If we know how to ensure that virtually every child will become a skillful, strategic, and enthusiastic reader, then it is criminal to let children fall behind and only then provide assistance. Neverstreaming, not mainstreaming or special education, should be the goal for all children who are at risk.

References

Bear, G. G., A. Clever, and W. A. Proctor. (1991). "Self-Perceptions of Nonhandicapped Children and Children with Learning Disabilities in Integrated Classes." *Journal of Special Education* 24: 409–426.

Campbell, F. A., and C. T. Ramey. (1994). "Effects of Early Intervention on Intellectual and Academic Achievement: A Follow-up Study of Children from Low-Income Families." *Child Development* 65: 684–698.

Carnegie Corporation of New York. (1991). *Starting Points: Meeting the Needs of Our Youngest Children.* New York: Carnegie Corporation of New York.

Clay, M. (1985). 3rd ed. *The Early Detection of Reading Difficulties.* Auckland, New Zealand: Heinemann Educational Books.

Comer, J. (1988). "Educating Poor Minority Children." *Scientific American* 259: 42–48.

Lyons, C. A. (1989). "Reading Recovery: A Preventative for Mislabeling Young 'At-Risk' Learners." *Urban Education* 24: 125–139.

Madden, N. A., R. E. Slavin, N. L. Karweit, L. J. Dolan, and B. A. Wasik. (1993). "Success for All: Longitudinal Effects of Restructuring Program for Inner-City Elementary Schools." *American Educational Research Journal* 30: 123–148.

Pinnell, G. S., D. E. DeFord, and C. A. Lyons. (1988). *Reading Recovery: Early*

Intervention for At-Risk First Graders. Arlington, Va.: Educational Research Service.

Pinnell, G. S., C. A. Lyons, D. E. DeFord, A. S. Bryk, and M. Seltzer. (1994). "Comparing Instructional Models for the Literacy Education of High-Risk First Graders." *Reading Research Quarterly 29,* 9–40.

Silver, A. A., and R. A. Hagin. (1990). *Disorder of Learning in Childhood.* New York: Wiley.

Slavin, R. E., N. A. Madden, N. L. Karweit, L. Dolan, B. A. Wasik, A. Shaw, K. L. Mainzer, and B. Haxby. (1991). "Neverstreaming: Prevention and Early Intervention as Alternatives to Special Education." *Journal of Learning Disabilities 24,* 373–378.

Slavin, R. E., N. A. Madden, N. L. Karweit, L. Dolan, and B. A. Wasik. (1992). *Success for All: A Relentless Approach to Prevention and Early Intervention in Elementary Schools.* Arlington, Va: Educational Research Service.

Slavin, R. E., N. A. Madden, N. L. Karweit, L. J. Dolan, B. A. Wasik, S. M. Ross, and L. J. Smith. (1994). " 'Wherever and Whenever We Choose. . .': The Replication of Success for All." *Phi Delta Kappan 75,* 8: 6399–6647.

Slavin, R. E., N. A. Madden, N. L. Karweit, L. Dolan, and B. A. Wasik. (1996). *Every Child, Every School: Success for All.* Newbury Park, Calif.: Corwin.

Smith, L. J., S. M. Ross, and J. P. Casey. (1994). *Special Education Analyses for Success for All in Four Cities.* Memphis, Tenn.: University of Memphis, Center for Research in Educational Policy.

Zigler, E. F., M. Finn-Stevenson, and K. W. Linkins. (1992). "Meeting the Needs of Children and Families with Schools of the 21st Century." *Yale Law and Policy Review 10,* 1: 69–81.

 Article Review Form at end of book.

If gifted students are not challenged educationally, what are some of the consequences? Why do parents of gifted students believe their children should have individualized learning plans similar to those of special education?

Educating the Very Brightest

A mother who battled to find programs for her son says the public schools have a lot to learn. Their story reflects a broader question—how to teach the highly gifted.

Amy Pyle
Times Education Writer

Times staff writer Nick Anderson contributed to this report.

Fitting the mind of an adult into the body of a 6-year-old is a tough squeeze.

Finding a place in the public school system that satisfies the needs of that mind and that body is tougher still.

This is the search that consumes Leila Levi, a former schoolteacher who refuses to accept second-best for her son, Levi Meir Clancy.

How smart is Levi? Testing him is complicated by his youth, but formal exams intended for older kids have pegged him above the 145 IQ range, one measure of the "highly gifted" designation, bestowed on fewer than 1% of Los Angeles Unified School District's students.

Reality hints at an even higher intelligence. At home in Venice, Levi reads novels in English and Spanish and adds three-digit numbers in his head. Boosted by pillows so he can reach the keyboard, he runs smoothly through sophisticated computer programs such as ClarisWorks. He wants to be a bio-engineer.

Nevertheless, the odds that such children will be sufficiently challenged in school are discouraging, experts say.

Educators throughout the nation are advocating "mixed ability" classes, and are struggling with the very word "gifted," sensitive to its anti-egalitarian overtones. Many districts do not even recognize "highly gifted" as a distinct category. LAUSD does, but its top gifted administrator stresses programs at the students' local schools—including creating independent-study programs for the most extraordinary children.

In Orange County, where administration of schools is divided among 27 districts, children classified as gifted receive various services depending on where they live.

Some are sent to magnet schools or are grouped in "gifted-only" classes. Some are pulled from mainstream classes periodically for special seminars or get independent study assignments. Others are clustered in groups of eight or 10 in mainstream classes.

"No one program's perfect," said Marge Hoctor, who works for Garden Grove schools and is president-elect of the California Assn. for the Gifted. "There are pros and cons to any program."

The Los Angeles district, whose sheer size gives it more options than smaller districts, offers fewer than 400 slots in special accelerated elementary school classes for its 1,600 elementary school-age youngsters who have been identified as highly gifted.

As a consequence, parents such as Leila Levi fear that these children will never reach their potential—growing up, instead, without brilliant peers, made to feel odd or ostracized, becoming discipline problems.

Among the experts who consider those fears valid is psychology professor Ellen Winner, who shocked gifted advocates in her 1996 book, "Gifted Children: Myths and Realities." She suggested that the "moderately gifted" belonged in regular classes.

Highly gifted children, by contrast, "are at risk," she said. "A lot get bored or teased in school and they tune out or become disinterested in their abilities and end up underachievers. They need to be in classes with other kids who are like them."

Many parents turn to special classes in desperation after other options fail horribly. Though there are so-called "gifted" programs of some sort in most of the district's schools, some provide as little as one hour a week of enrichment—hardly adequate to satisfy children like Levi.

The question of how to educate Levi is a metaphor for the broader question of how public schools—and society at large—should deal with our most intellectually gifted. For parents, it is a journey radically different, and far more chaotic, than the well-worn paths that have been smoothed for gifted athletes, musicians or artists.

Search Plagued by Obstacles

Leila Levi opted for one of the special programs—an LAUSD magnet school—only after two years of navigating.

They were two years in which she slammed into a succession of frustrating walls: The wall of the principal who doesn't believe in skipping grades, because that was how his son missed decimals; the wall of the first-grade teacher who never fulfilled another principal's proposed compromise of sending Levi next door for third-grade math and science; the wall of the district, which eventually offered Leila the choice of Eagle Rock Highly Gifted Magnet, but provides a bus for only half the trip.

Leila firmly believes her son's needs are as unique as those of a severely retarded youngster. She and some other parents of the very bright believe their children

should be provided a tailored learning plan similar to those required for special education students.

"It's their legal and moral responsibility," Leila said. "And what's more, he's a gift to society. They should want to do it."

By law, special education students must be tested, transported and closely monitored. No such standards apply to the highly gifted, or to the simply "gifted" students, who make up about 6% of the school population and generally fall in the above-125 IQ range.

It would be easy to dismiss parents such as Leila as pushy or unrealistic, or to point out that their children will probably succeed regardless of the education they receive, while disabled kids probably will not.

But such swift dismissal ignores the burning fears and frustration inside parents such as Westside resident Loren Grossman.

Grossman dragged her son, Max, from therapist to therapist trying to figure out why he was misbehaving at school. When the other kids were sitting on the classroom rug, Max would be crawling on the floor, picking up staples and dust particles. Though he seemed completely distracted, when the teacher would call on him, he would usually be up to speed.

One counselor diagnosed mild autism, another attention deficit disorder, still another a more obscure ailment. Each time, Grossman was both comforted and confused by the answers.

Then, she insisted Max be tested for giftedness and he scored off the charts. It was midyear, and the only highly gifted magnet openings were at San Jose Highly Gifted in the mid-

San Fernando Valley, where Grossman said the 8-year-old boy has excelled, causing her to launch a campaign to begin a highly gifted magnet closer to home.

"He went from being phobic and eccentric, crying all the time, basically clinically depressed and ended up the school year happy, thriving, he could not wait to get on the bus."

A Promising but Exhausting Start

Everyone wants a smart kid, but having a child so far out of sync with the norm can be scary.

As a baby, Levi barely slept, began walking at 5 months and spoke well at age 1, mixing English and the Spanish he heard from his bilingual mother. At age 3 he came to Leila while she was doing the dishes and solemnly suggested they needed to talk.

Leila recalls her only child saying: "Mommy, you have to learn another language because I have to learn another language. By the time I'm in the work force, being bilingual won't be good enough and the best way for me to learn another language is for you to learn it and teach it to me."

He thought maybe Chinese would be a good start.

For kindergarten, Leila chose the bilingual immersion program at Grandview Elementary in West L.A., figuring that reinforcing the two languages spoken at home would keep her son's mind busy.

The following summer, she enrolled him in a third-grade math class in Culver City Unified, then volunteered to help out. She said what she observed took her breath away: She had been a teacher for years but had never seen a student learn as quickly as her son.

Back at Grandview in the fall, Levi came home in tears, saying he was helping teach the first-grade class.

The state's top administrator for gifted education, Cathy Barkett, says such use is common, and unfair.

"Teachers tend to teach to the middle and . . . the students at the top often are misused by teachers," said Barkett, who moved her own children to an all-gifted class in suburban Sacramento. "The message to them is, 'You've met that standard, so help someone else.' "

Leila decided she needed ammunition if she was to get Levi what he needed. She asked to have him tested and was told he was too young. She insisted, and eventually won.

Usually, students are tested only if their teachers suggest it two years in a row, and even then months of delays stretch beyond the end of second grade—frequently too late to nab a coveted spot in the magnet gifted programs, most of which begin in third grade.

But Leila had an advantage over the average parent: She knows the ropes because she taught middle school art until 1996. She also knows how to take on L.A. Unified's bureaucracy, having once launched a State Department of Education investigation into treatment of limited-English speakers that ended with sanctions against the district this fall.

When Levi's impressive test results came back, Leila pressed for alternatives. First the psychologist who tested him recommended the Brentwood Science Magnet, which had set aside two

highly gifted classes. But when Levi arrived there, Leila discovered the accelerated classes did not begin until third grade, where he was not welcome to enroll at age 5, and an interim plan for him to spend part of his days in those classes never materialized.

In frustration, Leila pulled Levi out of school altogether and taught him herself for 10 months. She started with the basics—mostly math and English—but said he consumed most of the elementary school curriculum in just three months. During the course of the year, he read hundreds of books, including a 50-volume set on countries around the world, and began questioning his mom about such theories as group consciousness.!

Worried that she would accelerate Levi to the point where no public school could accommodate him, Leila tried to help him gain the experience to match his intellect. She took him to art openings and other cities, helped him learn to roller-blade and play chess, and took him with her to a computer graphics class at UCLA Extension.

Levi remembers it as a freeing time, when he could pursue interests at his own pace.

His mother has a different recollection.

"It was exhausting and it got to the point where there wasn't much I could do for him anymore," she said.

She realized she would have to try the district again this fall.

"When he asks a question, I always kind of gasp for air," she said. "I don't know if I can go there. . . . I have a master's degree, I've been a teacher for years, but I feel so inadequate."

A Long Commute to a Special Class

At 6:25 a.m., Levi is napping in the front seat of Leila's car as she pulls up in front of Hillcrest Elementary in the Crenshaw district, a 20-minute drive from their Venice condominium. The bus waiting for him there will bump over surface streets all the way to Eagle Rock, picking up four other children along the way, and Levi may not arrive home until nearly 5 p.m.

Just a month into the school year, Levi's accomplishments already are legendary.

Nine-year-old Jennifer Ho, who boards the bus in Chinatown, says in reverent tones: "Did you hear about him? He's 6 years old but he's in fourth grade!"

The mother and child chose Eagle Rock from the list of three elementary magnets for highly gifted children in LAUSD's "Choices" brochure, which was sent to all district parents for the first time last year.

Eagle Rock accepted Levi into its mixed second- through fourth-grade class and he now works with ease at the top of that continuum.

Not only is Levi the youngest in his class, but he is small for his age—a full head shorter than his classmates, with room to spare in his size 6 jeans. The classroom furniture is so big that his feet dangle and he has to stand up on his knees to write.

At first he felt oddest during recess, when the older kids didn't want him to play ball. But this brain magnet is a place where students actually talk about books during recess, too, and practice their parts for a Halloween performance of "Macbeth." A place where teacher Joyce Muraoka doesn't think twice about using words such as "perusing" and "eccentric."

In such an environment, Levi feels comfortable enough to share his thoughts without fear of being mocked. When Muraoka hands out a new math game originally developed by the Mayans, Levi raises his hand and asks whether she knew the Mayans sacrificed animals and, by the way, so did the Egyptians. And they also put animal heads on their Gods.

Acknowledging Levi's tangent, Muraoka tells the class about an Egyptian history museum in San Jose visited by magnet students on a parent-sponsored field trip several years ago.

Levi raises his hand again: Would she like to see a magazine he brought to school, which has some Egyptian royalty in it?

There are gaps in his learning that Muraoka must find and fill. When he digs in to his homework one night, he is so used to being able to do math in his head that he can't remember how to regroup for harder subtraction problems. Shown once, he zooms through the rest of the page like a human calculator.

Frustrated Parents Driven to Activism

Last spring, Leila unwittingly joined the gifted parents lobby when she attended her first meeting of the Committee on Gifted Education at school district head-

quarters. She went there on a personal mission: If lower-level administrators would not take responsibility for Levi's education, she would go to the top in a forum in which she could not be ignored.

At meeting's end, she shoved Levi's home-school notebook in front of Sheila Smith, the district's gifted-programs coordinator.

"I was so aggressive, I was almost embarrassed," Leila recalls.

That first meeting, she was stunned by how angry the other parents were. She felt irritated that all the attention seemed to be on high schools simply because most of the parents had older kids.

In the past, the committee has found little school board sympathy for its primary causes—to make testing routine and increase the number of special gifted classes to serve those identified. Last year members presented a plan to then-board President Jeff Horton and never heard back.

Horton acknowledges that is because he is torn on the issue-agreeing the system could be improved and worrying about equity issues, including the traditional underrepresentation of poor children.

Members are hopeful that times are changing because the new superintendent, Ruben Zacarias, prides himself on having increased the numbers of identified gifted students during his stint as an Eastside regional superintendent.

An unexpected flurry of activity occurred last spring: Applications far exceeded space at

North Hollywood's Highly Gifted magnet after the campus received heavy publicity for topping the local heap on Advanced Placement tests.

Parents complained about the lack of slots and the uprising "made the district aware of the need," said the district's high school director, Bob Collins.

Advanced programs were created at seven high schools around the city to accommodate the overflow though information was sent only to those turned away from North Hollywood.

"The joke in the district is these are the stealth programs—parents don't even know they exist," said founding committee member Carol Knee, who got involved in spring 1994, after she was informed that there was no room for her son in a gifted middle school, even though he had attended a gifted elementary.

Board member David Tokofsky, who took the helm of the board's curriculum committee during the summer, believes it will take such advocacy to bust through an administrative culture he claims favors "equity over excellence."

Tokofsky has never met Leila Levi, but describes her perfectly, always adamant, now angry.

"The thing is," she said, "I had the wherewithal to know where to look. I had a clue—and it was still impossible."

 Article Review Form at end of book.

Gifted programs for minority-language students should consider what factors? What types of assessment criteria should be used in identifying minority-language students as gifted?

Meeting the Needs of Gifted and Talented Minority Language Students

Linda M. Cohen

Students with special gifts and talents come from all cultural and linguistic backgrounds. Gifted students can be described as possessing an abundance of certain abilities that are most highly valued within a particular society or culture. Many minority language children have special talents that are valued within their own cultures; unfortunately, these students are often not recognized as gifted and talented.

Most procedures for identifying gifted and talented students have been developed for use with middle class children who are native English speakers. Such procedures have led to underrepresentation of minority language students in gifted and talented programs, which in turn prevents our schools from developing the strengths and abilities of this special population.

This digest explores the controversy surrounding the under-representation of minority language students in gifted and talented programs and makes recommendations for more suitable assessment techniques and program models.

Why Are Minority Language Students Underrepresented in Programs for Gifted and Talented Students?

Educators who work closely with minority language students argue that using standardized IQ tests as a primary measure of giftedness does not fairly accommodate the linguistic and cultural differences of those students. These educators look to identify the "able learner" rather than the more narrowly defined gifted student who scores in the top 3% on IQ tests. Able learners are defined by some educators as students in the top 10% of their class who have shown some extraordinary achievement in one or more areas such as science, mathematics, or the performing arts (Ernest Bernal, personal communication, September 13, 1988).

Reliance on IQ tests alone has greatly diminished the potential number of gifted students. Renzulli (1978) indicated that "more creative persons come from below the 95th percentile than above it, and if such cut-off scores are needed to determine entrance into special programs, we may be guilty of actually discriminating against persons who have the highest potential for high levels of accomplishment" (p. 182).

Three percent is a conservative estimate of the percentage of the population that is considered gifted. However, in Arizona, for example, only 0.14% of the students in gifted and talented programs come from language minority backgrounds (Maker, 1987). Using the 3% criterion, one would estimate that 2,900 limited-English-proficient (LEP) students in Arizona could be receiving

From *ERIC Digest,* #E480, 1990, Council for Exception Children, Reston, VA: ERIC Clearinghouse on Handicapped and Gifted Children, Reston, VA.

some type of services for giftedness. An assessment of needs, however, revealed that only 143 LEP children were participating in gifted programs, despite the fact that minority language students represent 16.17% (96,674) of the school-age population. Other studies indicate that the proportion of Blacks, Hispanics, and American Indians identified as gifted represents only half that expected (Chan & Kitano, 1986).

Table 1 (at the end of this digest)* illustrates that, nation wide, Caucasians and Asians are overrepresented, while the percentage of Blacks and Hispanics is only half what would be expected in gifted and talented programs. The concept of giftedness as it relates to culture and values can help explain why more gifted and talented Asian and Pacific-American students have been identified than any other group. Although these children comprise only 2.2% of the school-age population, they constitute 4.4% of the identified gifted students, twice the expected number (Kitano, 1986). (This figure is slightly lower than the statistic given in Table 1.)

Different learning styles may also contribute to the underrepresentation of gifted and talented minority language students. Native Americans are often caught between the schools' value of independence and the home and community value of interdependence. In school, students generally sit in rows and face the teacher, whereas in Native American culture, everyone would be seated in a circle and decisions would be made collectively.

Among many Hispanics, cultural differences may also produce manifestations of giftedness that differ from the traditional manifestations in the majority culture. In Puerto Rico, for example,

children learn to seek the advice of their family rather than act independently (Perrone & Aleman, 1983). Respect for elders is often valued more than precociousness, which can be seen as disrespectful. Similarly, the Mexican-American child who respects elders, the law, and authority becomes vulnerable in a school system that values individual competition, initiative, and self-direction.

What Are Some Commonly Used Techniques for the Identification of Gifted and Talented Minority Language Students?

Research on the identification of giftedness points to the lack of appropriate assessment procedures. Giftedness is not a trait inherent to native English speakers; however, there is a lack of instruments that can detect giftedness in minority language students (Gallagher, 1979; Llanes, 1980; Raupp, 1988; Renzulli, Reis, & Smith, 1981). Most tests rely on either oral or written language skills. Minority language students who are not considered gifted may, in fact, be very gifted, but unable to express themselves in English. Therefore, many researchers urge that great caution be exercised in using English standardized tests for the identification of linguistic and cultural minority students. These researchers also recommend selecting tests that reduce cultural and linguistic bias.

The identification and assessment of gifted and talented minority-language students is complex because it involves students who are both gifted and talented and from a language or cultural background different from that of mid-

dle class, native-English-speaking children. Many researchers and practitioners recommend multiple assessment measures to give students several opportunities to demonstrate their skills and performance potential.

Each school can establish its own relevant criteria to ensure that the screening process is appropriate for a specific target population. Moreover, an assessment team that is sensitive to their needs can represent the population to be served in the program. In addition, teachers can be brought into the identification process, because they have the opportunity to observe students in numerous academic and social situations.

An alternative to using English language standardized tests is the assessment of LEP students in their native language. These tests measure a variety of skills: creative thinking skills such as fluency, flexibility, originality, and elaboration; intellectual development based on Piaget's theory of development (Piaget, 1954; Piaget & Inhelder, 1973); language proficiency; and nonverbal perceptual skills of cognitive development.

Many school districts now include behavioral checklists or inventories, nominations, or related techniques to identify gifted and talented minority language students. Checklists usually compare or rate the student according to general descriptions or more specific examples of behavior deduced from characteristics of gifted persons. Many of these instruments are designed locally, are available from state departments of education, or are available commercially.

Other commonly used methods such as interviews, self-reports, autobiographies, and case histories can also be used to identify gifted and talented minority language students. Interviews are often scheduled as part of the identification or selection process to determine a candidate's general fitness for a program and provide information for instructional planning. The use of case studies to identify giftedness has been documented by Renzulli and Smith (1977) and is recommended because it relies on multiple sources of information about a student's performance. Although these procedures can be cumbersome, time consuming, and complex, they can provide the most valid basis for decision making.

What Types of Programs Are Available for Gifted and Talented Students, and Are They Suitable for Minority Language Students Who Are Selected to Participate?

There are many different types of programs and instructional models for gifted and talented LEP students as there are different views of intelligence. The program models discussed in this digest demonstrate a wide range of suggestions for choosing a program for gifted and talented students and can stimulate ideas about the types of program that can be implemented. However, each district must implement the program that will best meet the needs of its gifted and talented minority language students.

Jean M. Blanning, of the Connecticut Clearinghouse for Gifted and Talented (1980), suggests that, in general, programs for gifted and talented minority language students should allow their students to:

- pursue topics in depth at a pace commensurate with their abilities and intensity of interest;

- explore, branch out on tangents unforeseen when first beginning a study, without curriculum parameters confining them to a particular direction;

- initiate activities, diverge from the structured format, within a framework of guidance and resources appropriate for such exploration;

- ask questions about areas or aspects of studies and find answers which lead to more questions;

- experience emotional involvement with a project because it is based on interests and use of higher levels of ability;

- learn the skills, methodology, and discipline involved in intellectual pursuits and/or creative endeavors;

- think (interpretations, connections, extrapolations) and imagine (ideas, images, intuitive insights) to develop fully into their own products;

- experience the use of intellectual abilities and senses necessary in all creative endeavors.

Enrichment Programs

The most common program model for gifted and talented students is probably an enrichment program, in which students receive instruction in addition to their regular classroom instruction. Enrichment programs provide learning experiences designed to extend, supplement, or deepen understandings within specific content areas (Dannenberg, 1984). Some enrichment programs provide academic services and cultural opportunities for gifted and talented students.

Gifted and talented LEP students at Louis B. Brandeis High School in New York City (Cochran & Cotayo, 1983) attend operas and museums and, in this way, become a part of American culture. Students have said that the program has made them feel "special," because they visit places they ordinarily would not. Another example of activities in an enrichment program would be to have students studying the prehistoric era watch films on dinosaurs, draw pictures on them, and go to a natural history museum to see a dinosaur exhibit.

The decision as to whether or not to implement an enrichment program may be greatly influenced by the school district's concept of giftedness. If giftedness is considered a quality to be measured through IQ tests, then perhaps an enrichment program would be seen as a "frill," because it does not concentrate strictly on academics. On the other hand, this program may be particularly appreciated by gifted and talented minority language students, since they often do not receive this sort of exposure to the arts in a standard instructional program.

Resource Rooms

Another program model uses a resource room, which is usually staffed by a resource teacher. Students may visit the resource room to do special assignments or to check out various educational games or puzzles. In a kindergarten/first grade gifted and talented program in Albuquerque, New Mexico (Beam, 1980), parents are also able to check out items for their children. The resource room provides an excellent opportunity for parents and students to bridge the gap between home and school. However, in many inner-city schools, special programs may be needed to obtain the desired levels of parental support. Also, the establishment of a resource room usually requires physical space for the room, sufficient operating funds, and a resource teacher who has expertise in the area of gifted and talented students.

The Hartford, Connecticut, program "Encendiendo Una Llama" ("Lighting a Flame") has been in operation since 1979 and uses a resource room, an after-school program, and a regular classroom component to provide services for gifted and talented minority language students. This program emphasizes language development in English and Spanish, high-level thinking skills, independent work and study skills, and development of creative thinking. It is an integrated program in which English-dominant children also participate. In each of the participating Hartford schools, the bilingual gifted and talented program is the only gifted program in the school, and all children are eligible to participate, regardless of their language background.

Parent Involvement Programs

Many programs include a strong parent involvement component in which parents can help support their children's development at home while the school can be used as an additional resource. Although it is important for all parents to be involved in their children's education, it is particularly critical to develop a strong link between the home and the school for gifted and talented minority language children.

Many programs provide parents with checklists to help assess their children. In addition, programs often provide booklets of home activities through which parents can encourage critical thinking and creativity.

Acceleration or Honors Programs

Many people associate acceleration or honors programs with gifted and talented programs. These programs may include skipping grades, early entrance, early graduation, credit by examination, nongraded classes, and advanced placement classes (Dannenberg, 1984). Some gifted students who seem bored in school may benefit from an accelerated program that provides an academic challenge and keeps them involved in school. However, it may be difficult to identify these students, who initially may not be seen as gifted.

Some educators who adhere to the narrow definition of giftedness as high IQ may not feel that an honors program is appropriate for students who fit the broader definition of the able learner. This attitude is refuted in the film "Stand And Deliver," which is based on a true story about several minority language students at an inner-city school in Los Angeles. These students were not considered gifted by many of their teachers, yet they were the only students in their school to pass the Advanced Placement exams given by the Educational Testing Service for college credit in calculus. Their success can be attributed largely to their mathematics teacher, Jaime Escalante, who had very high expectations for them and refused to believe that they were unable to think critically simply because they were from low-income, minority language backgrounds. He encouraged their participation in these special advanced classes (held at night and on Saturdays in overcrowded, stifling classrooms) to prove to other students, the faculty, and themselves that they were intelligent. Moreover, these students gained new, strong, self-concepts, which inevitably improved their academic skills and gave them the courage and discipline to pursue a college education.

Mentor Programs

Another program model for gifted and talented education is the mentor program. Mentors provide role models for the students, giving them an opportunity to interact with adult professionals. Through the Higher Achievement Program in Washington, DC, elementary and junior high school students from low-income neighborhoods are tutored by volunteers 2 nights a week. To be eligible for the program, students must show a high level of motivation and pass a qualifying examination. One night each week is devoted to verbal skills such as reading comprehension, vocabulary, and writing; the second night is devoted primarily to mathematics and related skills. Critical thinking skills are stressed in all subjects.

The mentor program has many psychological and social benefits for the students and is a low-cost program if the school district recruits area professionals as volunteers. School districts located near universities can encourage them to establish a course in which official credit is given to university students who participate as mentors. If the mentors are sensitive to the needs of particular cultural and linguistic groups, they can provide positive role models for the students. The mentor program concept can be a solution to difficult budget constraints and has been used by numerous school districts around the country.

Recommendations for Change

The following recommendations may improve the assessment and educational programs of gifted and talented minority language students.

Broaden the Concept of Giftedness. Broadening the concept of giftedness to include able learners will allow for the identification of a greater proportion of gifted minority language students. A broader definition of giftedness may be the first essential step toward identifying and educating gifted and talented minority language students.

Expand Research on Giftedness and Minority Language Students. Although there is a large body of literature on gifted and talented students in general, there is much less literature on gifted and talented minority language students. This may be because many researchers in the past did not consider minority language students as gifted, based on the traditional measure of giftedness as a high IQ score. Further research is needed on all the able learners in our schools, including minority language students.

Employ More Well-rounded Assessment Techniques. If there is a lower-than-expected proportion of minority language students identified as gifted, then the identification and assessment process should be examined to determine why these students have not been identified. School districts may need to find creative solutions to the problem of how to identify gifted and talented minority language students by using nontraditional methods.

The identification of minority language students can include multiple criteria (with information from as many sources as possible) that are relevant to the needs of the population. Using multiple instruments can result in a more precise picture because it provides information about students from different perspectives. A combination of assessment instruments can help insure that a student's ability to participate effectively in a gifted and talented program is adequately measured.

Increase Staff Awareness of Their Potential for Developing a Gifted and Talented Program. Regardless of the program model selected for implementation, administrators must first examine the resources they have within their school system. Upon entering the school district, teachers could be asked to complete a questionnaire about their abilities and interests and whether or not they would be interested in participating in a gifted and talented program. For example, a teacher who has played piano for 10 years might be interested in teaching a course in music appreciation. Administrators need to be aware of the unique talents within their own staff as they identify local personnel who may be able to contribute their time, effort, and expertise to gifted and talented programs.

Explore Various Program Models. No single model can be recommended as the "best" instructional approach for gifted and talented minority language students, because each population is unique and each program has its own specific goals and objectives. The type of program implemented may depend on several issues such as the instructional model, the talents of the students, the number of gifted students identified, the talents of the professional staff, the availability of qualified personnel, the level of commitment of the school and school system, and budget constraints.

Increase Awareness of Different Ways Giftedness May Be Manifested in Different Populations. Many students are gifted or talented. Teachers face the challenge of identifying, developing, and supporting their students' talents. Although this may be a challenge, it is also a rewarding experience. Watching students grow to their fullest potential and knowing that, as the teacher, you have played an integral part in your students' growth are great personal and professional triumphs.

Conclusion

This digest highlights some of the current debates in the education of gifted and talented students focusing on the definition of giftedness, the assessment of gifted students, and the development and implementation of gifted programs. Providing appropriate gifted and talented programs for students from linguistically and culturally diverse backgrounds is a challenge that many school districts face. Since minority language students represent an increasing percentage of the total school population, meeting the educational needs of gifted minority language students is vital. All students, including minority language students, deserve the most challenging instruction possible.

References

Beam, G. C. (1980). "A kindergarten/primary program for culturally different potentially gifted students in an inner city school in Albuquerque, New Mexico" (Final Report). Grant Number G007901801. Project Number 562AH90290. Albuquerque: Albuquerque Special Preschool.

Blanning, J. M. (1980). *A Multidimensional Inservice Handbook for Professional Personnel in Gifted and Talented.* Hartford: Connecticut State Department of Education, Connecticut Clearinghouse for the Gifted and Talented.

Chan, K. S., & Kitano, M. K. (1986). "Demographic characteristics of exceptional Asian students." In M. K. Kitano & P. C. Chinn (Eds.), *Exceptional Asian Children and Youth* (pp. 1–11). Reston, VA: The Council for Exceptional Children.

Cochran, E. P., & Cotayo, A. (1983). *Louis D. Brandeis High School, Demonstration Bilingual Enrichment College Preparatory Program.* New York: New York City Public Schools.

Dannenberg, A. C. (1984). *Meeting the Needs of Gifted & Talented Bilingual Students: An Introduction to Issues and Practices.* Quincy: Massachusetts Department of Education. Office for Gifted and Talented.

Gallagher, J. J. (1979). "Issues in education for the gifted." In A. H. Passow (Ed.), *The Gifted and the Talented: Their Education and Development.* Chicago: University of Chicago Press.

Kitano, M. K. (1986). "Gifted and talented Asian children." *Rural Special Education Quarterly,* 8(1), 9–13.

Llanes, J. R. (1980, February–March). "Bilingualism and the gifted intellect." *Roeper Review,* 2(3), 11–12.

Machado, M. (1987, February). "Gifted Hispanics underidentified in classrooms." *Hispanic Link Weekly Report,* p.1.

Maker, C. J. (1987). *Project Discover; Discovering Intellectual Skills and Capabilities While Providing Opportunities for Varied Ethnic Responses.* Tucson: University of Arizona, Division of Special Education and Rehabilitation.

Piaget, J. (1954). *The Construction of Reality in the Child.* New York: Basic Books.

Piaget, J., & Inhelder, B. (1973). *Memory and Intelligence.* New York: Basic Books.

Raupp, M. (1988). *Talent Search: The Gifted Hispanic Student.* Quincy: Massachusetts Department of Education, Office for Gifted and Talented.

Renzulli, J. S. (1978). "What makes giftedness? Reexamining a definition." *Phi Delta Kappan, 60*(3), 180–184, 186.

Renzulli, J. S., Reis, S., & Smith, L. H. (1981). *The Revolving Door Identification Model.* Mansfield Center, CT: Creative Learning Press. Renzulli, J., & Smith, L. (1977). "Two approaches to identification of gifted students." *Exceptional Children 43,* 512–518.

Zappia. (1989). Identification of gifted Hispanic students: A multidimensional view. In C. J. Maker & S. W. Schiever (Eds.), *Defensible Programs for Gifted Students from Underserved Populations: Cultural and Ethnic Minorities* (pp. 10P26). Austin: Pro-Ed.

Article Review Form at end of book.

WiseGuide Wrap-Up

- Inclusion programs can be implemented to positively serve both special education and regular education students.

- Educators must ensure that reform strategies, such as those affecting academic standards, not threaten student-focused instruction delivery for special education students.

- Models for improving instruction to diverse learners in inclusive classrooms should include modification of curriculum, instruction, and assessment.

- Implementing early intervention programs to ensure that students are successful can minimize the need for special education services later.

- The failure to identify gifted of African-American, Hispanics, and Native American students can be corrected by implementing unbiased assessment practices.

- Meeting the educational needs of gifted minority-language students is important, since this population is growing in public schools.

R.E.A.L. Sites

Site name: The Council for Exceptional Children
URL: http://www.cec.sped.org/

Why is it R.E.A.L.? CEC is the largest international professional organization dedicated to improving educational outcomes for individuals with exceptionalities, students with disabilities, and the gifted. Includes information on governmental policies, professional standards, ERIC documents, and professional development. Resources include public policy and legislative information.

Key topics: special education, gifted, educational policy

Activity: Review "Public Policy and Legislative Information" on the website and prepare a report on current changes and possible implications for schools.

Site name: ERIC Clearinghouse on Disabilities and Gifted Education
URL: http://www.cec.sped.org/er-menu.htm

Why is it R.E.A.L.? Focuses on the professional literature, information, and resources relating to the education and development of persons with disabilities and/or gifted. Provides ERIC database searching capacity, as well as digests, fact sheets, and mini-bibliographies.

Key topics: special education, gifted

Activity: Using the section called "Search the Database" on the website, gather information for a current report or term paper related to the topic of gifted/special education.

Site name: Gifted and Talented Education
URL: http://www.edweek.org/context/topics/gat.htm

Why is it R.E.A.L.? Brief but thorough background essay. Includes links to definitions of related educational terms and to the most relevant stories from the *Education Week* and *Teacher Magazine* archives. It also includes a carefully selected and annotated list of pertinent sites on the World Wide Web, selected background readings, and a hyperlinked roster of related organizations.

Key topics: gifted, diversity

Activity: Review the archives of recent articles in *Education Week* regarding gifted and talented education. Use data collected in preparation for class presentation.

Spicing It Up: Cultural Diversity and Schooling

- Describe current research on culture and learning style and its appropriate use in instructional design and delivery, particularly with diverse learners.

- Compare and contrast past multicultural program efforts with newer practices in the delivery of instruction to all learners.

- Describe how 'multiple intelligence' theory compliments efforts in teaching all learners, with particular emphasis on diverse learners.

- Explain the components of the anti-bias/ecological model for multicultural education and describe its application in the classroom.

- Identify the purpose of 'deliberation' in education, describe its importance in a global society, compare deliberation with other forms of communication, and describe classroom/school activities that develop this process for students.

 **WiseGuide Intro**

Race and culture continue to be hot topics in America. The issues include increasing minority populations, growing cultural militancy, and increased affluence by previously underrepresented groups. In addition, social and political issues fuel controversies in our society, including continuing racism, debates on affirmative action, the English-only movement, bilingual education, and racial/cultural categorization to name a few.

As citizens, we struggle with these issues in our country and community. But more important, as educators we must work to succeed in providing effective education to all students. Our growing national diversity requires that we triumph in that effort. This section tackles the challenges we face in this regard. It reviews the research literature and exposes practices that promote stereotypes and limit students' capacity. This section presents exciting practices that hold promise in addressing the diversity of all our learners and promoting their full potential.

The section begins with an article reviewing more traditional cultural practices in "The Cultural/Learning Style Connection." A critical analysis of multicultural education is discussed in "The Goals and Track Record of Multicultural Education." A more recent educational practice based on current research is shared in "Multiple Intelligences, Culture, and Equitable Learning." A well-developed and comprehensive perspective on individual learners that addresses cultural diversity is reviewed in the article "Proposal: An Anti-Bias and Ecological Model for Multicultural Education." The section concludes with "The Art of Deliberation," a look at the purposes of promoting civility, respect, and working relationships in our diverse society.

? ? ? ? ? Questions ? ? ?

Reading 12. Linking culture and learning styles is controversial for what reasons? Explain why researchers believe that learning styles are neutral.

Reading 13. What are the two goals of multicultural education? Underachieving and special education students increase achievement as a response to what kind of teaching?

Reading 14. What are the three conditions for the development of a particular type of intelligence?

Describe how educational equity practices are addressed by using multiple intelligences and cultural influences in learning.

Reading 15. What traditional areas are addressed in most anti-bias curricula? How can the ecological model be used to examine factors that affect a student's set of experiences?

Reading 16. How does the author describe the skills of deliberation? What role can deliberation play in cultural diversity?

Linking culture and learning styles is controversial for what reasons? Explain why researchers believe that learning styles are neutral.

The Culture/Learning Style Connection
Educating for diversity

Pat Guild

Pat Guild is owner of Pat Guild Associates, P.O. Box 99131, Seattle, WA 98199.

Abstract: The teaching of multicultural education is plagued by sensitive issues concerning culture and the learning styles of children. Research studies have shown that students of different cultures exhibit varied ways of learning. It is important for educators to recognize these differences to make effective educational decisions and develop proper curricular materials. The differences in learning styles call for different approaches to prevent cultural conflict between the students. A better understanding of the relationship between culture and learning styles is the key towards successful multicultural education.

Cultures do have distinctive learning style patterns, but the great variation among individuals within groups means that educators must use diverse teaching strategies with all students.

Our ability to give every child a chance to succeed in school depends upon a full understanding of culture and learning styles. After all, effective educational decisions and practices must emanate from an understanding of the ways that individuals learn. Consequently, knowing each student, especially his or her culture, is essential preparation for facilitating, structuring, and validating successful learning for all students.

This imperative leads to three critical questions. Do students of the same culture have common learning style patterns and characteristics? If they do, how would we know it? And most important, what are the implications for educators?

These questions are both important and controversial. They are important because we need all the information we can get to help every learner succeed in school and because our understanding of the learning process is the basis for decisions about curriculum and instruction. They are important because success for the diverse populations that schools serve calls for continual reexamination of educators' assumptions, expectations, and biases. And they are important because, ultimately, every educational decision is evaluated according to its impact on individual students' learning.

One reason that the linkage between culture and learning styles is controversial is that generalizations about a group of people have often led to naive inferences about individuals within that group. Although people connected by culture do exhibit a characteristic pattern of style preferences, it is a serious error to conclude that all members of the group have the same style traits as the group taken as a whole.

A second source of controversy is the understandable sensitivity surrounding attempts to explain the persistent achievement differences between minority and nonminority students—it is all too easy to confuse descriptions of differences with explanations for deficits. Finally, the relationship between culture and learning styles is controversial because it brings us face to face with philosophical issues that involve deeply held beliefs. Debaters in the uniformity versus diversity dispute, for instance, differ over whether instructional equality is synonymous with educational equity. Another debate concerns the ultimate purpose of schooling. Is it "cultural pluralism" or the "melting pot"?

From Pat Guild, "The Culture/Learning Style Connection" *Educational Leadership,* Vol. 51 (8). May, 1994.
Reprinted with permission of Pat Guild

A highly public example of how sensitive these issues are occurred in 1987 when the state of New York published a booklet to help decrease the student dropout rate. A small section of the booklet described the learning styles typical of minority students and identified certain patterns associated with African-American students.

These descriptions became the subject of intense scrutiny and animated debate. Eventually, the descriptions were deleted from the booklet. Nonetheless, in the New York State Regent's Report, a review panel reiterated that:

> learning style and behavioral tendency do exist, and students from particular socialization and cultural experiences often possess approaches to knowledge that are highly functional in the indigenous home environment and can be capitalized upon to facilitate performance in academic settings (Claxton 1990).

How We Know That Culture and Ways of Learning Are Linked

There is very little disagreement that a relationship does exist between the culture in which children live (or from which they are descended) and their preferred ways of learning. This relationship, further, is directly related to academic, social, and emotional success in school.

These conclusions are not as simple or definite as they seem, however. Though many syntheses and surveys have discussed the interdynamics of different cultures and ways of learning, each comes from a very distinctive approach, focusing either on a specific learning style model or a particular cultural group. No work, to my knowledge, claims to be comprehensive on the topic of culture and learning styles.

In general, researchers have reported three kinds of information about culture and learning styles.

The first is the set of observation-based descriptions of cultural groups of learners. For the most part, people who are familiar with each group have written these descriptions to sensitize people outside the culture to the experiences of children inside the culture. They have often contrasted minority students' learning patterns with European-American students' ways of learning and the school practices designed for such students.

Researchers have identified typical learning patterns among African Americans (Hale-Benson 1986, Shade 1989, Hilliard 1989), Mexican Americans (Ramirez 1989, Vasquez 1991, Berry 1979, Cox and Ramirez 1981), and Native Americans (Bert and Bert 1992, More 1990, Shade 1989).

The reports conclude that Mexican Americans regard family and personal relationships as important and are comfortable with cognitive generalities and patterns (Cox and Ramirez 1981, Vasquez 1991). Such traits explain why Mexican-American students often seek a personal relationship with a teacher and are more comfortable with broad concepts than component facts and specifics.

Research about the African-American culture shows that students often value oral experiences, physical activity, and loyalty in interpersonal relationships (Shade 1989, Hilliard 1989). These traits call for classroom activities that include approaches like discussion, active projects, and collaborative work.

Descriptions indicate that Native-American people generally value and develop acute visual discrimination and skills in the use of imagery, perceive globally, have reflective thinking patterns, and generally value and develop acute visual discrimination and skills in the use of imagery (Shade 1989, More 1990, Bert and Bert 1992). Thus, schooling should establish a context for new information, provide quiet times for thinking, and emphasize visual stimuli.

In contrast, the observers describe mainstream white Americans as valuing independence, analytic thinking, objectivity, and accuracy. These values translate into learning experiences that focus on competition, information, tests and grades, and linear logic. These patterns are prevalent in most American schools.

A second way that we know about the links between culture and learning styles is data-based descriptions of specific groups. In this class of inquiry, researchers administer learning style/cognitive style instruments to produce a profile of a cultural group, compare this group with another previously studied one (usually white Americans), or validate a particular instrument for cross-cultural use.

The various formal assessment instruments that purport to measure learning styles detect differences in two general ways. In the category of instruments that looks for style preferences, respondents usually self-report their favored approaches to learning. The best known instrument of this kind is probably the Myers-Briggs Type Indicator. It infers learning style patterns from basic perceptual and judging traits.

Another type of assessment instrument tests style strengths, that is, the ability to do tasks with a certain approach. The Swassing-Barbe Modality Index, for example, asks test takers to repeat patterns given auditorily, visually, and tactilely. Another example is the well-known series of assessments that distinguishes between field-dependence and independence. In this series, the test taker tries to find a simple figure embedded in a more complex one. The results show differences in cognitive strengths, such as global, holistic learning in contrast to analytic, part-to-whole approaches.

Formal assessment data should be interpreted (though often, it is not) in the light of the kind of assessment used. An important fact about self-report instruments, for instance, is that they are language- and culture-specific. In other words, when test takers respond to specific words, they interpret the words through their cultural experiences.

Further, different assessments may yield conflicting results. For instance, someone might self-report a preference for learning something in a certain way and yet test out in a different way on a task involving strengths. It is equally possible for descriptions based on observations to conflict with self-reported preferences.

These inconsistencies do not invalidate the usefulness of each of the ways of assessing learning styles. They do point out, however, that understanding learning patterns is a complex task and that the scope of the diagnostic tool used imposes limits on generalizations that can be drawn on the basis of it. Further, the characteristics of the assessment instruments used often account for the seemingly contradictory information reported about groups of learners.

The third way we know about the relationship of learning and culture is through direct discussion. Shade (1989), for instance, comments that:

. . . perceptual development differs within various ethnocultural groups. It is therefore an erroneous assumption in the teaching-learning process to assume children "see" the same event, idea, or object in the same way.

Cognitive styles research, Ramirez (1989) believes, could help accommodate children who see things differently. The research findings, he notes, provide "a framework to look at and be responsive to diversity within and between cultures."

Bennett (1986) warns that ignoring the effects of culture and learning styles would depress learning among nonmainstream students:

If classroom expectations are limited by our own cultural orientations, we impede successful learners guided by another cultural orientation. If we only teach according to the ways we ourselves learn best, we are also likely to thwart successful learners who may share our cultural background but whose learning styles deviate from our own.

Accepted Conclusions about Culture and Learning Styles

Those who study culture and those who study learning styles generally agree on at least five points.

1. Educators concur that students of any particular age will differ in their ways of learning. (Guild and Garger 1985). Both empirical research and experiences validate these learning style differences, which in their cognitive, affective, and behavioral dimensions, help us to understand and talk about individual learning processes.

2. Most researchers believe that learning styles are a function of both nature and nurture. Myers (1990) asserts that:

Type development starts at a very early age. The hypothesis is that type is inborn, an innate predisposition like right- or left-handedness, but the successful development of type can be greatly helped or hindered by environment.

Some researchers downplay the innate aspects of learning style, preferring to focus on the impact of environment. Many place great importance on the early socialization that occurs within the family, immediate culture, and wider culture.

3. Most researchers also believe that learning styles are neutral (Guild and Garger 1985). Every learning style approach can be used successfully, but can also become a stumbling block if applied inappropriately or overused.

This concept in the learning styles literature says a great deal about the effects of different learning approaches with different school tasks. Without question, for example, an active, kinesthetic learner has a more difficult time in school because of the limited opportunities to use that approach, especially for the development of basic skills. Nonetheless, the kinesthetic approach is a successful way to learn, and many adults, including teachers and administrators, use this approach quite effectively. Howard Gardner's (1983, 1991) identification of various intelligences has helped people appreciate the strengths of various approaches to learning.

4. In both observational and data-based research on cultures, one consistent finding is that, within a group, the variations among individuals are as great as their commonalities. Therefore, no one should automatically attribute a particular learning

style to all individuals within a group (Griggs and Dunn 1989).

This subtle point is often verbally acknowledged, but ignored in practice. Cox and Ramirez (1981) explain the result:

Recognition and identification of . . . average differences have had both positive and negative effects in education. The positive effect has been the development of an awareness of the types of learning that our public schools tend to foster. . . . The negative effect . . . is that the great diversity within a culture is ignored and a construct that should be used as a tool for individualization becomes yet another label for categorizing and evaluating.

5. Finally, many authors acknowledge the cultural conflict between some students and the typical learning experiences in schools. When a child is socialized in ways that are inconsistent with school expectations and patterns, the child needs to make a difficult daily adjustment to the culture of the school and his or her teachers. Hale-Benson (1986) points out the added burden this adjustment places on black youngsters:

Black children have to be prepared to imitate the "hip," "cool" behavior of the culture in which they live and at the same time take on those behaviors that are necessary to be upwardly mobile.

Debates about Applying Theory on Culture and Learning Styles

The published literature recommends caution in applying knowledge about culture and learning styles to the classroom. This prudence seems advisable because, despite the accepted ideas, at least five differences of opinion persist.

1. People differ, for instance, on whether educators should ac-quire more explicit knowledge about particular cultural values and expectations. Proponents say that such knowledge would enable educators to be more sensitive and effective with students of particular cultures. Certain states even mandate such information as part of their goals for multiculturalism.

Other authors argue, however, that describing cultures has resulted in more stereotyping and may well lead to a differentiated, segregated approach to curriculum. For example, Cox and Ramirez (1981) note that "the concept of cognitive or learning styles of minority and other students is one easily oversimplified, misunderstood, or misinterpreted." The authors go on to say that misuse of the concept has led to stereotyping and labeling rather than the identification of educationally meaningful differences among individuals.

2. Authors also debate the proper response to the fact that the culture-learning styles relationship affects student achievement. Evidence suggests that students with particular learning style traits (field-dependent, sensing, extraversion) are under-achievers in school, irrespective of their cultural group. Students with such dominant learning style patterns have limited opportunities to use their style strengths in the classroom.

Even more disheartening is the practice of remediating problems so that the learner conforms to school expectations, rather than structuring school tasks in ways that respond to students' strengths. With the current emphasis on the inclusion of all learners in classrooms, it seems essential to change that practice.

Another achievement problem is the serious inequity that results when certain cultures value behaviors that are undervalued in school. Will increased attention to culture and learning styles eradicate this problem?

Hilliard (1989) thinks not:

I remain unconvinced that the explanation for the low performance of culturally different "minority group" students will be found by pursuing questions of behavioral style. . . . Children, no matter what their style, are failing primarily because of systemic inequities in the delivery of whatever pedagogical approach the teachers claim to master—not because students cannot learn from teachers whose styles do not match their own.

Bennett (1986) agrees that accommodating learning styles won't solve all problems:

We must be careful . . . not to view learning styles as the panacea that will eliminate failure in the schools. To address learning styles is often a necessary, but never sufficient, condition of teaching.

3. Another unresolved issue is how teachers working from their own cultures and teaching styles can successfully reach diverse populations. Bennett (1986) sums up the problem this way:

To the extent that teachers teach as they have been taught to learn, and to the extent that culture shapes learning style, students who share a teacher's ethnic background will be favored in class.

Some argue, though, that teachers properly play a special role in representing their own culture. Hale-Benson (1986), for example, says:

It is incumbent upon black professionals to identify the intelligences found especially in black children and to support the pursuit of their strengths.

Yes, that seems sensible. But we have all learned successfully from teachers who were neither like us in learning style or in culture. Often, these were masterful, caring teachers. Sometimes our own motivation helped us learn in spite of a teacher. Clearly, neither culture nor style is destiny. Just as clearly, though, teachers of all cultures and styles will have to work conscientiously to provide equitable opportunities for all students.

4. How cultural identity and self-esteem are related remains an open question, too. Many large city school systems are wrestling with the appropriateness of ethnically identified schools, such as an African-American academy. Bilingual programs continue to debate the value of instruction in the students' first language.

I would add to this discussion a remark of Carl Jung's: "If a plant is to unfold its specific nature to the full, it must first be able to grow in the soil in which it is planted" (Barger and Kirby 1993). This comment has led me to argue against the approach to learning so prevalent in our schools (especially in special education programs), which emphasizes the identification and remediation of deficiencies.

An acceptance of learning styles demands an approach that develops skills through strengths. Should the same not be said of cultural identity?

5. Perhaps the most weighty of the application issues has to do with ways to counteract our tendency toward instructional pendulum swings. This oscillation has become so predictable in schooling in our country. Today it's phonics. Tomorrow whole language. The day after that, phonics again. We are always seeking one right way to teach, and when we accumulate evidence that a strategy is effective with some students, we try to apply it to every student in every school.

A deep understanding of culture and learning styles makes this behavior seem naive. If instructional decisions were based on an understanding of each individual's culture and ways of learning, we would never assume that uniform practices would be effective for all. We would recognize that the only way to meet diverse learning needs would be to intentionally apply diverse strategies. As Bennett (1986) says, equitable opportunities for success demand "unequal teaching methods that respond to relevant differences among students."

Ideas about culture and learning styles can be of great help to teachers as they pursue such intentional instructional diversity. A teacher who truly understands culture and learning styles and who believes that all students can learn, one way or another, can offer opportunities for success to all students.

Not Easy, but Crucial

While the culture/learning styles relationship is deceptively simple and the issues surrounding it are complex, it is a crucially important idea to contemplate. We should not be reluctant to do so for fear of repeating past mistakes. With a better understanding of these missteps, we can avoid them in the future. As Hilliard (1989) assures us:

Educators need not avoid addressing the question of style for fear they may be guilty of stereotyping students. Empirical observations are not the same as stereotyping, but the observations must be empirical and must be interpreted properly for each student.

As we try to accommodate students' cultural and learning differences, it is most important to deeply value each person's individuality. If we believe that people do learn—and have the right to learn—in a variety of ways, then we will see learning styles as a comprehensive approach guiding all educational decisions and practices. The ideas will not become ends in themselves, which would merely support the uniformity found in most schools.

Using information about culture and learning styles in sensitive and positive ways will help educators value and promote diversity in all aspects of the school. This task will not be easy, but then teaching is not a profession for the faint of heart. It requires courage and a willingness to grapple with real questions about people and their learning. Many students stand to benefit from that effort.

References

Barger, N J., and L. K. Kirby. (Fall 1993). "The Interaction of Cultural Values and Type Development: INTP Women Across Cultures." *Bulletin of Psychological Type 16*: 14–16.

Bennett, C. (1986). *Comprehensive Multicultural Education, Theory and Practice.* Boston: Allyn and Bacon.

Berry, J. W. (1979). "Culture and Cognitive Style." In *Perspectives on Cross-Cultural Psychology,* edited by A. Marsella, R. Tharp, and T. Ciborowski. San Francisco: Academic Press.

Bert, C. R. G., and M. Bert. (1992). *The Native American: An Exceptionality in Education and Counseling.* (ERIC Document Reproduction Service No. ED 351 168)

Claxton, C. S. (Fall 1990). "Learning Styles, Minority Students, and Effective Education." *Journal of Developmental Education 14*: 6–8, 35.

Cox, B., and M. Ramirez III. (1981). "Cognitive Styles: Implications for Multiethnic Education." In *Education in the '80s,* edited by J. Banks, Washington, D.C.: National Education Association.

Gardner, H. (1983). *Frames of Mind.* New York: Basic Books.

Gardner, H. (1991). *The Unschooled Mind: How Children Think and How Schools Should Teach.* New York: Basic Books.

Griggs, S. A., and R. Dunn. (1989). "The Learning Styles of Multicultural Groups and Counseling Implications." *Journal of Multicultural Counseling and Development 17:* 146–155.

Guild, P., and S. Garger. (1985). *Marching to Different Drummers.* Alexandria, Va.: Association for Supervision and Curriculum Development.

Hale-Benson, J. E. (1986). *Black Children: Their Roots, Culture, and Learning Styles,* Rev. ed. Baltimore: Johns Hopkins University Press.

Hilliard, A. G., III. (January 1989). "Teachers and Cultural Styles in a Pluralistic Society." *NEA Today:* 65–69.

More, A. J. (1990). "Learning Styles of Native Americans and Asians." Paper presented at the Annual Meeting of the American Psychological Association, Boston. (ERIC Document Reproduction Service No. ED 330 535)

Myers, I. B. (1990). *Gifts Differing,* 2nd ed. Palo Alto, Calif.: Consulting Psychologists Press.

Ramirez, M., III. (1989). "Pluralistic Education: A Bicognitive-Multicultural Model." *The Clearinghouse Bulletin 3:* 4–5.

Shade, B. J. (October 1989). "The Influence of Perceptual Development in Cognitive Style: Cross Ethnic Comparisons." *Early Child Development and Care 51:* 137–155.

Vasquez, J. A. (1991). "Cognitive Style and Academic Achievement." In *Cultural Diversity and the Schools: Consensus and Controversy,* edited by J. Lynch, C. Modgil, and S. Modgil. London: Falconer Press.

 Article Review Form at end of book.

What are the two goals of multicultural education? Underachieving and special education students increase achievement as a response to what kind of teaching?

The Goals and Track Record of Multicultural Education

Rita Dunn

Rita Dunn is Professor, Division of Administrative and Instructional Leadership, and Director, Center for the Study of Learning and Teaching Styles, St. John's University, Grand Central and Utopia Parkways, Jamaica, NY 11439. She is the author of 17 books, including ASCD's How to Implement and Supervise Learning Style Programs (1996).

Paying attention to the varied learning styles of all students will do more to accomplish the goals of multicultural education than misguided programs that often divide children.

Because multicultural education is a volatile political issue— one with articulate proponents and antagonists on both sides— the research on this topic needs to be examined objectively. Many practices that schools promote make little sense in terms of how multiculturally diverse students learn. Thus, we need to examine the data concerning how poor achievement has been reversed among culturally diverse students in many schools.

What Is Multicultural Education?

Multicultural education originated in the 1960s as a response to the long-standing policy of assimilating immigrants into the melting pot of our dominant American culture (Sobol 1990). Over the past three decades, it has expanded from an attempt to reflect the growing diversity in American classrooms to include curricular revisions that specifically address the academic needs of students. In recent years, it has been distorted by some into a movement that threatens to divide citizens along racial and cultural lines (Schlessinger 1991). Generally, multicultural education has focused on two broad goals: increasing academic achievement and promoting greater sensitivity to cultural differences in an attempt to reduce bias.

Increasing Academic Achievement

Efforts intended to increase the academic achievement of multicultural groups include programs that (1) focus on the research on culturally based learning styles as a step toward determining which teaching styles or methods to use with a particular group of students; (2) emphasize bilingual or bicultural approaches; (3) build on the language and culture of African- or Hispanic-American students; and (4) emphasize math and science specifically for minority or female students (Banks 1994). Programs in each of these categories are problematic.

- Culturally based learning styles. So long as such programs include reasonable provisions for language and cultural differences, they can help students make the transition into mainstream classes. In that sense, they may be considered similar to other compensatory programs that are not multicultural in their emphasis. As a researcher and advocate of learning styles, however, I would caution against attempting to identify or respond to so-called cultural learning styles. Researchers have clearly established that there is no single or dual learning style for the members of any cultural, national, racial, or religious group. A single learning style does not appear even within a family of four or five (Dunn and Griggs 1995).

- Bilingual or bicultural approaches. Attention to cultural and language differences can be done appropriately or inappropriately. Bi- and trilingualism in our increasingly interdependent world are valuable for, and should be required of, all students. An emphasis on bilingualism for only non-English-speaking children denies English-speaking students skills required for successful interactions internationally. Today, many adults need to speak several languages fluently and to appreciate cultural similarities and differences to succeed in their work.

- Another problem arises in those classrooms in which bilingual teachers speak English ungrammatically and haltingly. Such teachers provide a poor model for non-English-speaking children, who may remain in bilingual programs for years, unable to make the transition into English-speaking classes. Ultimately, this impairs the ability of these children to

move into well-paying professions and careers—the ultimate goal of most of their parents.

- Selective cultural programs. Building on the language and culture of selected groups and not of others suggests bias and bigotry. Parents should teach their children to appreciate and respect their native cultures; schools should teach children to appreciate and respect all cultures. If the need exists to expand attention to more cultures, let us do that. But let us stop promoting one culture over another with the inevitable result of dividing our children and diminishing their sense of belonging to the dominant culture that is uniquely American intentionally a combination of the best of all its citizens.

- Minority- and gender-based grouping for math and science. Emphasizing math and science specifically for minority or female students may be based on good intentions, but it ignores the fact that minority students and female students all learn differently from one another and differently from their counterparts—whether those be high- or low-achieving classmates. Providing resources and methods that help all students learn rapidly and well should be the focus for teaching math and science—and every other subject. Are there not males and majority students who fail those subjects? The answer is to change how those subjects are taught, not to isolate certain groups and teach them as though they all have the same style of learning.

Sensitizing Ourselves to Social Agendas

Some multicultural education programs are specifically designed to increase cultural and racial tolerance and reduce bias. These are intended to restructure and desegregate schools, increase contact among the races, and encourage minorities to become teachers; and they lean heavily on cooperative learning (Banks 1994). Sleeter and Grant (1993) describe these programs as emphasizing human relations, incorporating some compensatory goals and curricular revisions to emphasize positive contributions of ethnic and cultural groups, and using learning styles to enhance students' achievement and reduce racial tensions.

Some of these programs emphasize pluralism and cultural equity in American society as a whole, seeking to apply critical thinking skills to a critique of racism and sexism. Others emphasize multilingualism or examine issues from viewpoints other than those of the dominant culture.

In my judgment, these focuses are more political than educational or social. Critical thinking is a requirement for all—not a select few. In addition, whose thinking prevails in these programs, and what are their credentials? Being a minority member or having taken a course does not automatically make a person proficient in teaching minority or female students, or in critiquing social issues. Political debate is helpful to developing young minds; one-sided, preconceived viewpoints are not.

Curriculum and Multicultural Achievement

In the debate over New York's "Children of the Rainbow" curriculum, the ideas of multicultural education captured almost daily headlines. Opponents argued that curriculum change would not increase student achievement, whereas proponents insisted that culturally diverse students performed poorly in school because they could not relate to an American curriculum.

Drew, Dunn, and colleagues (1994) tested how well 38 Cajun students and 29 Louisiana Indian students, all poor achievers, could recall story content and vocabulary immediately and after a delay. Their recall differed significantly when they were instructed with (1) traditional versus multisensory instructional resources and (2) stories in which cultural relevance matched and mismatched students' identified cultural backgrounds. Each subject was presented with four story treatments (two culturally sensitive and two dominant American) and tested for recall immediately afterward and again one week later. The findings for Cajun subjects indicated significant differences between instructional treatments, with greater recall in each multisensory instructional condition—Cultural-Immediate, Cultural-Delayed, American-Immediate, and American-Delayed. The main effect of instructional treatment for Louisiana Indian subjects was significant as well. Recall scores were even higher when they used multisensory materials for American stories. No significant main effect emerged for test interval with either group.

This study demonstrated that what determined whether students mastered the content was how the content was taught, not the content itself. The culturally sensitive curriculum did not produce significantly higher achievement for these two poorly achieving cultural groups; the methods that were used did.

Teaching Methods and Multicultural Achievement

Other studies of teaching methods revealed even more dramatic results. Before being taught with methods that responded to their learning styles, only 25 percent of special education high school students in a suburban New York school district had passed the required local examinations and state competency tests to receive diplomas. In the first year of the district's learning styles program (1987–88), that number increased to 66 percent. During the second year, 91 percent of the district's special education students were successful, and in the third year, the results remained constant at 90 percent—with a greater ratio of "handicapped" students passing state competency exams than regular education students (Brunner and Majewski 1990).

Two North Carolina elementary principals reported similarly impressive gains as a result of their learning styles programs. In an impoverished, largely minority school, Andrews (1990) brought student scores that had consistently been in the 30th percentile on the California Achievement Tests to the 83rd percentile over a three-year period by responding to students' learning styles. Shortly thereafter, Stone (1992) showed highly tactual, learning

disabled (LD) elementary school students how to learn with Flip Chutes, Electroboards, Task Cards, and Pic-A-Holes while seated informally in rooms where levels of light matched their style preferences. The children were encouraged to study either alone, with a classmate or two, or with their teacher—based on their learning style strengths. Within four months, those youngsters had achieved four months' reading gains on a standardized achievement test—better than they ever had done previously and as well as would have been expected of children achieving at normal levels.

Many professional journals have reported statistically higher scores on standardized achievement and attitude tests as a result of learning style teaching with underachieving and special education students (Dunn, Bruno, Sklar, Zenhausern, and Beaudry 1990; Dunn, Griggs, Olson, Gorman, and Beasley 1995; Klavas 1993; Lemmon 1985; Perrin 1990; Quinn 1993). Indeed, a four-year investigation by the U.S. Office of Education that included on-site visits, interviews, observations, and examinations of national test data concluded that the Dunn and Dunn Learning Styles Model was one of only a few strategies that had had a positive effect on the achievement of special education students throughout the nation (Alberg, Cook, Fiore, Friend, and Sano 1992).

What Have We Learned?

Research documents that underachieving students—whether they are from other cultures or from the dominant U.S. culture—tend to learn differently from students who perform well in our schools (Dunn and Griggs 1995; Milgram, Dunn, and Price 1993). As indicated in the examples cited earlier, schools with diverse populations reversed academic failure when instruction was changed to complement the children's learning style strengths.

In our book, Multiculturalism and Learning Style (Dunn and Griggs 1995), my coauthor and I summarize research findings on each of the major cultural groups in the United States: African Americans, Asian Americans, European Americans, Hispanic Americans, and Native Americans. The research clearly shows that there is no such thing as a cultural group style. There are cross-cultural and intracultural similarities and differences among all peoples. Those differences are enriching when understood and channeled positively.

Given this information, I believe it is unwise for schools with limited budgets to support multicultural education in addition to—and apart from regular education. Instead, schools need to make their instructional delivery systems responsive to how diverse students learn (Dunn 1995).

Educational programs should not separate young children from one another. Any separation becomes increasingly divisive over time and is likely to produce the opposite of what multicultural education is intended to accomplish. Segregated children begin to feel different from and less able than the larger groups of children they see—but are apart from. These feelings can lead to emotional insecurity and a dislike of others.

The United States was founded as a nation intended to absorb people from many nations. Monocultural education in the guise of multicultural education offends the cornerstone of those intentions. The melting pot concept does not diminish one's heritage. It unites the strengths of many cultures into a single, stronger blend of culture to reflect the best of all.

References

Alberg, J., L. Cook, T. Fiore, M. Friend, and S. Sano. (1992). *Educational Approaches and Options for Integrating Students with Disabilities: A Decision Tool.* Triangle Park, N.C.: Research Triangle Institute.

Andrews, R.H. (July–September 1990). "The Development of a Learning Styles Program in a Low Socioeconomic, Underachieving North Carolina Elementary School." *Journal of Reading, Writing, and Learning Disabilities International 6,* 3: 307–314.

Banks, J.A. (1994). *An Introduction to Multicultural Education.* Boston: Allyn and Bacon.

Brunner, C.E., and W.S. Majewski (October 1990). "Mildly Handicapped Students Can Succeed with Learning Styles." *Educational Leadership 48,* 2: 21–23.

Drew, M., R. Dunn, P. Quinn, R. Sinatra, and J. Spiridakis. (1994). "Effects of Matching and Mismatching Minority Underachievers with Culturally Similar and Dissimilar Story Content and Learning Style and Traditional Instructional Practices." *Applied Educational Research Journal 8,* 2: 3–10.

Dunn, R., J. Bruno, R.I. Sklar, R. Zenhausern, and J. Beaudry. (May–June 1990). "Effects of Matching and Mismatching Minority Developmental College Students' Hemispheric Preferences on Mathematics Scores." *Journal of Educational Research 83,* 5: 283–288.

Dunn, R., S.A. Griggs, J. Olson, B. Gorman, and M. Beasley. (1995). "A Meta-Analytic Validation of the Dunn and Dunn Research Learning Styles Model." *Journal of Educational Research 88,* 6: 353–361.

Dunn, R. (1995). *Educating Diverse Learners: Strategies for Improving Current Classroom Practices.* Bloomington, Ind.: Phi Delta.

Dunn, R., and S.A. Griggs. (1995). *Multi-culturalism and Learning Styles: Teaching and Counseling Adolescents.* Westport, Conn: Praeger Publishers, Inc.

Klavas, A. (1993). "In Greensboro, North Carolina: Learning Style Program Boosts Achievement and Test Scores." *The Clearing House 67,* 3: 149–151.

Lemmon, P. (1985). "A School Where Learning Styles Make a Difference." *Principal 64,* 4: 26–29.

Milgram, R.M., R. Dunn, and G.E. Price, eds. (1993). *Teaching and Counseling Gifted and Talented Adolescents: An International Learning Style Perspective.* Westport, Conn.: Praeger Publishers, Inc.

Perrin, J. (October 1990). "The Learning Styles Project for Potential Dropouts." *Educational Leadership 48,* 2: 23–24.

Quinn, R. (1993). "The New York State Compact for Learning and Learning Styles." *Learning Styles Network Newsletter 15,* 1: 1–2.

Schlessinger, A., Jr. (1991). "Report of the Social Studies Syllabus Review Committee: A Dissenting Opinion." In *One Nation, Many Peoples: A Declaration of Cultural Independence,* edited by New York State Social Studies Review and Development Committee. New York: Author.

Sleeter, C.E., and C.A. Grant. (1993). *Making Choices for Multicultural Education: Five Approaches to Race, Class, and Gender,* 2nd ed. New York: Merrill.

Sobol, T. (1990). "Understanding Diversity." *Educational Leadership 48,* 3: 27–30.

Stone, P. (November 1992). "How We Turned Around a Problem School." *Principal 71,* 2: 34–36.

 Article Review Form at end of book.

What are the three conditions for the development of a particular type of intelligence? Describe how educational equity practices are addressed by using multiple intelligences and cultural influences in learning.

Multiple Intelligences, Culture and Equitable Learning

Judith C. Reiff

"Knowing that a relationship exists between cultures and education is a prerequisite to effective teaching, but continuing to teach with styles and strategies appropriate only for middle-class Anglo learners fails to meet the needs of culturally diverse children and adolescents" (Baruth & Manning, 1992, p. 332).

The high drop-out rates and low academic achievement of some young adolescents are indications that middle level educators' teaching practices need to be more culturally responsive. Instruction and assessment strategies that promote educational equity should reflect research on how multiple intelligences, as well as cultural backgrounds, affect young adolescents' learning. Educators often expect all learners to assimilate middle-class, Anglo American perspectives. This "culturally assaultive" perspective can adversely affect young adolescents' development, academic achievement and overall school progress. Educators can promote educational equity practices by addressing both students' multiple intelligences and cultural influences on learning.

Multiple Intelligences

Howard Gardner's theory of multiple intelligences (1983, 1993) provides a solid foundation upon which to identify, value and develop students' abilities. Gardner based his multiple intelligences theory on brain research, previous developmental work with young children, experiments with animals, psychological testing, cross-cultural studies and the works of Dewey, Bruner, Piaget and Eisner. Gardner (1983) maintained that intelligence is biologically based and can represent itself in multiple ways. He believes every individual has a least seven intelligences to some degree:

logical-mathematical: enjoys solving problems, finding patterns, outlining, calculating

linguistic: relates to the meaning, rhythms and sounds of words

spatial: likes to design, invent, imagine and create

bodily kinesthetic: learns through physical movement, mimicking and touching

musical/rhythmic: enjoys the human voice, as well as environmental and instructional sounds

interpersonal: understands others' feelings

intrapersonal: understands one's own emotions, motivations and moods.

The Effects of Culture

The concept of multiple intelligences has gained increased attention because of the discrepancy that often exists between school tasks and children's "spectrum of intelligences" (Gardner, 1983). In addition, culture significantly influences the development of learners' intelligences by defining what is valued for every individual. Too often, schools have developed elaborate systems for identifying and labeling students according to their deficiencies, rather than building on their strengths, intelligences and cultural backgrounds.

Educators of diverse populations will find Gardner's work on multiple intelligences especially relevant. Gardner (1994) believes American society suffers from three biases . . . "westist," "testist" and "bestist." He suggests a broader view of intelligence that allows students to solve problems in culturally meaningful ways and create products that reflect their cultural perspectives. The development of a particular type of intelligence requires three conditions: 1) the individual must have the opportunity to learn, 2) the culture must place value on the intelligence's development and 3) the individual must place value on developing intelligence.

When a student's cultural style differs from the school culture, cultural incompatibility, or dissonance, often occurs. Fortunately, culturally responsive teaching methods and activities can address the needs of diverse learners (Baruth & Manning, 1992). Every middle school curriculum should include authentic assessments that reflect different intelligences, strengths, learning styles, and cultural backgrounds and interests. As Armstrong (1994) suggested, it would be wrong for teachers to ask students to participate in a wide variety of multiple intelligence activities and then test their learning by using a standardized test. Teachers should rely on intelligence-fair and curriculum-embedded assessments, including process folios, portfolios, observations, journals, performance-based projects, open-ended questions and domain-related projects.

Application of Multiple Intelligences

By applying multiple intelligences teachers can actively involve students in learning experiences, help develop particular intelligences that individual students may lack (yet are important for future success), and design culturally responsive approaches to reach students who have trouble learning. Individualized and culturally responsive learning experiences allow students to achieve at their own pace, provide positive reinforcement and help them reach their full potential (Teele, 1990).

Gardner (1983, 1993, 1994) says that educators do not have to address all of the intelligences in everything they teach. Different projects can give students the option to explore a topic using their strongest intelligence. Some students might make a model, write or illustrate content, for example. Students must learn about a topic in a manner that is appropriate for them.

Gardner's (1993) insightful conclusions regarding multiple intelligences provide a sound basis on which middle school educators can build teaching-learning practices. Still, this translation of theory into practice often challenges educators. Rather than focusing on the whole class, teachers should begin assessing multiple intelligences by specifically focusing on one to three students. The teacher should develop intelligence profiles for these students that exemplify their strengths and weaknesses, as related to Gardner's seven intelligences. Draw up an intelligence profile for each student by brainstorming a list of seven to ten observable characteristics. Finally, brainstorm a list of three to five things that capitalize on dominant intelligences and develop weaker ones.

Consider an upcoming lesson or unit. Select an activity for each intelligence that will help you achieve your objective for the lesson or unit. Then write down step-by-step procedures for implementing the lesson or unit, incorporating the activities you have chosen into the teaching and learning process (Lazear, 1991a, 1991b).

As previously suggested, promoting equitable educational experiences through multiple intelligences also requires culturally responsive assessment. David Lazear (1994) identified several key principles when providing instruction that reflects multiple intelligences and culturally responsive assessment:

Assessment design and execution should include educators who work with the students.

Assessment requires time and effort; educators should be given appropriate time to create and administer instruments.

Assessment should be authentic and central to the education process.

Assessment should drive the curriculum.

Assessment practices should be designed for students' benefit.

Assessment practices should mirror assessment in the "real world."

Assessment should be individualized and developmentally appropriate.

Assessment requires that students become active partners in demonstrating learning.

Summary

Research on multiple intelligences suggests that middle school educators should rethink current instructional and assessment practices. Planning, teaching and assessment should be based upon learners' individual needs and intelligences. Overall, educational experiences should reflect an understanding of each learner's culture, especially since a relationship exists between multiple intelligences and culture (Reiff, 1993, 1996).

Rather than expecting all young adolescents to use the same intelligences, middle school educators can devise culturally appropriate strategies and assessment. The following learning activities, developed and implemented by students in the author's Teaching/Learning Styles course, show how middle school educators can incorporate multiple intelligences into the curriculum. The different formats demonstrate how middle school teachers can be flexible when planning such activities—as long as they reflect multiple intelligences.

References

Armstrong, T. (1994). *Multiple Intelligences in the Classroom.* Reston, VA: Association of Supervision and Curriculum Development.

Baruth, L. G., & Manning, M. L. (1992). *Multicultural Education of Children and Adolescents.* Boston: Allyn and Bacon.

Gardner, H. (1983). *Frames of Mind* (rev. 1993). New York: Basic Books.

Gardner, H. (1993). *Multiple Intelligences: The Theory in Practice.* New York: Basic Books.

Gardner, H. (1994). *Intelligences in Theory and Practice: A Response to Elliott W. Eisner,* Robert J. Sternberg, and Henry M. Levin. Teachers College Record, 95(4), 567–582.

Lazear, D. (1991a). *Seven Ways of Knowing: Teaching for Multiple Intelligences.* Palentine, IL: Skylight Publishing.

Lazear, D. (1991b). *Seven Ways of Teaching: Teaching for Multiple Intelligences.* Palentine, IL: Skylight Publishing.

Lazear, D. (1994). *Multiple Intelligence Approaches to Assessment: Solving the Assessment Conundrum.* Tucson, AZ: Zephyr Press.

Reiff J. (1993, February). *Learning Styles and Culture: Promises and Problems.* Paper presented at the annual meeting of the National Association for Multicultural Education, Los Angeles, CA.

Reiff, J. (1996, April). *Bridging Home and School Through Multiple Intelligences.* Paper presented at the annual meeting of the Association for Childhood Education International, Minneapolis, MN.

Teele, S. (1990). *Teaching and Assessment Strategies Appropriate for the Multiple Intelligences* (rev. 1992). Riverside, CA: University of California.

 Article Review Form at end of book.

What traditional areas are addressed in most anti-bias curricula?
How can the ecological model be used to examine factors that affect
a student's set of experiences?

Proposal
An anti-bias and ecological model for multicultural education

Francis Wardle

Francis Wardle is Director, Resource Development & Training, Children's World Learning Centers, and Adjunct Faculty, University of Phoenix, Arizona.

The early childhood community has led efforts to develop materials and resources to support children's unique heritages and diverse experiences (Derman-Sparks, 1989; Neugebauer, 1992; York, 1991). While recognizing that education programs should validate all children and their families, educators have relied on a traditional multicultural model that limits their ability to explore the full range of diversity. It is time to propose a new model—one that recognizes the differences among traditional racial and cultural groups, acknowledges the variability within these groups and enables us to explore the uniqueness of people whose heritages and experiences do not fit into any traditional racial or cultural category.

Traditional Model

The traditional model of anti-bias and multicultural education views the child as the product of

culture (Figure 1). Or, to put it another way, children's sets of experiences and their world outlook are totally predetermined by their culture. "Culture forms the prism through which members of a group see the world and create shared meaning" (Bowman, 1989, p. 2). Children's values, traditions and expectations are predetermined by their religion, attitudes about family and, sometimes, a long history of persecution and oppression.

Children are then viewed as a product of their community's culture: African American, Native American, Asian, Hispanic or European. According to this model, all black children are supposedly the products of a collective black cultural context and Native Amer-

ican children all "see the world" in the same way. This model stresses culture, group membership and shared attributes. Individual identity and self-esteem are based on a sense of belonging to and pride in one's cultural group.

The traditional multicultural education model in the United States teaches children about the values, celebrations, histories, traditions and art forms of five traditional cultural groups: European, African American, Latino, Asian American and Native American (Ramirez & Ramirez, 1994). Teachers are urged to help each child connect with his/her heritage, and to help each child feel positive about the group to which he/she belongs. Multicultural curricula include books and other

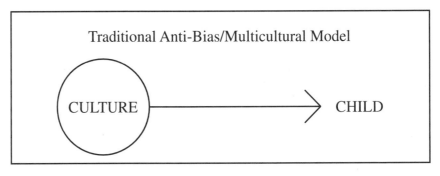

Traditional Anti-Bias/Multicultural Model

CULTURE ——————————————> CHILD

Figure 1

materials that reflect each of these groups (Ramirez & Ramirez, 1994). The child develops a sense of self-esteem and identity through knowledge of and identification with his/her cultural group.

This traditional model has many shortcomings. It perpetuates stereotypes: if every child from the same culture sees the world through the same prism, then all children from one culture must be the same. The traditional model does not allow for the tremendous diversity to be found within traditional cultural groups (Wardle, 1994a; West, 1992). A child who can trace his/her heritage directly to the original Spanish settlers of northern New Mexico has a different cultural context from a Latino child living in inner-city Los Angeles. A black child whose family has just immigrated to the United States from Belize has a very different set of experiences from a child of black college professors at Harvard.

Many Latin Americans have parents who are German, Polish, Austrian or Swiss. They speak Spanish and live in a Hispanic culture, yet are blond and have blue eyes. A member of Argentina's current national soccer team, for example, is a third-generation Irish descendent with red hair and freckles. Other residents of these Hispanic countries belong to specific minority groups.

William Cross (1985) questions the notion that young minority children's self-esteem is based on pride in and a sense of belonging to their cultural and racial group. Cross's research shows that positive self-esteem is more likely to be based on how the child sees himself as an individual, not how he sees himself in reference to racial groups or communities. Personal identity reinforced by positive responses to the individual child is more important than group identity.

Also, it is impractical, if not impossible, to teach about the multitude of cultures in our world (Gomez, 1991). According to Valeria Lovelace (1994), this difficulty is the reason *Sesame Street*'s "Race Project" does not explore the identities of biracial children. Clearly, Lovelace adheres to the traditional model of multicultural education. Furthermore, some children's experiences do not fit into any of the traditional cultural groups. Transracially adopted children, biracial children and some foreign children, for example, cannot be placed into any of the five traditional groups (Wardle, 1988a, 1993, 1994b). Curricula that use the traditional model as the basis for classroom activities and material selection do not reflect these children's experiences, and sometimes actually force them to deny part of their heritage (York, 1991).

Many people claim multicultural education is divisive, and that it creates ethnocentric curricula, segregation and alternative histories. Most books that address multicultural education portray a power conflict between whites and people of color (McCracken, 1993; Ramirez & Ramirez, 1994). The traditional model lends itself to these criticisms, and sometimes does create hostility among students from different cultural groups. Furthermore, it gives ammunition to those who believe the sole purpose of multicultural education is to devalue the majority culture.

Finally, the problem of content must be addressed. Educators should not assume that *what* they teach is more important than *how* they teach. A traditional focus on content led to the development of state-mandated curricula and national social science texts that did not represent the backgrounds of non-white student and children of recent immigrants. Consequently, discussions about multicultural education are often debates about what content should and should not be taught (e.g., the current debate on the national standards for social science content and Colorado's new state standards).

Focusing on the content of traditional multicultural groups can result in a "tourist approach" (Derman-Sparks, 1987) to multicultural education and very inappropriate teaching methods (Bredekamp, 1987). This focus emphasizes the cultures, leading to arguments concerning which culture is most important and who is competent to teach each culture. Consider the debate about who should teach bilingual Spanish/English classes. In a California district, for example, protests erupted when bilingual teachers were hired from Spain. And what happens if a conflict exists between two minority groups? Such jockeying for a favored position tends to make the child's needs secondary, even though multicultural education's purpose is to support the total heritage of each child.

We should instead focus on recognizing the unique set of experiences each child brings to school, and learning how we can utilize those experiences to help him or her achieve the utmost self-esteem and academic success. When we let adult content and political ends become more important than children's needs, we fail as educators.

The Anti-Bias and Ecological Model

An anti-bias and ecological model requires educators to present a multicultural foundation that teaches all children to accept one another (Gomez, 1991). It should enable each child to associate positive feelings with multicultural experiences and to feel included and valued (Dimidjian, 1989). It also provides a much simpler framework for teaching with a multicultural perspective.

In this model, the child is the focus, rather than the culture. Educators should recognize the variety of contexts that affect each child's experiences and point of view. The individual child exists within his/her own dynamic context, or milieu, which includes a variety of experiences that interact with each other to produce a unique environment (Johnson, 1990). This model is built on previous models by Jones (1985) and Wardle (1992), which themselves were developed to study the psychological functioning of African Americans and biracial children, respectively.

The resulting model recognizes that children clearly experience integrated contexts, not a series of distinct, opposing factors (Jones, 1987; Wardle, 1992). The overlapping circles depicted in Figures 2 and 3 represent the weight, or power, of each contextual factor that differs from situation to situation, from child to child, and is dependent on the interaction between two or more factors. This model assumes that children interact on their contextual environments. Thus, each child will experience the same context differently.

Factors/Contexts

Two groups of significant factors come into play. Group A factors are the traditional areas addressed in most anti-bias curricula (Derman-Sparks, 1989; Neugebauer, 1992; York, 1991): race, culture, gender and disability (see Figure 2). Our society has traditionally viewed these factors as having a preferred side, and one or more sides that can be inferior, dominated and/or persecuted. They are also individual characteristics that cannot be changed.

Group B factors are what Bronfenbrenner (1989) calls ecological components: family, community and social-economic status (S.E.S.) (see Figure 3). These factors have a powerful effect on the other factors' influence. Anti-bias activities must be directed toward these factors. Children cannot change their race, culture, gender or disability. Family, school and community, however, can help them feel positive about these personal characteristics.

It should not be assumed that A factors are more important than B factors. All the factors interact in a variety of unique ways, and their influence changes as children develop. Factors group together in

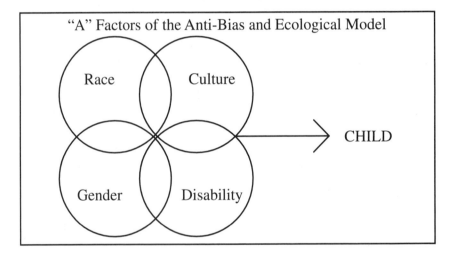

Figure 2

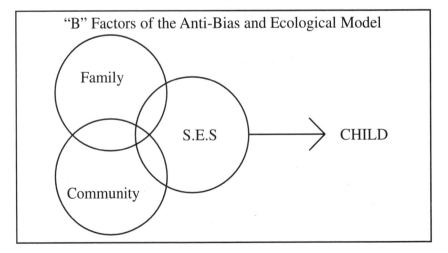

Figure 3

different ways to affect children's development in different ways. For example, race, gender and S.E.S. can have such a strong impact on a child's development that they sometimes override other factors.

Group A Factors (Figure 2)

Race/Ethnicity. Although racial groups do not represent pure biological categories, society does attach significance to differences of physiognomy (Wilson, 1984). The assumption is that racial contexts affect an individual's identity (Wilson, 1984). Until quite recently, however, scholars studied race and culture separately. Many countries still separate race and culture (Wilson, 1984).

Culture. Culture includes family traditions, religion, holidays, heroes, music, ideals and beliefs, primary language and national origin. Cultures operate as contexts because they fix meanings over time, and each culture has the capacity to fix meaning differently (Johnson, 1990). The separation of the cultural category from the racial category allows for distinctions among American blacks, first-generation blacks from Africa and Caribbean blacks; direct descendants of original Spanish settlers, Puerto Rican immigrants in New York, first-generation immigrants from Brazil and Mestizos from Mexico; third-generation Chinese Americans and first-generation Hmongs, Cambodians and Vietnamese. It also allows us to appreciate the rich differences in the customs, religions, art, dance, houses and languages of the various Native American nations (Sample, 1993).

Gender. This distinction is obvious. Many cultures still respond very differently to girls and boys, beginning in infancy. Early childhood programs, curricula and experiences treat the genders in distinct ways (Wardle, 1990). More boys are diagnosed with learning disabilities, and girls are less likely to succeed in math and science. The students in special education programs are predominantly boys.

Disability. For the purposes of this article, disability is what a child views as a disability—in him/herself and/or others. This includes obvious physical disabilities along with speech problems, mental challenges, learning disabilities and behavioral issues.

Group B Factors (Figure 3)

Family. In the language of Johnson (1990), the family clearly is a context. The most critical influence on young children is the family (Wardle, 1992). Family diversity can mean two working parents, teen parents, adoptive parents (including transracial adoption), foster parents, single parents (male or female), blended families, interracial and interethnic families, families that combine divergent religious beliefs, extended family support, grandparents raising their grandchildren and gay families. Parenting style (authoritarian, authoritative or permissive) and family dysfunction or abuse are also included in this factor.

Technology also affects this ecological component—primarily TV, movies and music videos, but also home computers. TV's influence can be totally absent (Amish and Hutterite children and some poor children), controlled (in terms of content and amount) or uncontrolled, developmentally inappropriate and dominating.

While religion is placed under the cultural factor in this model, the family is the prime vehicle through which children receive their religious context. Families that mix religions (Jewish/Protestant, etc.) have a different effect on children from those that do not, or families that practice no religion.

Social-Economic Status. It could be argued that this factor belongs under the A factors in recognition of the tremendous discrimination that exists against the poor. It could also be argued, however, that this status can and does change, either improving or worsening.

Poverty clearly has a long-standing impact—thus the term, "culture of poverty." Welfare status, middle-class culture and professional households (regardless of income) all act as strong ecological factors. Some families have been welfare recipients for generations; others have a long heritage of college education. Homeless children's experiences are distinct from those of an Appalachian child from a poor family.

Community. Community encompasses a vast array of factors. It includes a child's geographical location and type of community (rural, urban, suburban, etc.). A Native American reservation, a bedroom community, and integrated and segregated neighborhoods represent different community contexts, as do intentional religious communities—Hutterite, Amish, Mennonite and New Age.

Schools, child care centers, churches, Head Starts, colleges, recreational opportunities, health centers, gangs and soccer teams help identify a community. Media also plays a part.

Advantages of the Anti-Bias and Ecological Model

The anti-bias and ecological model allows us to concentrate on each individual child. It acknowledges that every child has a unique culture (Gomez, 1991), and ensures that each child will feel included and valued (Dimidjian, 1989). By concentrating on the child, the family and the family's education expectations, we can begin to tailor and individualize multicultural programs for each child. This approach is totally consistent with the individual perspective advocated by developmentally appropriate practice (Bredekamp, 1987). It also discourages stereotyping and prevents expectations that children who belong to the same cultural groups will act the same way, share the same interests and play with children from their "group" (Wardle, 1988b).

Role of Teacher and School

How can a teacher respond to all these factors, and the range within factors? How can the school environment be arranged to support children whose set of experiences can differ so dramatically? How can we provide child care settings that are responsive to such a range of diversity? And how can we teach our children to respect and appreciate the variability of other children, both inside and outside the classroom?

We must always go back to the child. . . . Instead of trying to learn everything about every community, culture and home, the teacher should combine an enlightened knowledge of cultural, gender and individual differences with a constant ability to "read" the child. If a child does not seem to respond to certain stories or is uneasy in certain activities, find out why.

This approach will require a radical change in teaching methods and in the way many teachers are trained. Traditionally, we expect children to adapt to the needs of the classroom, curricula and teacher. If something did not work, we tried to change the child or labeled the child with a disability (Wardle, 1990). Now we must change our entire approach. The teacher must also "read" the family and community. What encourages a family to come to the program? What keeps them away? What do they expect the program to do for their child? What materials do they want their children to use? (York, 1991).

A good teacher must be able to use the framework of this model to effectively support each child in the classroom and challenge his/her own cultural and individual framework. This model can be effectively used by a sensitive, well-trained teacher. Clearly this model challenges the notion that a black teacher is the only person who can adequately teach black children and only a Native American teacher can teach a Native American child. That notion leads to segregated classrooms; in one instance, a Head Start teacher from one Native American tribe was considered an inappropriate teacher for children from another tribe (Wardle, 1991).

Clearly, society has strong biases toward each factor of this model—from race to income to community to religion. Thus, any program adapting this model must engage, to some extent, in anti-bias activities and consciousness raising (Derman-Sparks, 1989).

Schools and child care centers must know about the children, community and families they are serving before purchasing curriculum materials. Furthermore, because curriculum materials still tend to support socially accepted points of view, program administrators may have to develop their own materials.

Curriculum materials, classroom activities and community outings must address all seven factors in a way that conveys the variability within each factor. A lesson about communities, for example, can focus on the dynamics of a small farm community, a Native American reservation, integrated segments of a large city or a Mexican neighborhood. As part of this activity, a class might study various dwellings, including apartments, mobile homes, hogans and homeless shelters.

Equal value should be given to all aspects of any factor. When teaching about the various religions in a community, each religion—be it Quaker, Jewish, atheist or Methodist—must be taught with the same respect and deliberation. The program must support exploration of the variability within each factor, regardless of whether the program is religiously, ethnically, racially or economically homogeneous or diverse.

Conclusion

The traditional multicultural model has served well to heighten the recognition that all children should be exposed to the rich contribution of all Americans, and that we must support the history, heritage and culture of each child in our programs. We have been sensitized to the injustices and biases that have hurt people from specific cultural, gender and disability groups. We were inspired to develop curricula that celebrate each of these traditional cultures. Now, however, we must move beyond this traditional model. The anti-bias and ecological model described in this article enables us to see the child as a product of important factors, including—but not limited to—culture. We can examine every factor that affects the child's set of experiences, and allow each of our children to develop to their full potential.

References

Bowman, B. T. (1989). Educating language—minority children. *ERIC Digest.* Urbana, IL: ERIC Publications.

Bredekamp, S. (Ed.). (1987). *Developmentally appropriate practice in early childhood programs serving children birth through age 8* (rev. ed.). Washington, DC: National Association for the Education of Young Children.

Bronfenbrenner, U. (1989, April). *The developing ecology of human development.* Paper presented at the biannual meeting of the Society for Research in Child Development, Kansas City, KS.

Cross, W. (1985). Black identity: Rediscovering the distinction between personal identity and reference group orientation. In M. B. Spencer, G. K. Brooklin, & W. R. Allen (Eds.), *Beginnings: The social and affective development of black children* (pp. 155–172). Hillside NJ: Lawrence Erlbaum.

Derman-Sparks, L. (1989). *Anti-bias curriculum: Tools for empowering young children.* Washington, DC: National Association for the Education of Young Children.

Dimidjian, V. J. (1989). Holiday, holy days, and wholly dazed. *Young Children, 44*(6), 70–75.

Gomez, R. A. (1991). Teaching with a multicultural perspective. *ERIC,* EDO-PS-91-11.

Johnson, S. (1990). Toward clarifying culture, race, and ethnicity in the context of multicultural counseling. *Journal of Multicultural Counseling and Development, 18,* 41–50.

Jones, A. (1985). Psychological functioning in Black Americans: A conceptual guide for use in psychotherapy. *Psychotherapy, 22,* 363–369.

Lovelace, V. (1994, April). Personal communication with F. Wardle.

McCracken, J. B. (1993). *Valuing diversity: The primary years.* Washington, DC: National Association for the Education of Young Children.

Neugebauer, B. (1992). *Alike and different.* Washington, DC: National Association for the Education of Young Children.

Ramirez, G., & Ramirez, J. L. (1994). *Multiethnic children's literature.* Albany, NY: Delmar.

Sample, W. (1993). The American Indian child. *Child Care Information Exchange, 90,* 39–44.

Wardle, F. (1988a). Kids benefit from exposure to other cultures. *Denver Parent, 2,* 20.

Wardle, F. (1988b). Who am I? Responding to the child of mixed heritage. *PTA Today, 13*(7), 7–10.

Wardle, F. (1990). Are we shortchanging boys? *Child Care Information Exchange, 79,* 48–51.

Wardle, F. (1991). *Problems with Head Start's multicultural principles.* Unpublished paper. Denver, CO.

Wardle, F. (1992). *Biracial identity: An ecological and developmental model.* Denver, CO: Center for the Study of Biracial Children.

Wardle, F. (1993). Interracial families and biracial children. *Child Care Information Exchange, 90,* 45–58.

Wardle, F. (1994a). Diversity module. In F. Wardle (Ed.), *Staff training modules for CDA candidates in Children's World Learning Centers.* Golden, CO: Children's World Learning Centers.

Wardle, F. (1994b). What about the other kids in the neighborhood? *New People, 4*(5), 10–19.

West, B. (1992). Children are caught—between home and school, culture and school. In B. Neugebauer (Eds.), *Alike and different.* Washington, DC: National Association for the Education of Young Children.

Wilson, A. (1984). Mixed race children in British society: Some theoretical considerations. *British Journal of Sociology, 35*(1), 42–61.

York, S. (1991). *Roots and wings.* St. Paul, MN: Toys 'n Things Press.

Article Review Form at end of book.

How does the author describe the skills of deliberation? What role can deliberation play in cultural diversity?

The Art of Deliberation

Schools and their diverse populations

Walter C. Parker

Walter C. Parker is Professor of Education at the University of Washington, 122 Miller Hall, Seattle, WA 98195-3600.

With their diverse populations and social and academic problems, schools are unique arenas for learning how to thrive in a civilized society. Educators must seize the teaching opportunity.

"A school is not a private place, like our homes," writes kindergarten teacher and moral philosopher Vivian Gussin Paley. "The children I teach are just emerging from life's deep wells of private perspective: babyhood and family. Then, along comes school. It is the first real exposure to the public arena" (1992).

Paley's observation is insightful, and the implications are far reaching. For most children, school is the first sustained, daily experience of public life. For this reason, schools are ideal places to nurture the public habits and values (sometimes called civic virtue or civility) that are crucial for democratic living in diverse societies.

Diversity on Common Ground

Schools are places where diverse children are gathered together. Their diversity often runs the gamut from language and religion to ability and intelligence to race and social class. The diversity of students is increasing more rapidly than ever. It is estimated that by 2026, the Hispanic and nonwhite student enrollment in U.S. schools will reach 70 percent, the inverse of today's proportion (Garcia and Gonzalez 1995).

This buzzing variety does not exist, as Paley notes, in a "private place, like our homes." It exists where diverse people congregate, where people from numerous private worlds are brought together on common ground, where private perspectives and personal values are brought face-to-face around mutual problems and concerns.

Compared to life at home, schools are like crossroads, marketplaces, village squares, and cities themselves. When aimed at democratic ends, interaction in schools can help children develop the habits of behavior and character necessary for public life: the courtesies, manners, tolerance, respect, sense of justice, and knack for forging public policy with others, whether one likes them or not. Without these qualities, anything approaching a vigorous civic life is impossible. As Plato asked, "Are there not some qualities of which all the citizens must be partakers if there is to be a city at all?"

How to Nurture Civility?

To clarify the distinction between private and public place, we could contrast life in a criminal gang with life in a public school. This is what John Dewey did in 1916 when American society was also roiling in a new wave of diversity. In the gang, Dewey wrote, "we find that the ties which consciously hold the members together are few in number;" they are almost entirely reducible to defense, offense, and crime. Such ties "isolate the group from other groups with respect to the give-and-take of the values of life" (1916). A gang is ingrown. Its members are so similar and their shared interests and reference points so few, and of such a nature, as to partition them from exchange with the broader congregation. Because they are removed from the soil in which civility might grow, bigotry and decay—both personal and social—grow instead.

A public school, by contrast, has members who are not so similar; the common school movement of the last century and Supreme Court decisions in this century saw to that. Students cluster into cliques and peer groups, of course, but they also share many interests that bring them face-to-face with others outside these groups. The great task for teachers, administrators, and parents is to seize the opportunity afforded by this diverse congregation and channel it to help children develop the habits of behavior and character necessary for civilized public life.

Ours is certainly not the first generation to ask how to nurture civility. Looking back through the historical record and across the cultural landscape, three actions seem to be key:

1. Increase the variety and frequency of interaction among students who are different from one another.

2. Orchestrate these contacts to foster deliberation about two common kinds of problems: those that arise from the friction of interaction itself and those grounded in the academic controversies at the core of each discipline.

3. Clarify the distinction between deliberation and blather. In other words, expect, teach, and model competent deliberation that is rooted in knowledge.

Increasing Interaction

One can deepen and expand the opportunities for interaction in two arenas: the classroom and the common areas of the school. In both, students should be mixed in various kinds of groups. These groups should be temporary and task-oriented. Why? Because separating students permanently, for whatever reason—ability, prior knowledge, behavior—does not build civic health (Slavin 1995, Radencich and McKay 1995). The isolated group lacks the multiple reference points, and hence the give-and-take, of public life. Here are a few examples of interaction in both arenas.

Classroom interaction: (1) Primary grade children sit in a group around the teacher to share their work with one another; (2) students in a science class, who have been taught cooperative skills, work in teacher-assigned cooperative learning groups to compose biographies of Galileo; (3) middle school children work in teacher-assigned pairs to practice a skill, recite a poem, or interpret a chart or essay; and (4) middle and high school students gather for band and choir classes.

Schoolwide interaction: (1) Students gather in after-school clubs and teams, in assemblies, and at school events and presentations—dances, plays, pageants, athletic games, band and choir concerts; and (2) students are assigned to cross-grade teams to care for an area of the school they have adopted. (A team may, for example, consist of five children, one each from

grades 1–5, with the 5th grader as leader.) This is a time-honored activity in Japan, where it is considered part of the "moral education" program.

Fostering Deliberation

It is one thing to attend a Friday night dance with a diverse group of classmates, but quite another to plan the dance together. Students need such opportunities to deliberate together. (Note that the word deliberate comes from the Latin word libra for scale. It means "to weigh," as when weighing alternative courses of action or which policy would be best for all concerned.)

Elementary and middle school students are in the perfect setting to deliberate classroom and school policies. High school students should be doing this, too, but also deliberating divisive and complicated domestic and foreign policy questions—from environmental issues to dilemmas of international trade and resource distribution.

Deliberation should not be confused with debate, where people who have already formed their opinions gather to advocate and defend them. Nor is deliberation the same as alternating monologues, where there is sequential talking but no real listening, let alone empathy.

What I call the "deliberative arts" include a host of skills: listening as well as talking, taking turns, striving to understand points of view different from one's own, criticizing ideas rather than persons, admitting ignorance, slowing the rush to judgment so as to reframe the problem or gather more information, courageously asserting unpopular views, supporting claims with reasoning, drawing analogies, and appreciating Voltaire's principle: "I disapprove of what you say, but I will defend to the death your right to say it."

This is difficult work, of course, but so is democracy. It is what schools are for (Greene 1996). Here are a few examples.[1]

Classroom deliberation: (1) Primary grade children sit in groups around the teacher to consider a classroom rule that the teacher has proposed (Paley 1992); (2) students research and deliberate academic controversies in U.S. history, such as the causes of the Salem witchcraft hysteria or Supreme Court civil rights cases (Johnson and Johnson 1988); (3) students in teacher-assigned cooperative learning groups gather information on an assigned topic after deciding on the fairest and most effective division of labor; (4) students hold weekly homeroom meetings to weigh classroom and school policies on cheating, stealing, violence, and vandalism (They rotate the role of discussion moderator); and (5) high school seniors take a rigorous course called "Senior Problems," in which they deliberate pressing domestic and international policy questions.[2]

Schoolwide deliberation: (1) A vigorous student council has rotating delegates from homerooms who meet in order to decide policies and plan activities; (2) classrooms in each wing of the school congregate as "houses" within the larger school, planning joint projects, setting policy, and solving common problems (see Kohlberg's "Just Community" model [Power et al. 1989]); and (3) cross-grade teams decide on and plan a community service project.

Expanding Knowledge

Knowledge is the intellectual capital that a liberally educated student can bring to deliberation; it is what distinguishes deliberation from bull sessions. For this reason, early and continuous education in the liberal arts—history, the social and natural sciences, mathematics, literature, philosophy—is fundamental to the development of civility.

Perhaps no one has argued the point better, and for the American context particularly, than W.E.B. DuBois (1903) in The Souls of Black Folk, an historic critique of Booker T. Washington's work at the turn of the century. Washington advocated vocational education for recently emancipated African Americans. But DuBois warned that this would be a disabling education of "adjustment and submission" because it would be shorn of disciplinary knowledge—great ideas, theories, visions, and struggles. Therefore vocational education would be damaging to both the people subjected to it and the public spaces they might have created together. These arguments still provide us with an object lesson in high and low achievement expectations (Darling-Hammond).

During deliberation, a rich fund of knowledge will reveal itself in numerous ways: how a student frames a problem, searches for related information, uses reference materials and databases, seeks diverse viewpoints, judges the strength of arguments, interprets charts and primary documents, adjudicates competing interpretations, and weighs alternative courses of action. Studies of experts at work reveal the almost seamless interaction of substantive knowledge and problem-solving abilities (Glaser 1984, Wineburg 1991). Of course, the possession of such knowledge does not guarantee its deft application, but certainly no application is possible without it.

Let us elaborate on the first three examples above to show how relevant knowledge and deliberation are interdependent.

Children are gathered on the rug to deliberate a proposed rule that would forbid a child from telling other children that they cannot join in a game. Some children bring an array of examples and observations to the discussion, using these to construct a more elaborate understanding of the proposed rule than their peers are able to do (Paley 1992).

High school juniors are weighing the possible causes of the witchcraft accusations in Salem in order to decide on the most probable cause. Some students are able to bring substantial historical knowledge to the topic. They draw analogies to the Spanish Inquisition, the McCarthy anticommunist hearings, and anti-Semitic hysteria in Germany.

Students are assigned to cooperative "Jigsaw" teams to create a museum exhibit on the Salem witchcraft phenomenon. They are deciding on a division of labor and their knowledge of the topic is a key factor in how they divide the work. For example, if they studied world history the year before and know of the European

---

1. For curriculum models, see W.C. Parker, ed., Educating the Democratic Mind (Albany: State University of New York Press, 1996); R. Soder, ed., Democracy, Education, and the Schools (San Francisco: Jossey-Bass, 1996); J.T. Dillon, ed., Deliberation in Education and Society (Norwood, N.J.: Ablex, 1994); and A. Gutmann, Democratic Education (Princeton, NJ: Princeton University Press, 1987).

2. Helpful, inexpensive curriculum materials for launching such a course are Choices for the 21st Century Education Project (Providence, R.I.: Brown University, 1960); and National Issues Forum (Dubuque, Iowa: Kendall/Hunt, 1996).

witchcraft craze that occurred at about the same time, they may have a team member compare the American and European cases. Or, if in studying the Holocaust they learned something about the relationship between economic insecurity and scapegoating, they might gather socioeconomic data on the Salem accusers and victims.

Fertile Teaching Arenas

In sum, schools are public places in which diversity and mutual problems (policies, vandalism, racism, theft, and so on) come with the territory. In addition, every topic addressed in class is loaded with genuine problems of interpretation and explanation. Teachers should seize upon both types of problems to teach the deliberative arts.

Included in the deliberative arts are the many facets of joint problem solving—listening as well as talking, grasping others' points of view, and using the common space to forge positions with others rather than using it only as a platform for expressing opinions. Acquired long before, this blend of skills, dispositions, and knowledge is what enables a diverse group of people—young or old to peacefully discuss divisive issues in order to forge an intelligent and just decision that is binding on all. Such education in schools helps children develop the public virtues needed "if there is to be a city at all."

References

Darling-Hammond, L. (1996). "Democracy and Access to Education." In *Democracy, Education, and the Schools,* edited by R. Soder. San Francisco: Jossey-Bass, pp. 151–181.

Dewey, J. (1916). *Democracy and Education.* New York: MacMillan, p. 89.

DuBois, W.E.B. (1903, reprinted in 1990). *The Souls of Black Folk.* New York: Vintage, p. 42.

Garcia, E.E., and R. Gonzalez. (1995). "Issues in Systemic Reform for Culturally and Linguistically Diverse Students." *Teachers College Record 96,* 3: 420.

Glaser, R. (1984). "Education and Thinking: The Role of Knowledge." *American Psychologist,* pp. 93–104.

Greene, M. (1996). "Plurality, Diversity, and the Public Space." In *Can Democracy be Taught?,* edited by A. Oldenquist. Bloomington, Ind.: Phi Delta Kappa, p. 28.

Johnson, D.W., and R.T. Johnson. (May 1988). "Critical Thinking through Structured Controversy." *Educational Leadership 45,* 8.

Paley, V. (1992). *You Can't Say You Can't Play.* Cambridge, Mass.: Harvard University Press, p. 16.

Power, F.C., A. Higgins, and L. Kohlberg. (1989). *Lawrence Kohlberg's Approach to Moral Education.* New York: Columbia University.

Radencich, M.C., and L. McKay. (1995). *Flexible Grouping for Literacy in the Elementary Grades.* Boston: Allyn and Bacon.

Slavin, R.E. (1995). "Cooperative Learning and Intergroup Relations." In *Handbook of Research on Multicultural Education,* edited by J.A. Banks and C.A. McGee Banks. New York: Macmillan, pp. 628–634.

Wineburg, S. (1991). "Historical Problem Solving: A Study of the Cognitive Processes Used in the Evaluation of Documentary and Pictorial Evidence." *Journal of Educational Psychology 83*: 73–85.

Article Review Form at end of book.

WiseGuide Wrap-Up

- Multiple intelligence theory in consideration of cultural influences is a valid foundation for promoting effective learning.

- Traditional multicultural education models fail to recognize variability

- within cultural groups and tend to perpetuate stereotypes.

- New models for addressing diverse learners should contain multiple factors, including race, culture, gender, family, community, and social-economic status.

- Strengthening our diverse community through civility, respect, and acceptance can be facilitated by promoting the process of 'deliberation' in schools and classrooms.

R.E.A.L. Sites

This list provides a print preview of typical **coursewise** R.E.A.L. sites. (There are over 100 such sites at the **courselinks**™ site.) The danger in printing URLs is that Web sites can change overnight. As we went to press, these sites were functional using the URLs provided. If you come across one that isn't, please let us know via email to: webmaster@coursewise.com. Use your Passport to access the most current list of R.E.A.L. sites at the **courselinks**™ site.

Site name: ERIC Clearinghouse on Urban Education

URL: http://eric-web.tc.columbia.edu/

Why is it R.E.A.L.? A national information service and database funded by the U.S. Department of Education. Sections on equity and cultural diversity, urban teachers, curriculum and instruction, compensatory education, and administration and finance. Information about school reform, school safety, and technology in urban education. Features digests, short bibliographies, parent guides, key abstracts (short summaries), and other publications.

Key topics: urban education, culture, poverty, educational equity

Activity: Review featured digests (which change regularly) for preparation of a report or term paper.

Site name: Multicultural Pavilion

URL: http://curry.edschool.virginia.edu/go/multicultural/

Why is it R.E.A.L.? Resources for teachers, including reviews of children's music, multicultural activities, and on-line literature archives. Multicultural research resources including statistical data archives, on-line article archives, and links to on-line libraries, E-journals, and research organizations.

Key topics: multicultural education, cultural diversity

Activity: Visit the "Teachers Corner" and review instructional strategies for teaching diverse populations with regard to preparing lesson plans.

Site name: Intercultural E-Mail Classroom Connections

URL: http://www.stolaf.edu/network/iecc/

Why is it R.E.A.L.? Mailing lists are provided by St. Olaf College as a free service to help teachers and classes link with partners in other countries and cultures for e-mail classroom pen-pal and project exchanges.

Key topics: cultural diversity, multicultural education

Activity: Contact the website and develop a partnership between students in your classroom and another classroom in the world related to current curriculum or thematic units.

section 4

Speaking the Lingo: Diverse Language Learners

Learning Objectives

- Summarize the purpose, intent, and results of the Bilingual Education Act of 1968 and the Lau v. Nichols Supreme Court decision of 1974.

- Compare and contrast the instructional programs of bilingual education and English as a second language.

- Describe the techniques for using first-language skills in developing English language proficiency.

- Identify content-centered language learning methods for effective English instruction with language-minority students.

- Describe how programs in English language acquisition can be adjusted to suit the characteristics and goals of a particular school/community.

 **WiseGuide Intro**

"Words are but pictures of our thoughts." (Dryden) About 3.2 million limited-English-proficient (LEP) children attend U.S. public schools, and their numbers are increasing. Few districts will remain unchanged by the nation's changing demographics. The challenge of addressing the learning needs of this linguistically diverse population is one faced by educators across the country.

Most LEP students are young. Two-thirds are in grades K–6, 18% are in grades 7–9, and 14% are in grades 10–12. Spanish is the native language of approximately three out of four LEP students. Four percent speak Vietnamese, followed by Hmong, Cantonese, Cambodian, and Korean (2% each). One of twenty-nine different Native American languages is spoken by 2.5% of LEP students.[*]

Educators are feeling the pressure of such profound linguistic diversity, especially with the increasing realization of the role language plays in the development of student learning, culture, and self-concept. This section provides readings for this critically important, highly controversial, and politically charged topic.

Setting the stage for this section is "Bilingual Education Program Models: A Framework for Understanding." Roberts reviews the theory and practice of bilingual education, with a close analysis and presentation of how community goals and nationalist perspectives drive program development. Instructional strategies for educators to use with minority-language students in the classroom are discussed in "Content-Centered Language Learning." This section concludes with parent, community, and cultural groups in the forefront of criticism of past practices and some suggestions for the future on this publicly debated educational topic. These controversial perspectives are presented in three different articles: "Bilingual Education Theory and Practice: Its Effectiveness and Parental Opinions," "Hooked on Ebonics," and "Children in Prison (Hispanic Parents Fight Bilingual Education)."

[*]H. L. Fleischman and P.J. Hopstock, *Descriptive Study of Services to Limited English Proficient Students* (Arlington, VA: Development Associates, 1993).

? ? ? ? Questions

Reading 17. Describe the difference between "additive" and "subtractive" bilingual programs in the United States. Describe how assimilationist vs. pluralistic goals influence the various bilingual education models.

Reading 18. Krashen's theory of second-language acquisition indicates that a second language is most effectively acquired under what conditions? According to Cummins, what are the two basic types of language proficiency?

Reading 19. What claims does the author make regarding parental preferences in language instruction? What are the differences in effectiveness between bilingual education programs and English as a second language (ESL) programs?

Reading 20. What is the Standard English Proficiency (SEP) training program? How can Ebonics be used to enhance students' educational performance?

Reading 21. According to the author, why are some students placed/kept in bilingual classes against parental wishes? Why is instruction in English as a second language used for most non-Spanish-speaking students instead of bilingual education?

Describe the difference between "additive" and "subtractive" bilingual programs in the United States. Describe how assimilationist vs. pluralistic goals influence the various bilingual education models.

Bilingual Education Program Models
A framework for understanding

Cheryl A. Roberts
University of Northern Iowa

Abstract: *Bilingual education remains a controversial topic of discussion in the United States locally and nationally. Issues of educational benefits need to be kept separate from political issues; both must be informed by understanding of the larger society. In this paper I describe different possible bilingual education models and comment on the educational costs and benefits associated with each.*

Introduction

Bilingual education continues to fuel debate in the national as well as local arenas. Some believe passionately that use of any language other than English in the U.S. creates divisiveness; others believe that freedom to speak whatever language one chooses is a fundamental human right. Yet others feel that other languages in education are a luxury that cannot be afforded in difficult economic times. As recent demographic projections show (see editors' introduc-

tion), the number of children classified as limited English proficient (LEP) will continue to grow; thus, bilingual education is likely to continue to be a topic of debate.

In order to understand the contentiousness of this issue, it may be helpful to briefly consider assumptions and questions underlying some of the more commonly articulated arguments related to bilingual education. First, many appeal to national unity as a prime reason to reject bilingual education. An equally passionate view relates to language rights, and notes that as the Constitution does not endorse one religion, neither does it proclaim one language. A third perspective is that bilingual education is a generous attempt to help less fortunate non-native English speakers that simply is not affordable in difficult economic times.

Common to all three of these divergent views is the assumption that bilingual education is intended to promote bilingualism, and that it does in fact produce students who are either bilingual or whose English is less devel-

oped than that of their native English-speaking peers. Both assumptions can be challenged; bilingual programs are so diverse that it is problematical to make generalizations. In fact, efforts to review the efficacy of bilingual education programs, the most famous example of which is the AIR report (Hakuta, 1986), are criticized for failure to take into account the significant variations in programs. Labeling a program as transitional bilingual education, for example, does not ensure that the program is transitional nor that it is bilingual. The students served, languages spoken, grades and ages involved, number of teachers, their specializations and languages, subject matter taught, hours in program, and so on are all variables that make each program distinct. The program descriptions in this issue demonstrate this very well.

Yet it is possible to provide a framework for systematically investigating bilingual educational programs, and it is the intent of this paper, along with the collection of papers following, to provide a framework for investigation and discussion. In order to provide this framework, I will briefly discuss a range of societal, linguistic, and educational goals and outcomes of bilingual education programs. Next, I will identify and comment on specific program models, with their typical goals and outcomes. Finally, I will review the importance of considering bilingual education programs as specific responses to local conditions, in a national context. The programs described in the rest of the papers may then be seen as variations on a particular model.

Bilingual Education Goals and Outcomes

Goals

Goals can be examined with respect to national or societal goals, linguistic goals, and educational goals. In general, national goals are of two types: assimilationist and pluralistic (Baker, 1993). Assimilationist goals seek to assimilate minority language speakers into the majority language and culture; in doing so, the minority language would become less important or even disappear. These goals characterize images of a "melting pot" culture and suggest that failure to assimilate may lead to separatism. Pluralistic goals typically affirm individual and group language rights, and are seen as support for group autonomy, which may or may not be viewed as a threat to larger group unity.

Assimilationist and pluralistic goals reflect ideological and philosophical differences; however, it must be noted that many, more specific goals, might not be identifiably either. For example,

an individual's desire to learn more than one language may be related to improved job opportunities, to reinforcement of religious beliefs (Hebrew or Arabic, for example), personal travel, maintenance of historical family connections, personal enrichment, and so on. In the case of bilingual education, an important educational goal of using a minority language is to promote ability in the majority language (through transfer of skills and knowledge, improved emotional support, and so on). Thus, while considering the goals of the program type, we must keep in mind that groups and individuals, both majority language speakers and minority language speakers, will bring to the discussion group and individual goals.

Outcomes

Outcomes are typically categorized as that which results from bilingual education programs, or even from bilingualism as a result of societal forces. Wallace Lambert (1975) first identified two possible outcomes: additive bilingualism and subtractive bilingualism. Additive bilingualism is what results from a program in which students maintain their first language and acquire their second language. Subtractive bilingualism characterizes the situation in which students lose their first language in the process of acquiring their second language. According to Cummins (1981), students who experience additive bilingualism will show cognitive benefits. These might include greater metacognitive ability and greater mental flexibility. Subtractive bilingualism typically has a negative effect on students' educational experience.

It should be noted that programs may have the stated goal of additive bilingualism, but for a variety of reasons may not achieve that goal. Furthermore, the community's support and resources may be inadequate to support additive bilingualism. For these reasons, goals and outcomes should be looked at independently as well as together.

Program Models

Submersion

The submersion model, sometimes mistakenly identified as the immersion model in the U.S., mainstreams non-native English speaking students into regular English-speaking classrooms.

The goals of this model are assimilationist; that is, the goal is to have the non-native speaker learn English and assimilate to North American society. Since the first language is not supported, it is frequently lost and so the model is also considered subtractive. Cummins (1981) asserts that subtractive bilingualism leads to negative cognitive effects, and experience shows that learners who receive neither L1 support nor ESL have a difficult time succeeding in school. Such students frequently feel marginalized and drop out before finishing high school.

Submersion is not a legal option for schools with non-native English speakers; however, oversight and enforcement are lax, and many smaller schools with low populations of NNS students are simply unaware that they are required to provide some sort of services to these students. Parents of these children, for cultural and other reasons, tend not to demand the services their children are entitled to; thus it is not uncommon to find submersion in U.S. public schools.

ESL Pullout

In this model, students are "pulled out" of some other classes in order to receive an English as a second language class. They are mainstreamed into other classes. ESL Pullout is also assimilationist in its goals, and subtractive bilingualism is the usual outcome. Students in this model may receive as little as twenty minutes or as much as several hours or more (often these programs are called language intensive) but students may still fall behind in content areas as they struggle to learn English.

ESL pullout is commonly found in areas with students of a variety of language backgrounds, making it difficult to find enough bilingual teachers and aides, and in areas where resources, particularly financial, are limited. It is also not uncommon to find pullout programs in somewhat homogeneous communities where assimilationist attitudes prevail, although it is certainly not limited to those types of communities.

The issue of which class to release children from should be thoughtfully considered; generally, it makes sense to release children from English Language Arts for native speakers. It is less appropriate to take children from content classes or from classes in which they can form friendships with native speakers of English, such as P.E., music, or art.

A related program type is the sheltered model, in which ESL and content area classes are combined, and taught either by an ESL-trained subject area teacher or by a team. These classes are designed to deliver content area instruction in a form more accessible than the mainstream. They may use additional materials, bilingual aides, adapted texts and so on to help students of diverse language backgrounds acquire the content as well as the language. Sheltered programs, or classes, are also assimilationist.

Transitional Bilingual Education

Transitional bilingual education provides content area support in the native language while teaching the student English. Initially, the learner is taught content classes in the native language, is taught English as a Second Language, and may also take music, P.E., art, and similar classes in English, partly because these classes require less language proficiency and also because it is important that the learner know English speaking students (for language and social development).

The transitional model serves as a bridge for students, helping them move from their native language to English, and any given program may do so more quickly or more slowly. Federal guidelines now suggest that 3 years is the target amount of time for learners to receive L1 support, in spite of studies showing that 5–7 years is a more realistic time frame for learners to reach levels comparable to their native English speaking peers (See Collier, 1989; Krashen et al., 1982).

The goals of transitional bilingual education are still assimilationist, and the outcome is generally subtractive bilingualism. Still, it is hoped that these programs will provide the content area support which will enable these students to remain in school.

These programs are often found in communities with significant populations of non-native English speakers, particularly of one or two language backgrounds. This makes it easier and more desirable in terms of community attitudes to find bilingual teachers. The U.S. government, through Title VII grants, funds transitional programs.

Maintenance Bilingual Education

Maintenance bilingual programs differ significantly from the previous models in both goals and outcomes. In maintenance programs, the learners are transitioned into English content classes, and are given support in their first language, as in transitional programs. However, they also receive language arts in their native language, enabling them to become literate in that language, and they continue to receive content area classes in their first language as well, so that they become literate in both languages.

The goal of maintenance bilingual programs is to promote bilingualism and biliteracy; rather than as assimilationist goal, this model promotes pluralism. Languages other than English are seen as resources. Because it promotes the development of two languages, the outcome is additive bilingualism, which is associated with positive cognitive benefits (Cummins, 1981).

Maintenance programs exist where there are sufficiently large numbers of students of one language background to make it possible to hire bilingual teachers and where there is interest and support in the community for having a bilingually educated population. While the financial investment may not be much more than for a transitional program, it is essential that the community and school staff, both speakers of majority and minority languages, support a maintenance program. It may be possible for a maintenance program to succeed with limited support on the part of the minority language community as long as the majority language speakers do not actively object. However, without support from the minority language community, such a program is unlikely to exist. There are minority language speakers who object strongly to the use of languages other than English in the public school system, and again care must be taken to address parent and community goals as an important determinant of educational goals.

Enrichment, Two-way, or Developmental Bilingual

Enrichment bilingual education in the U.S. involves not only non-native speakers of English but also native English speakers. (Enrichment programs in Canada can be immersion programs, discussed below. These do not include both minority and majority language speakers in the same classes in the early grades). While the non-native English speakers are essentially in a maintenance program, the native English speakers are in a similar maintenance program in the second language. From the start and continuing throughout, the learners serve as resources for each other. While there are segregated ESL or L1 content classes initially, the goal is to have the students of both language backgrounds studying content classes in both languages.

Like maintenance bilingual education, the goal of enrichment bilingual education is pluralistic: the development of biliterate and bilingual individuals. Both (or several) languages are valued. Outcomes of enrichment bilingual programs are additive bilingualism, not just for one ethnic group but for majority and minority speakers.

In order to ensure a balance of languages, several alternatives are possible. For example, classes taught in the morning might be taught in one language, while classes taught in the afternoon might be taught in the other. It is recommended that the languages switch slots periodically, as students are said to be more alert in the morning. Another possibility is to teach one content class such as math in one language, and then teach the next math class in the other language the following semester. These two possibilities are identified as alternate because languages are alternated by time or by subject matter.

A second approach is known as concurrent, in which classes are simultaneously taught in both languages in a team teaching approach, where one teacher represents English and the other represents another language. In the preview-review technique of concurrent language teaching, one teacher previews the lesson in his/her language, the other teaches the lesson in the other language, and the first reviews the lesson in the first language. Unfortunately, team teaching can have several drawbacks. First, though the goal is to provide a balance of input in both languages, it has been found that English tends to dominate (v. Ovando & Collier, 1985, p. 83). In addition, there can be a great deal of repetition, which may waste time. Finally, students who know they will hear the material in both languages may simply not pay attention until the teacher begins using their preferred language. (Wong-Fillmore, 1980; cited in Ovando & Collier, 1985). These obstacles can be overcome when there is a commitment to the goals of the program.

Enrichment bilingual education programs require a high level of community support and involvement, both financial and human, by both majority and minority speakers. They are more complicated to set up, and the scheduling of students, teachers, and classes requires more effort. However, the results are highly promising for those who feel that the non-English languages spoken in the U.S. and Canada are valuable resources for the future.

Immersion (Canadian Model)

The immersion model was originally developed in Canada, and was and is used successfully with English speakers learning French as well as with growing numbers of minority language children (Taylor, 1992). Though nothing in the definition of immersion bilingual education excludes minority language children, it may happen in practice.

When immersion is used with majority English speakers learning French, immersion bilingual education is generally pluralistic and promotes additive bilingualism. Learners become biliterate and bilingual in two languages. However, when minority language speakers are immersed in the majority language, the goal is frequently assimilationist and results in subtractive bilingualism.

A variety of immersion models are used with majority English speakers in Canada, from early to late total immersion and from partial to full immersion; differences in outcomes between these models seem to be relatively minor (Swain, 1978).

Again, due to confusion in the usage of the terms, it is critical to differentiate between submersion for minority students in English-speaking classrooms and French immersion for minority students in French-speaking classrooms: the difference relates to L1 or L2 oriented pedagogy. That is, "minority language students in an English-medium class with mother tongue speakers of English experience pedagogy intended for L1 speakers; hence, English is not presented as an L2, neither is pedagogy necessarily appropriate for L2 learners. In a L1 classroom, on the other hand, minority and majority children alike are not expected to speak French as an L1; hence, the program is entirely geared to L2 learning and the pedagogy is geared to L2 learners" (Taylor, 1995, personal communication).

Conclusion

Although each program is unique, it is generally possible to identify an underlying basic program model. Variations can and should occur, as a program is adjusted to suit the characteristics of a particular school and community. As the following papers show, there are as many designs as there are programs. In looking at possible models, and in reading about actual programs, the reader should be aware of the goals and outcomes of different programs, as well as the details of implementation.

References

Baker, C. (1993). *Foundations of bilingual education and bilingualism.* Philadelphia: Multilingual Matters.

Collier, V. P. (1989). How long? A synthesis of research on academic achievement in a second language. *TESOL Quarterly, 23*(3), 509–531.

Cummins, J. (1981). The role of primary language development in promoting educational success for language minority students. In California State Department of Education (Ed.), *Schooling and language minority students: A theoretical framework* (pp. 3–49). Los Angeles: Evaluation, Dissemination and Assessment Center, California State University.

Ferguson, C. A., Houghton, C., & Wells, M. H. (1977). Bilingual education: An international perspective. In B. Spolsky & R. Cooper (Eds.), *Frontiers of bilingual education* (pp. 159–194). Rowley, MA: Newbury House.

Krashen, S., Long, M., & Scarcella, R. (1979). Age, rate, and eventual attainment in second language acquisition. *TESOL Quarterly 13*(4), 573–582.

Lambert, W. E. (1975). Culture and language as factors in learning and education. In A. Wolfgang (Ed.). *Education of Immigrant Students.* Toronto: O.I.S.E.

Ovando, C. J. & Collier, V. P. (1985). *Bilingual and ESL classrooms: Teaching in multicultural contexts.* New York: McGraw-Hill.

Swain, M. (1978). Bilingual education for the English-speaking Canadian. In J.E. Alatis (Ed.), *International Dimensions of Bilingual Education.* Washington, D.C.: Georgetown University Press.

Taylor, S. (1992). Victor: A case study of a Cantonese child in early French immersion. *Canadian Modern Language Review, 48*(4), 736–759.

 Article Review Form at end of book.

Krashen's theory of second-language acquisition indicates that a second language is most effectively acquired under what conditions? According to Cummins, what are the two basic types of language proficiency?

Content-Centered Language Learning

JoAnn Crandall

Although estimates of the number of language minority students in U.S. schools vary, there is consensus that the numbers are rising dramatically. "Increasingly, the American classroom is multiethnic, multiracial, and multilingual at all levels" (Crandall, 1992). In response, a number of program models have been developed to meet the needs of language minority students, many involving the integration of language and content instruction. In addition, attention to the lack of foreign language proficiency among Americans has led to the development of a number of foreign language programs that integrate academic content into language instruction. In this approach, the second or foreign language is used as the medium of instruction for mathematics, science, social studies, and other academic subjects; it is the vehicle used for teaching and acquiring subject specific knowledge.

This Digest discusses the rationale for integrating language and content instruction and provides an overview of some of the program models and teaching techniques that focus on this approach.

Why Use Content-Centered Instruction?

In the United States, Krashen's theory (1982) of second language acquisition has influenced the development of integrated instruction at all levels. Krashen suggests that a second language is most successfully acquired when the conditions are similar to those present in first language acquisition: that is, when the focus of instruction is on meaning rather than on form; when the language input is at or just above the proficiency of the learner; and when there is sufficient opportunity to engage in meaningful use of that language in a relatively anxiety-free environment. This suggests that the focus of the second language classroom should be on something meaningful, such as academic content, and that modification of the target language facilitates language acquisition and makes academic content accessible to second language learners.

Cummins (1981) argues that individuals develop two types of language proficiency: basic interpersonal language skills and cognitive academic language proficiency. He suggests that these two types of proficiency vary according to the degree of context available to the individual and the degree of cognitive challenge of the task. Social language can be acquired in 1 to 2 years, but the level of proficiency needed to read social studies texts or solve mathematics word problems can take 5 to 7 years to develop (Collier, 1987).

Integrated language and content instruction offers a means by which English as a second language (ESL) students can continue their academic or cognitive development while they are also acquiring academic language proficiency. It also offers a means by which foreign language students can develop fuller proficiency in the foreign language they are studying. In foreign language or two-way bilingual immersion programs, in which a portion of the curriculum is taught through the foreign language, some type of integrated language and content instruction appears to be essential.

From *ERIC Digest*, #ED367142, January 1994, ERIC Clearinghouse on Languages and Linguistics, Washington, D.C.

This report was prepared with funding from the Office of Educational Research and Improvement, U.S. Dept. of Education, under contract no. RR93002010. The opinions expressed do not necessarily reflect the positions or policies of OERI or ED.

Program Models

Content-based Language Instruction. In this approach—also called integrated language and content instruction—ESL, bilingual, or foreign language teachers use instructional materials, learning tasks, and classroom techniques from academic content areas as the vehicle for developing language, content, cognitive, and study skills. The second language is used as the medium of instruction for mathematics, science, social studies, and other academic subjects. Instruction is usually given by a language teacher or by a combination of the language and content teachers.

Sheltered Subject Matter Teaching. This approach involves adapting the language of texts or tasks and use of certain methods familiar to language teachers (demonstrations, visuals, graphic organizers, or cooperative work) to make instruction more accessible to students of different English proficiency levels. This type of instruction is also called sheltered English or language-sensitive content instruction and is given by the regular classroom or content teacher, or by a language teacher with special expertise in another academic area (Brinton, Snow, & Wesche, 1989).

Theme-based. In these programs, a language curriculum is developed around selected topics drawn from one content area (e.g., marketing) or from across the curriculum (e.g., pollution and the environment). The goal is to assist learners in developing general academic language skills through interesting and relevant content.

Sheltered Instruction. Here, a content curriculum is adapted to accommodate students' limited proficiency in the language of instruction. This model was originally developed for elementary foreign language immersion programs to enable some portion of the curriculum to be taught through the foreign language (Genesee, 1987). It is commonly used in immersion and two-way bilingual programs (Met, 1991) and has been adapted for use in second language programs with large numbers of limited English proficient students of intermediate or advanced English proficiency.

Language Across the Curriculum. This is the name given to content-centered instruction that involves a conscious effort to integrate language instruction into all other curricular offerings. This may include the development of integrated curricula and some kind of paired or team teaching.

In schools where enough students share a common first language, bilingual programs using sheltered instruction have been developed. In one program, students more from content instruction in their first language to sheltered-content instruction in English, and then to mainstream classes where they are integrated with English-speaking peers. They receive content-based ESL as well (Freeman, Freeman, & Gonzales, 1987).

For schools with insufficient numbers of language minority students to create sheltered language programs, the techniques for sheltering instruction can be implemented in classes with both native and non-native English-speaking students.

Adjunct Model. This model links a specific language learning course with a content course in which both second language learners and native English speakers are enrolled. The courses share a content base, but the focus of instruction differs. The language teacher emphasizes language skills, such as academic reading or writing, while the content teacher focuses on traditional academic concepts. This model requires substantial coordination between the language and content teacher; usually the ESL teacher makes the extra effort of becoming familiar with the content. An adjunct program is usually limited to cases where students have language skills that are sufficiently advanced to enable them to participate in content instruction with English speaking students.

Cognitive Academic Language Learning Approach. (CALLA). This approach combines language, content, and learning strategy instruction into a transitional ESL approach for upper elementary and secondary students of intermediate or advanced English proficiency (Chamot & O'Malley, 1987).

Teaching Methods

There are a variety of strategies and techniques used in content-centered second language instruction. Here, the discussion will be limited to four types of strategies—cooperative learning and other grouping strategies, task-based or experiential learning, whole language strategies, and graphic organizers—that increase attention to academic language learning, contribute to content learning, and encourage development of thinking and study skills. (See Crandall, 1992, for additional information.)

Cooperative Learning. In this method, students of different linguistic and educational backgrounds and different skill levels work together on a common task for a common goal in either the language or the content classroom. Cooperative groups encourage students to communicate, to share insights, test hypotheses, and jointly construct knowledge. Depending on their language proficiency, students can be assigned various roles as facilitator, recorder, reporter, or illustrator. Other grouping strategies involve peer tutoring or pairing a second language learner with a more English-proficient peer.

Task-based or Experiential Learning. In this approach, appropriate contexts are provided for developing thinking and study skills as well as language and academic concepts for students of different levels of language proficiency. Students learn by carrying out specific tasks or projects: for example, "doing science" and not just reading about it (Rosebery, Warren, & Conant, 1992).

Whole Language Approach. The philosophy of whole language is based on the concept that students need to experience language as an integrated whole. It focuses on the need for an integrated approach to language instruction within a context that is meaningful to students (Goodman, 1986). The approach is consistent with integrated language and content instruction as both emphasize meaningful engagement and authentic language use, and both link oral and written language development (Blanton, 1992). Whole language strategies that have been implemented in content-centered language classes include dialogue journals, reading response journals, learning logs, process-based writing, and language experience stories (Crandall, 1992).

Graphic Organizers. These provide a "means for organizing and presenting information so that it can be understood, remembered, and applied" (Crandall, 1992). Graphs, realia, tables, maps, flow charts, timelines, and Venn diagrams are used to help students place information in a comprehensible context. They enable students to organize information obtained from written or oral texts, develop reading strategies, increase retention, activate schema as a pre-reading or pre-listening activity, and organize ideas during the prewriting stage (Crandall, 1992).

Conclusion

Although this Digest has focused on content-centered language instruction in the United States, similar interest in integrated language and content instruction is evident in many parts of the world, especially in countries where English serves as the medium of instruction for part of the educational program.

Among the issues facing content-centered language instruction in the United States is the need for research to evaluate the effectiveness of integrated instruction, specifying optimal conditions for various programmatic effects, including the timing of integrated instruction, the relative effectiveness of different program models, and the use of various instructional strategies, texts, and assessment measures. Teacher training is another concern as the number of second language learners in U.S. classrooms increases. To accommodate this diverse student population, content-area teachers need to know how to shelter their instruction, and language teachers need to learn how to integrate academic language and content better in their classrooms (Crandall, 1992).

References

Blanton, L.L. (1992). "A Holistic Approach to College ESL: Integrating Language and Content." *ELT Journal, 46,* 285–293.

Brinton, D.M., Snow, M.A., & Wesche, M.B. (1989). *Content-Based Second Language Instruction.* New York: Harper & Row.

Chamot, A.U., & O'Malley, J.M. (1987). "The Cognitive Academic Language Learning Approach: A Bridge to the Mainstream." *TESOL Quarterly, 21,* 227–249.

Collier, V.P. (1987). "Age and Rate of Acquisition of Second Language for Academic Purposes." *TESOL Quarterly, 21,* 617–641.

Crandall, J. (1992). "Content-Centered Learning in the United States." *Annual Review of Applied Linguistics, 13,* 111–126.

Crandall, J. A. (1993). "Diversity as challenge and resource." In *ESL Students in the CUNY Classroom: Faculty Strategies for Success.* New York: City College of New York and Kingsborough Community College.

Cummins, J. (1981). The Role of Primary Language Development in Promoting Educational Success for Language Minority Students. In *Schooling and Language Minority Students: A Theoretical Framework.* Los Angeles: California State University, Evaluation, Dissemination, and Assessment Center.

Genesee, F. (1987). *Learning through Two Languages: Studies of Immersion and Bilingual Education.* Cambridge, MA: Newbury House.

Freeman, D., Freeman, Y., & Gonzales, G. (1987). "Success for LEP Students: The Sunnyside Sheltered English Program." *TESOL Quarterly, 21,* 361–67.

Goodman, K. S. (1986). What's Whole *about Whole Language? A Parent/Teacher Guide to Children's Learning.* Postsmouth, NH: Heinemann.

Krashen, S. (1982). Principles and Practice in Second Language Acquisition. Oxford: Pergamon.

Met, M. (1991). "Learning Language through Content; Learning Content through Language". *Foreign Lanuage Annals, 24,* 281–95.

Rosebery, A. S., Warren, B., & Conant, F. R. (1992). "Appropriating Scientific Discourse: Findings from Language Minority Classrooms." Santa Cruz, CA and Washington, DC: National Center for Research on Cultural Diversity and Second Language Learning.

 Article Review Form at end of book.

What claims does the author make regarding parental preferences in language instruction? What are the differences in effectiveness between bilingual education programs and English as a second language (ESL) programs?

Bilingual Education Theory and Practice

Its effectiveness and parental opinions

Linda Chavez and Jorge Amselle

Linda Chavez is president and Jorge Amselle is communications director of the Center for Equal Opportunity in Washington, D.C.; Chavez is former director of the U.S. Commission on Civil Rights. Readers may continue the dialogue on the Internet at **comment @ceousa.org,** *and may access CEO's Web site at* **http://www.ceousa.org.**

Schools around the country have seen an explosion in the number of students needing help with English in recent years. Although this is a problem that mostly affects urban schools, even small rural schools are having to deal with language minority students, many for the first time. For almost 30 years the preferred program

Editor's note: CEO released "The Importance of Learning English: A National Survey of Hispanic Parents, " in September 1996. The survey may be ordered from CEO at 815 15th Street, NW, Suite 928, Washington, DC 20005; shipping and handling is $5. The main findings of the survey may be viewed on CEO's Web site.

for teaching Limited English Proficiency (LEP) children has been bilingual education.

The theory behind bilingual education is that children must first fully develop their native language before they can achieve academic proficiency in a second language—a process that takes five to seven years, say proponents. In practical terms, this means children must be taught to read and write in their native language before they are taught those skills in English.

The theory further claims that children will transfer their reading and cognitive skills from their native language to the new language. Of course, they must be taught all their academic courses in their native language during this period so they do not fall behind their English-speaking peers. Unfortunately for the theory, however, the actual classroom experience of bilingual education has been largely negative.

What Does the Research Say?

Bilingual education research is extensive, with literally hundreds of studies available. The best of them do little to support bilingual education theory. This is a problem that has plagued supporters of bilingual education for years. In his 1986 book, *Mirror of Language*, Stanford University professor of education and passionate bilingual education proponent Kenji Hakuta admitted:

There is a somber truth that even the ardent advocate of bilingual education would not deny. Evaluation studies of the effectiveness of bilingual education in improving either English or math scores have not been overwhelmingly in favor of bilingual education . . . An awkward tension blankets the lack of empirical demonstration of the success of bilingual education programs. Someone promised bacon, but it's not there.

Most studies are so flawed that they do not meet minimum methodological standards—a problem that has long plagued the supporters of bilingual education. In 1992 the National Academy of Sciences issued a report of their review of two major Department of Education studies that sought to compare bilingual education to other methods of educating LEP students, such as English as a Second Language (ESL). This report, *The Case of Bilingual Education Strategies,* concluded that the studies were so scientifically flawed as to render them useless.

Professor Christine Rossell of Boston University and former Department of Education researcher Keith Baker conducted the most thorough review of bilingual education research ever done for their 1996 book, *Bilingual Education in Massachusetts: The Emperor Has No Clothes.* They examined more than 300 program evaluations and studies and found that only 72 met minimum methodological standards. Of these, 78 percent showed bilingual education was either no different—or actually worse—for LEP students than doing nothing at all in terms of improving student performance in English reading and math tests.

Problems with Bilingual Education

The problem is not just with bilingual education research; implementing the program is also a problem. Under increasing pressure to provide bilingual education, schools face a severe shortage of qualified bilingual teachers. The problem is especially acute in non-Spanish languages, although the heavy demand for Spanish-language instructors has created many problems as well.

School districts must pay a premium to attract bilingual teachers and some have even gone to foreign countries to try and recruit teachers, which has created additional problems. The Houston Independent School District, for example, recruited teachers from Mexico only to discover that dozens of them had falsified college degrees and teaching certificates, many had cheated on competency exams, several were working in the United States in violation of their visas, and more than a few spoke no English.

Today, there are close to 3 million LEP students in U.S. schools. According to the National Center for Education Statistics, 58 percent of all LEP students were born in the United States and 74 percent are Spanish speakers. In fact, the next-largest language group are the Vietnamese with a mere 3.9 percent. Although "bilingual" programs for non-Spanish language groups can be found, few actually teach children to read and write in their native languages before teaching them these skills in English. These programs are bilingual only in the sense that they contain some measure of native-language support.

Only Spanish-speaking children receive true bilingual education, and they get it mainly for political reasons. Hispanic advocacy groups are the chief lobby for bilingual education and have insisted that Hispanic children be taught in Spanish. For many years the Hispanic lobby openly argued that the purpose of bilingual education was to develop Spanish proficiency among Hispanic children and to teach such children about their own ethnic heritage.

The vast majority of non-Spanish-speaking LEP students receive English as a Second Language (ESL) instruction rather than bilingual education. ESL focuses on rapid English language development through intensive English instruction by a teacher specially trained in second-language acquisition. It should come as no surprise that studies show—in El Paso, Tex., and in New York City—students learn English better and faster in ESL than in bilingual education programs that focus on native language development.

When bilingual education began in 1968 it was a small federal program for Mexican-American students in the Southwest. The idea was to provide some native-language instruction to try and lower dropout rates among Hispanic children. In 1974, the U.S. Supreme Court ruled in *Lau* v *Nichols* that schools were required to provide LEP students with equal educational opportunity. The Court did not specify what type of program was required to accomplish this, allowing for the use of several different approaches.

The Department of Education's Office of Civil Rights (OCR), however, interpreted the decision to mandate native-language instruction and instituted the Lau Remedies. Over the next several

> Only Spanish-speaking children receive true bilingual education, and they get it mainly for political reasons.
> In school districts and states across the country, parents, teachers and school administrators are becoming increasingly vocal and organized against the bilingual education policies that have failed so many.

years OCR was successful in convincing states and school districts to implement full-fledged bilingual education programs or face a possible cut-off of federal education funds.

What Parents Want

One reason OCR was so adamant in favor of this one approach was heavy lobbying on the part of various Hispanic advocacy organizations. In fact, for years the public and educators have been told that bilingual education is what Hispanic parents want for their children.

The Center for Equal Opportunity, however, learned differently when it commissioned a random national survey of Hispanic parents with school-aged children in five cities with heavy Hispanic concentrations and bilingual education programs: Los Angeles, San Antonio, Houston, Miami, and New York. Parents were asked if they preferred that their children be taught Spanish before English or English first. Sixty-three percent wanted their child to learn English as soon as possible; fewer than 17 percent preferred Spanish first.

Parents were also asked to rank five educational goals in order of importance: learning English, learning Spanish, learning academic subjects, learning about Hispanic culture, and learning extras like art or sports. Learning to read, write, and speak English was overwhelmingly ranked as most important, followed by learning academic subjects. More than 80 percent of parents also preferred that their child's academic courses be taught in English if it meant more time spent learning English.

Recent events show that Hispanic parents are beginning to realize their best interests are not being served by the bilingual education establishment. In Bethlehem, Pa., school superintendent Thomas Doluisio recently ended his district's failed experiment with bilingual education and instead implemented an English-intensive ESL program. Although this change first met with howls of protests from the bilingual education lobby and Hispanic organizations, Doluisio stuck to his plan. After just one year, the ESL program produced better results than years of bilingual education. Bethlehem surveyed Hispanic parents at the end of the first year of the new program and found that the vast majority (82 percent) described the new program as "good" or "very good."

Last year, more than 100 Hispanic parents in Los Angeles' immigrant-heavy garment district actually pulled their children from school and protested in front of the Ninth Street School. This boycott lasted for nearly two weeks until school officials finally agreed to give children more English classes. These parents were tired of seeing their children go through the bilingual program and graduate without sufficient English skills to succeed in high school.

Despite the legal guarantee in California state law that parents have the right to request all-English instruction for their children, the rights of these parents had been denied. It took national and statewide news media exposure, as well as the involvement of the mayor of Los Angeles and his law firm, to embarrass school administrators into doing the right thing.

When one Hispanic parent in Denver, Colo., requested that her child be removed from the bilingual program there, officials denied her request by claiming they were under a court order to place Hispanic children in the bilingual program. "The kids were doing work well below the regular grade level," said Rita Montero. In fact, officials did not tell Montero that she had the legal right to remove her child from this program. Montero was finally able to move her son out of the program by placing him in another school, but according to her, "only through determination and anger did I get my son in the class where he belonged."

In New York City, a group of 150 mostly Latino families calling themselves the Bushwick Parents Organization sued the New York State Commissioner of Education to try and remove their children from disastrous bilingual education programs. These programs had trapped many of their children for six, seven, or more years in dead-end programs.

One assistant high school principal testified that the students in his school's bilingual program were being allowed to graduate completely illiterate in either English or Spanish. He also testified that students were not allowed to exit the program, even when they requested it themselves.

Parent after parent testified that years in the bilingual education program had confused their children, many of whom were functionally illiterate in both English and Spanish. They complained about bilingual education teachers who could not speak English and said many children had been placed in the program simply because they had Spanish surnames, *even though they could not speak Spanish.* Despite the clear violations of the rights of these parents and children the judge dismissed the case. The Bushwick parents are appealing.

In school districts and states across the country, parents, teachers, and school administrators are becoming increasingly vocal and organized against the bilingual education policies that have failed so many. We have spoken with dozens of parents, teachers, school board members, and district supervisors from California, Texas, Colorado, New Mexico, Massachusetts, New York, New Jersey, Illinois, and Pennsylvania who are determined to change the system that promotes bilingual education.

Rosalie Pedalino Porter is one of these. For 10 years she co-ordinated the bilingual education programs for the Newton, Mass., public schools. Porter eventually became disillusioned with the program and exposed its failures in her 1990 book *Forked Tongue: The Politics of Bilingual Education.* She now serves as the director of the READ Institute and advises school districts around the country how to implement successful programs for English learners. She is just one of several teachers who have realized that bilingual education does not work and have started organizations to deal with this issue.

School districts and administrators should realize that bilingual education has failed to live up to its promise and must look at alternative methods of educating LEP students. The evidence collected during the past 30 years is clear: English instruction is what leads to success among LEP students. What is more, parents place a top priority on programs that teach their children English sooner rather than later.

If schools want to provide the best services possible for this growing population of students, they should start listening to students and parents rather than the self-interested bilingual education lobby that has so long dominated debate on this issue.

 Article Review Form at end of book.

What is the Standard English Proficiency (SEP) training program?
How can Ebonics be used to enhance students' educational
performance?

Hooked on Ebonics

John Leland and Nadine Joseph

With Steve Rhodes in Chicago

Abstract: The Dec. 18, 1996, decision by the Oakland, CA, school board to treat black English as a second language aroused an unexpected controversy nationwide. Officials responded by denying they will apply for bilingual education funds, and cited solid research documenting the methods's effectiveness.

A muddled plan to teach black English in the schools made outraged headlines, but the actual teaching methods may make sense.

In her brightly decorated classroom at Parker Elementary School in Oakland, Calif., Cleo Shavies reads her second graders a book called "Flossie and the Fox." The student body here is 90 percent African-American, from one of the poorest areas of the city. Two years ago, Shavies enrolled in a state Standard English Proficiency (SEP) training program to sensitize teachers to students who spoke black English. In a classroom decked with posters of black achievement, she applies the SEP techniques to "Flossie and the Fox." Flossie is an African-American girl who speaks in a vernacular that has been called Ebonics, from the words "ebony" and "phonics." The fox speaks standard English. Shavies might pull words from the text, pointing out differences in syntax. "I be Flossie Finley," Flossie says. Or "How do a fox look?" Shavies will ask, "Is this written in Ebonics or standard English?" The technique is called "contrastive analysis," and Shavies is impressed by its results. "I can already see the improvement in oral language skills," she says. "I'm building on what the children know."

Since Dec. 18, when the Oakland school board passed a muddled resolution to treat Ebonics as a second language, the quiet experiments of classrooms like Shavies's have been lost under a swell of rhetoric. By unanimous decision, the board voted to recognize Ebonics as the "primary language" of many of its students, and to teach students in their primary language in order both to maintain the "legitimacy and richness" of the language and to help students master standard English. Describing Ebonics as "genetically based," the resolution suggested that schools might seek federal funds earmarked for bilingual programs. What this meant for Oakland's students was anybody's guess. The board merely charged the superintendent to develop a program.

But for talking heads and holiday party-goers the board's announcement, however vague, meant a chance to tee off. Who didn't have an opinion? An America Online poll about Ebonics drew more responses than the one asking people whether O. J. Simpson was guilty. Jesse Jackson quickly lambasted the decision as "an unacceptable surrender borderlining on disgrace. NAACP president Kweisi Mfume called it "a cruel joke." California Gov. Pete Wilson vowed not to fund what his press secretary Sean Walsh called "a ridiculous theory" (an odd bit of posturing, since the state's own SEP program, using black English, operates in about 300 schools). From Washington, Secretary of Education Richard Riley fired a pre-emptive strike, restating a Reagan-era policy that black English is a dialect, not a distinct language, and therefore not eligible for bilingual-education moneys.

"Ebonies," first coined in 1973, refers to a grammatically consistent and rich African-American speech pattern with roots in West Africa. Key components include not conjugating the verb "to be" ("I be joking") and dropping final consonants from words ("hand" becomes "han"). Linguists have long debated whether it constitutes a distinct language or a dialect, often dividing along ideological lines. A language, runs an adage, is merely a dialect with an army.

The Oakland school board was quick to take up the controversy. Black students form a slight majority in the district and have performed below every other group, eking out a 1.8 average on a scale of 4. Against this underachievement, the board has groped for solutions. In 1991 it rejected a state-approved social-studies textbook series as racist and simplistic. It hunched an Afrocentric curriculum in one high school. It requires school uniforms for elementary- and junior-high-school students. The Ebonies resolution itself came with 18 pages of recommendations covering everything from hiring more black teachers to mentoring black males.

When the backlash came, the board hired a publicist and clarified—or hedged—its position. It did not intend to teach kids how to speak black English. Instead, it called for teachers to accept Ebonics as a native lan-guage and teach students to translate into standard English, rather than correct them for speaking wrongly. The board denied any intention to seek bilingual funds. And the phrase "genetically based," according to a statement, referred to linguistic genesis, not racial DNA. Jesse Jackson then repositioned himself, telling *Newsweek* the measure would help to "detect the problem without demeaning the students, and build a bridge to English proficiency."

The board has some evidence on its side. Since the 1980s a small body of research has suggested that black students learn better when schools use Ebonics to teach standard English. A 1989 study of inner-city college students, for example, found that those who used texts contrasting Ebonics with standard English included fewer Ebonics constructions in their own writing than those who just studied standard English. "The limited data is all positive," says Stanford linguistics professor John Rickford. "It's clearly a shortcut process to standard English that works."

But for the school system as troubled as Oakland's, Ebonics seems a small corrective. "It's like trying to put out a house fire with an eyedropper," says linguist John McWhorter of the University of California. Some students are skeptical. "They're afraid they would be taught in Ebonics, which would be insulting," says Nicole Thompson, 18, a senior at Oakland Tech. Test scores at the Parker school remain among the lowest in the district. State authorities point to bigger problems in Oakland: crowded classrooms, dilapidated schools, too few computers and—until a strike last year—some of the lowest teachers' salaries in the county. These deficiencies, which shadow low student performance around the country, don't make the talk-show and holiday-party circuit. And there may lie the real shame—and much bigger challenge—of the Oakland school district.

 Article Review Form at end of book.

According to the author, why are some students placed/kept in bilingual classes against parental wishes? Why is instruction in English as a second language used for most non-Spanish-speaking students instead of bilingual education?

Children in Prison

Diane Ravitch

Diane Ravitch is a historian and a Fellow at the Manhattan Institute of New York City.

Bilingual education has been a fixture in American public schools for nearly 30 years. It never has been popular with the public, which stubbornly failed to understand why public schools were teaching immigrant children their native language instead of English. Now the program is under fire from a new quarter: Hispanic parents in New York and California, who complain that their children are trapped in a "bilingual prison." They want out, and the system says no.

When Congress passed the Bilingual Education Act in 1968, its supporters claimed that children who were taught their native language and cultural heritage would gain higher self-esteem, better attitudes toward school and improved achievement.

Education experts persuaded congressmen that it was the best route to learning English. Senator Ralph Yarborough (D–Tex.) said, "Unless a child becomes very fluent in English, he will rarely reach the top in American cultural life. He might as a baseball player, but not as a performer on radio; he could not in law; he could not in medicine; he could not in any of the professions or in business." In 1974 the Supreme Court ruled against the San Francisco school system for failing to provide English-language instruction to Chinese students. The high court did not order the district to provide bilingual education, but told it to teach the students in English or Chinese or whatever else that would "rectify the language deficiency."

In the years since then, ethnic activists have used the political process to turn bilingual education into a program in which children take all their subjects in their native language. Bilingual educators scorn the principal alternative, called English-as-a-Second-Language (ESL), which emphasizes English-language instruction.

What they cannot so easily scorn is the anger of Hispanic parents. In Brooklyn a parents' organization sued the state, and in Los Angeles parents pulled their children out of school. The parents are angry, first, because they want their children to learn English; and second, because the system is rigged to make it hard to remove their children from bilingual programs.

In New York City a 1974 consent decree required that every child with a Spanish surname and every child from a home in which anyone speaks a non-English language must take an English proficiency test. Any child who scores in the bottom 40% is automatically placed in a bilingual class, even if English is the primary language spoken at home and even if the child knows more English than Spanish. In short, the system is programmed to fill the bilingual classrooms.

The results of bilingual education, contrary to the activists' promises, have been dismal. A 1994 New York City study revealed that children in bilingual classes are slower to join the regular English-language curriculum than children in ESL classes, and do not perform as well as youngsters who learned English in ESL. State law requires that children receive no more than three years of bilingual education. Asian and Russian children move quickly into English classes, but most Hispanic children are retained in bilingual programs for several years.

Parents who want to remove their children from bilingual classes get a bureaucratic runaround. Most parents are themselves recent immigrants who lack the skill to negotiate the political maze. They must get permission from the principal and the bilingual coordinator, who do not want to lose the extra funds that flow to bilingual classrooms. And a shrinkage of the bilingual enrollment would mean fewer jobs for bilingual teachers.

The federal government spends "only" $150 million on bilingual education, but the nation spends $5.5 billion. (New York City alone spends $400 million.)

Parents who want to remove their children from bilingual classes get a bureaucratic runaround.

Yet bilingual education has failed Hispanic students (children from other ethnic groups enroll mainly in ESL because of a shortage of teachers in the many other languages spoken by newcomers). Among youngsters 16 to 24 years of age, precisely the group likeliest to have experienced bilingual education, the dropout rate for Hispanics is 30%, more than double the rate for blacks and four times the rate for whites.

The parents in Brooklyn and Los Angeles say that their children need to learn English. They are more qualified to judge than are the educators and judges who have built the "bilingual prison."

Article Review Form at end of book.

WiseGuide Wrap-Up

- English-as-a-second-language programs vary significantly from bilingual programs in purpose, design, instruction, and assessment.

- Using teaching techniques that utilize students' skills in their first language enhances English proficiency.

- Two types of language proficiency (basic interpersonal and cognitive academic) take varying lengths of time to acquire.

- Bilingual education programs vary in their goals based on assimilation vs. pluralistic perspectives as well as additive vs. subtractive outcomes.

- Content-centered language-program models and teaching methods can effectively improve English language acquisition.

R.E.A.L. Sites

This list provides a print preview of typical **coursewise** R.E.A.L. sites. (There are over 100 such sites at the **courselinks**™ site.) The danger in printing URLs is that Web sites can change overnight. As we went to press, these sites were functioning using the URLs provided. If you come across one that isn't, please let us know via email to: webmaster@coursewise.com. Use your Passport to access the most current list of R.E.A.L. sites at the **courselinks**™ site.

Site name: Summing up the Lau decision

URL:
http://ourworld.compuserve.com/homepages/JWCRAWFORD/summing.htm

Why is it R.E.A.L.? Two decades after the Supreme Court's Lau decision, the court's promise to non-English-speaking students remains to be fulfilled. A child entering school without English today is still unlikely to receive a first-class education. While a sink-or-swim policy is no longer officially tolerated, more subtle forms of neglect persist. This article chronicles the path of educational services to linguistically diverse students.

Key topics: language minority students, bilingual education, cultural diversity, Lau v. Nichols

Activity: Review and describe how the intent, direction, and implementation of the Lau v. Nichols decision has changed since 1974.

Site name: National Clearinghouse of Bilingual Education

URL: http://www.ncbe.gwu.edu/

Why is it R.E.A.L.? Funded by the U.S. Department of Education—collects, analyzes, and disseminates information relating to the effective education of linguistically and culturally diverse learners in the United States. Includes an online library, databases, weekly news bulletin, lesson plans, links to other schools, and so on.

Key topics: bilingual education, English as a second language, cultural diversity

Activity: Develop lesson plans for your classroom from activities and reference information on the website under "Fun Languages."

Site name: National Clearinghouse for ESL Literacy Education

URL: http://www.cal.org/ncle/

Why is it R.E.A.L.? This site offers online access to ERIC digests on ESL education, e-mail forums, annotated bibliographies, digest, and newsletters. Updated by the Center for Applied Linguistics.

Key topics: English-as-a-second-language

Activity: Use the ERIC digests in preparing a class presentation or report.

section 5

Rich Man, Poor Man, Knocking on Heaven's Door: Educating the Poor and Homeless

Learning Objectives

- Identify the challenges and needs faced by homeless/poor students and families which affect student learning.

- Describe changes to current classroom practices that improve the learning opportunities for homeless/poor students.

- List school policy changes that encourage homeless students' participation and attendance.

- List the services for homeless/poor students that could be provided by creating school-agency partnerships.

- Detail the benefits and uses of a directory of community services for homeless and poor students.

- Describe the role that school nurses, counselors, and other school support professionals can play in addressing the needs of homeless students.

WiseGuide Intro

One simple sentence (author unknown) sums up the importance of this section: "You can judge a society by how it treats its weakest members." Surely the poor are our weakest members in American society. Lacking life's most basic necessities—food, shelter, safety, clothing—they face challenges for the future that are quite foreign to most of us. Yet, as educators, we strive to provide educational services to individuals and families who, at times, don't seem to take full advantage of what is being offered.

A closer look at the needs and hurdles faced by the poor provides a focus for developing effective educational services for them. For example, homeless students face limitations in simply doing their homework. This includes a lack of materials, study space, or uninterrupted time. By understanding the comprehensive situation in which the poor/homeless find themselves, educators are better prepared to redesign learning environments, develop partnerships for services, and advocate for individuals who have little voice in public and educational policy.

Section 5 presents a variety of readings exploring the conditions and challenges of educating America's poor and homeless. It begins with addressing teachers' skills in the classroom in "Teacher Strategies for Supporting Homeless Students and Families". This section moves from focusing on the classroom to focusing on the school in "Hope in Chicago," which reviews schoolwide activities emphasizing success for the poor. Both "Teamwork for Tough Times" and "School-Community Partnerships and the Homeless" reflect the growing tendency for schools to develop partnerships with other agencies to address the broad social, physical, and emotional needs of the poor in order to assure success in school. The section concludes with bold recommendations for changing classroom and school policy to meet the unique needs of the poor in "Homeless Students, Heroic Students."

? ? ? ? Questions ?

Reading 22. Name some of the proactive strategies teachers can use to assist homeless students. Name some proactive strategies schools can implement to assist homeless students.

Reading 23. What two reasons does the author cite for student success in the Academy? What strategies have been used in the Academy to encourage school attendance?

Reading 24. What kind of agencies are joining together with schools to provide services to low-income families/students? What does it mean to transform a school into a "one-stop shopping center"?

Reading 25. What specific services were provided to the school by business and service groups? How were volunteers used to assist the needs of the homeless?

Reading 26. In what way can schools be more flexible to help effectively educate homeless students? Describe how a teacher might use a detailed manual that lists the available community resources for homeless students. What specific services for homeless students could be provided?

Name some of the proactive strategies teachers can use to assist homeless students. Name some proactive strategies schools can implement to assist homeless students.

Teacher Strategies for Supporting Homeless Students and Families

Kevin J. Swick

Kevin J. Swick is a professor in the Department of Instruction and Teacher Education, College of Education, University of South Carolina, Columbia.

Teachers are exploring new strategies to further their understanding and support of homeless students and families. Through a collaboratively organized professional development course (involving the local school district and community agencies, the state education department, and the University of South Carolina), teachers in Richland School District One in Columbia, South Carolina, are using several means to strengthen their efforts to better respond to the needs of homeless students. They are acquiring accurate information on the strengths and needs of the homeless; identifying specific needs of homeless students and parents; engaging in collaborative school/community service projects; using class discussions and reflective journals to clarify their views regarding homeless students and parents; and working with community agencies and groups that serve homeless families.

Developing Strategies

A central question posed by teachers at the outset of the professional development course was, What strategies can we develop that will support homeless students (and their families) in having successful school experiences? Teacher projects carded out as a part of the course served as a primary means of exploring the various dimensions of this question. Each teacher conducted a "project" in which he or she explored some aspect of school and community strategies to support homeless students and families. Descriptions of two teachers' projects highlight the value of the focus on strategies.

Child Care for Children of Abused Mothers

One action-project focused on working with children at the Sister Care Center for abused mothers. The center is a temporary housing shelter that includes counseling, peer-group network-

ing, relocation support, respite from the stress of abuse, referral to needed agencies, and long-term guidance. The mothers at the center participate in peer-group and parenting sessions. Child care is provided so that mothers can devote their time to discussing and dealing with their problems. The teacher in this project volunteered as one of the child-care-givers during the sessions for mothers and learned first-hand about this facet of homelessness. She met and talked with the mothers, cared for their children, and became a part of their lives. Twice a week for two hours she coordinated the child care, and at other times she returned to visit with some of the mothers and assist them with specific services. Two of the children were in her school, and thus she became a link for their families to the school. She plans to continue working at the center.

In sharing her experience in class, this teacher broadened other teachers' perceptions of homelessness and its complexity.

From *Clearing House,* Volume 69, Issue 5, p. 293–296, May/June 1996. Reprinted with permission of the Helen Dwight Reid Educational Foundation. Published by Heldref Publications, 1319 Eighteenth St., N.W., Washington, D.C. 20036-1802. Copyright © 1996.

For many of the teachers, realizing that middle class mothers are homeless brought the issue closer to reality. Gaining a sense of what abused mothers go through in trying to reframe their lives was also enlightening. Over half of the class, for example, had been unaware of the existence of the Sister Care Center.

Advocates for Homeless Students in Each School

Children who are homeless or in highly isolated and non-sustaining environments need teachers who are more than alert to their cognitive functioning (McCormick and Holden 1992). Several members of the class used the course project assignment to develop various advocacy strategies for supporting homeless children in their schools. For example, one teacher became the liaison for homeless children and families in her school. She visited a nearby shelter and set up a study area, visited with two parents at the shelter, increased faculty awareness of this problem in her school, and met with the school counselor to develop a more formalized approach for the next school year.

Another teacher did a survey of the school staff to see what needs they were aware of regarding homeless children in the school. Some staff said they had not known that any children in the school were homeless. Another teacher developed a supportive, mentoring relationship with a homeless middle school student. She tutored him, made sure the shelter he was in had a study area, provided him with needed study materials, and checked with him often to see how he and the family were doing.

Those individual efforts prompted the larger group to take steps that are resulting in districtwide efforts to improve the system for helping homeless students and families. The class invited the district's coordinator of special services to discuss existing and needed services for homeless students and families. The group also set up contact people at different schools in order to meet the needs of homeless students, developed a resource guide that lists community services for the homeless, and increased the awareness of their colleagues regarding homelessness and how it can be addressed in schools. Districtwide plans are now under way to involve all teachers in an annual workshop on the needs of homeless students.

New Teacher Perspectives

All participants kept a journal about their experiences during the course, particularly as related to their projects. The journals show the transformation of teachers in their understanding of homeless students and families and their development of strategies for better supporting homeless students. The transformation process encompassed five thematic areas: perceptions of the meaning of homelessness, understanding of the particular needs of homeless students (and their families), awareness of local community resources that serve the homeless (and the complexity of using those resources), self-assessment regarding one's attitudes toward homeless people, and a new feeling of empowerment regarding the teachers' ability to take action to support homeless students and families.

Changed Perceptions of Homelessness. Journal entries showed that a majority of teachers (eighteen of twenty-four) believed that their views of homelessness had changed and that their involvement in the project played a major role in bringing about that change. Entries such as the following were common.

I was astounded to learn that a majority of homeless families have very young children! This is alarming and a real danger to our future. I must admit that I thought most homeless people were single men who just didn't like to work.

Until tonight, it never hit home that homelessness occurs in middle-class families. With sudden unemployment and family stress happening more often, I can now see that my views of homelessness were pretty limited.

Special Needs of Homeless Students. Although the participants had had some insight into the unique needs of homeless students, course experiences stimulated them to think more analytically in that regard. Here are two journal entries that illustrate that change in thinking.

I never thought of the reality that these children do not have a place to study or lack basic resources to work with. Imagine not being able to do your homework when you really want to. I can see now how some of my students really struggle with this problem.

Motivation to study is certainly hindered when one moves to more than four schools in one year. Not only is the child disrupted constantly but must spend much energy just on survival issues. I'll think twice before responding too quickly to a homeless student's failure to do homework.

Awareness of Community Resources. Class discussions and visiting speakers highlighted the community resources, as well as school resources, that are available to homeless students and families. Journal notes reveal the new level of resource awareness that many teachers reached.

It was good to hear that our district has a liaison person working with the shelters and that steps are being taken to set up study rooms and that computers are being placed in these rooms.

The Children's Garden is great! What a fine way to reach homeless families before their problems become a pattern of living. I was really happy to see that our district was providing the space free of charge.

Changing Attitudes toward the Homeless. Journal entries show that many of the teachers made major attitude changes toward homeless students and their families. Three new attitudes were most prevalent: (1) homeless students and families are or can be capable when supported; (2) connecting homeless students and families to needed services can change the direction of their lives; and (3) homelessness is interrelated with many other social problems and needs to be viewed in a comprehensive manner. Journal entries highlight those themes as follows:

I gained a new respect tonight for the complexities of being homeless. I can see now that many who are homeless are capable people (or have the desire to be so) and with some help can get things going in the right direction.

Services like Centerplace, Sister Care, Children's Garden, and the tutoring program are powerful ways of helping people help themselves. These programs need our support.

Class discussion on the subject of the teachers' understanding of homelessness were rich and elaborate. The teachers' changed attitudes were evidenced in comments on the number of people who were homeless due to factors beyond their control, how services for the homeless had reached a limit, and how success stories showed the promise of homeless families being helped.

Empowered Teachers Take Action. Helping other people to achieve new power in their lives reinforces the belief of teachers that their influence reaches beyond the classroom doors. Teachers' journal notes reveal the way they felt empowered by their experiences.

I never thought I would learn so much by just helping make food packets at the Food Bank. Realizing these packets were being delivered to shelters that day and that homeless people were right beside me helping out changed my thinking more than anything.

My tutoring of Jan (a third grader) has done more for me than her—I think. Seeing her make such notable improvements in school has renewed my faith in my own abilities as a teacher. I see a new dimension in myself too!

Empowerment comes in many forms, and the teachers learned some new ways to help others and, at the same time, to increase their own human competence.

Teacher Strategies

The teachers developed a number of proactive strategies as a result of their work in the course. A synthesis of the strategies includes the following:

- Establish a liaison for homeless students at each school in the district.

- Develop close working relationships with area shelters where homeless students and parents are living.

- Provide homeless students with "mentors" who help them solve problems related to being successful in school.

- Individualize instruction so that learning problems of homeless students are addressed early in the school year.

- Provide homeless students with needed learning materials for doing school work and homework.

- Develop close relationships with parents through contacts at local shelters, meeting parents at shelters, and providing parents with transportation to school.

- Establish a "family service referral system" within the school that is linked to the community's available social and educational services.

- Educate other teachers and staff in each school about the unique needs of homeless students and families.

Plans for Change

Real teacher renewal is continuous, taking shape in the development and use of new ideas and strategies. Educators need to build a new system for thinking about and acting upon changed perspectives. Teacher brainstorming prompted several new ideas for connecting what was initiated in the course to future efforts for teachers and the school district.

- Distribution of a resource guide to all teachers for helping homeless students and families.

- Further development of the district's efforts to establish liaisons in each school to work with homeless shelters.

- Initiation of mentoring and tutoring projects for homeless students in several targeted schools in the district.

- Formalization of awareness information for all teachers on the problem of homelessness in the community.

- Continued development of the district's efforts to place computers and other learning materials in local shelters.

- Advocating on behalf of the multiple needs of homeless students and families in the community.

- Projects by individual teachers in several community sites, such as the Children's Garden, Center Place, the Salvation Army, Sister Care, and the Harvest Hope Food Bank.

- Further use of the graduate course on homeless students and families, using participant-teachers as resources and teacher-leaders in the second year.

Collaborative Efforts

The collaborative effort of the school district, state department of education, and university provided the framework for a successful professional development course that expanded teachers' understanding of and involvement with homeless students and families. Multiple perspectives, participants' involvement in goal setting, use of varied and relevant instructional strategies, and opportunities for applying acquired knowledge in community and school settings were the key means for achieving success.

The best use of local and global resources in any teacher renewal and development program can only be realized through collaborative planning among all stake holders. That collaboration process must be continuous, systematic, and connected to specific issues and needs. The blend of people engaged in the planning and implementation of the course on homeless students and families "enlarged" the vision of, and the system for, creating a framework for teacher change. Of particular importance were the following recommendations for those who engage in such collaboration:

- Share planning and discussion among state leaders, school administrators, teachers, and community leaders directly involved in serving homeless students and their families.

- Institute across-grade-level teacher participation that nurtures sharing of common and unique concerns related to homeless students, parents, and families.

- Involve school administrators in the course and have them participate in planning tutoring, mentoring, and liaison projects.

- Seek the participation of the state coordinator of educational and support services for homeless students and families.

Teachers can have a positive influence on homeless students and families. Collaborative efforts within schools can promote services such as after-school tutoring, easier access to school resources, provisions for needed study materials, increased involvement of homeless students in school activities, and the development of teacher liaisons to local shelters. Partnerships with agencies and groups that serve homeless families can extend that effort through the organization of several important services: teacher visits to families at shelters, development of study areas in the shelters, special transportation arrangements for students and parents, and school-community coordination of service councils. Teacher advocacy and direct action can also strengthen the community's system for effectively responding to the immediate and long-range needs of homeless students and families.

References

Bassuk, E. 1991. Homeless families. *Scientific American* (Dec.): 66–74.

Bassuk, E., and L. Rosenberg. 1990. Psychosocial characteristics of homeless children and children with homes. *Pediatrics* (March): 257–61.

Chauvin, V., J. Duncan, and M. Marcontel. n.d. Homeless students of the '90s: A new school population. Paper prepared by the authors in their work at the Dallas Independent School District, Dallas.

Coontz, S. 1995. The American family and the nostalgia trap. *Phi Delta Kappan* (March): Kl–K10.

Johnson, A., and L. Krueger. 1989. Toward a better understanding of homeless women. *Social Work* (Nov.): 537–40.

Klein, T., B. Calley, and J. Molnar. 1993. No place to call home: Supporting the needs of homeless in the early childhood classroom. *Young Children* (Sept.): 22–31.

McCormick, L., and R. Holden. 1992. Homeless children: A special challenge. *Young Children* (Sept.): 61–67.

Quint, S. 1994. *Schooling homeless children*. New York: Teachers College Press.

Solomon, C., and P. Jackson-Jobe. 1992. *Helping homeless people: Unique challenges and solutions*. Alexandria, Va.: American Association for Counseling and Development.

Tower, C., and D. White. 1989. *Homeless students*. Washington, D.C.: National Education Association.

Vissing, Y., D. Schroepfer, and F. Bloise. 1994. Homeless students, heroic students. *Phi Delta Kappan* (March): 535–39.

Wright, J. 1989. *Address unknown: The homeless in America*. New York: Aldine de Gruyter.

Ziesemer, C., L. Marcoux, and B. Marwell. 1994. Homeless children: Are they different from other low-income children? *Social Work* (Nov.): 658–68.

Article Review Form at end of book.

What two reasons does the author cite for student success in the Academy? What strategies have been used in the Academy to encourage school attendance?

Hope in Chicago

Carolyn R. Pool

Momma Hawk (Corla Hawkins) is lead teacher and Executive Director of the Recovering the Gifted Child Academy in Chicago, Illinois. She may be reached at P.O. Box 19683, Chicago, IL 60619 (e-mail: momma.hawk@rgca.cps.k12.il.us). Carolyn R. Pool is Senior Editor of Educational Leadership.

Success for inner-city children, excellence in school, love in the midst of desperation. Here is a real-life hero and the middle school she founded.

At the Recovering the Gifted Child Academy on Chicago's West Side, everyone knows founder and executive director Corla Hawkins as "Momma Hawk"—particularly the kids in this public alternative middle school. Momma Hawk has received local and national recognition for her work with children—from community awards to feature articles in major publications and mass media.

What is Momma up to? What is her school all about?

Founded in 1990, the academy is small—only 45 students in grades 4–7. The students come from poverty and have not been successful in elementary school, for many reasons—behavior problems, truancy, disrupted family life, homelessness, drugs, child abuse—the panoply of difficulties

facing many children living in the inner city. Currently, all the children in this school are African Americans. A waiting list of 120 students includes children from all ethnic backgrounds and even from other states. Parents are drawn to the school's high success rate: increased reading scores, higher test scores, greater retention, and higher graduation rates when the students reach high school.

Children have extended school hours—from 8:15 a.m. to 5 p.m., plus school. Saturday classes. The academy is run like a business—business dress, business time cards, business "paychecks" with school money, real student-run businesses that earn real money, business partnerships, business contracts.

The school benefits from the Recovering the Gifted Child Foundation, whose mission is "to provide early intervention in the lives of disadvantaged children to prevent them from falling prey to gangs, drugs, violence, and other dangers" in their environment. Hawkins established the foundation in 1992 to extend the care that staff members have for every child and every parent. This care is not only institutionalized in the form of hot meals at school, food, clothing, bank accounts, and laun-

dry and kitchen facilities but is personalized to the extent of providing temporary places for children in crisis to live.

According to Momma Hawk, caring is most likely the greatest reason for the success of the academy, as well as what is most needed in public schools. Another reason for the school's success is parent involvement—which is mandated.

Parent Involvement and Perfect Attendance

Hawkins relates a terrifying incident that happened at her former school, Bethune Elementary. An angry parent, accompanied by a group of toughs, came to school and attacked a teacher, rendering him permanently disabled. Hawkins says, "There was a big fight in the office, and I was petrified." She discovered that the parent was outraged over what turned out to be a lie his child had told about the teacher.

Hawkins reasoned that if parents were in the classroom every day, they would know what was going on. At the academy, she decided to get parents involved and quickly. She states, "This developed protection in the school for the teachers, because we could verify every story with the parents who were there that day."

So Hawkins tells parents: "If you want us to save your child, you'll come in here and support us, or your child will be transferred." The parents want the children at the academy, because students are not suspended from this school. Attendance is almost perfect, and parents volunteer in the classroom, in Saturday School, in the Life Skills Lab. In the lab, for example, students learn how to dress for success—and more:

We have a survival kit with clean underwear, clean socks, deodorant, toothpaste, and toothbrush. The kids just use the kits; when we see they're empty, we just buy more. They can take whatever is in the kit; we don't care. We're trying to teach them how to care for themselves. If kids come to school dirty, we clean them up. If kids are hungry, we feed them—three meals a day. I always say to them, "You can be as smart as Einstein, but if you don't know how to brush your teeth, comb your hair, and put on a clean outfit, you're going nowhere. No one will hire you."

Not only does Hawkins bring parents into the classroom; she has also been known to take the class to the parents—anything to get kids to school (and at 99.2 percent, the Academy has the highest attendance record in the district):

The first time a group of children is absent without an excuse, I take the whole class to the neighborhood and pick the absent children up. We walk up the street, go to the children's houses, and I say, "Oh, I realize that you don't want to be absent. It must be that you're scared to walk through the neighborhood—so you get a bodyguard. We have come to get you."

So all the neighbors watch us coming to get the kids, and the kids are embarrassed. These children tell the other students, "Next time, you can't be absent, because Momma is

going to come get you." Yes, indeed, I intimidate them to come to school. Momma means business.

School Means Business

The philosophy of the Recovering the Gifted Child Academy is that every child has gifts. And it is the teacher's job to help children develop those gifts. One way to do this, according to Hawkins, is to view school as the children's business. This is not just a metaphor. Business permeates the school community—from the way the children dress (dress pants or skirts, blazers, dress shoes), to the corporations the students run, to the paychecks they get and the savings accounts they maintain. Hawkins explains how it works:

The kids clock in every morning at eight, and they clock out every day at five. They get paid $10 a day in "school money" for attendance. If they stay after school to work on their individual educational program, they get paid time-and-a-half. They can get paid only if they've figured out how much they have earned. So, if you work time-and-a-half for three hours, I ask you, "How much are you supposed to get paid?"

Now, if you don't know what it is, you don't get paid. Maybe I'll offer $30, and you say, "That's not right." Then I say, "Well, you have to tell me how much you should get. You're always supposed to know how to figure your own paycheck." The kids can exchange their earnings at the school store for snacks, books, clothing, and other items.

In addition to earning school money, the students earn real money through their corporations at the real-life mini-mall they run. Set up in a converted classroom, the mall has many shops—and even real customers from outside the school. Hawkins states:

We teach kids how to put in stock, how to mark it up or down, how to record profits or losses. The kids pay

rent for their stores, they pay electricity, they pay somebody to clean up, and they pay an accountant and an auditor. They even pay the person who decorates the mall. We created all kinds of jobs that it takes to run a shopping mall, and everybody gets paid out of a percentage of the kids' (real) money.

Once a month our mall is sponsored by a corporation, whose employees are invited in to shop. That's where the kids get their cash— and 30 percent of that has to go into their savings accounts.

In the mini-mall, students learn entrepreneurial skills, along with reading, math, civics, economics, art, and other subjects. Hawkins says that she is the wholesaler, but the kids do everything else:

The younger children are the distributors, and the older students are the retailers. So before the mall is open, the retailers have to go to market (in a hallway), where the 5th graders sell them all the things they've made for the retailers to resell at the mall. And that's how the 5th graders make their money. That's their business. And then the children in the other grades run the mall. We teach the kids how to restock, which relates to reading and math. They have to tell me when they are making money or losing it as businesspeople.

Mall stores include a doll shop, "Just Like Me," selling handmade dolls: a shop called "My Heritage," selling items made out of African fabrics; a secondhand baby clothes store, "Bundles of Joy"; "Forever Denim," marketing items made from recycled jeans; and "A Tisket a Basket," selling recycled, cleaned-up, redecorated baskets filled with fruit or various holiday items. Other shops sell T-shirts air-brushed in art class, handmade ties, handkerchiefs, hair bows, and other gift items. Parents and community volunteers—as well as a dedicated staff—are essential to the business, and school isn't over on Friday afternoon.

Saturday School and Self-Esteem

Important to the academy's success is what goes on outside of school hours. Not only do staff members and their families provide sanctuary for children in their homes—Momma says, "I had 12 children at my house one recent weekend"—but the whole community participates in Saturday School. Business volunteers, parents, teachers, and students catch up on assignments, work in one-to-one tutoring pairs, participate in life-skills training, and enjoy Geography Club or choir.

Saturday School is for children who didn't get all their assignments completed because they weren't focused—for whatever reason. A lot of corporate volunteers come on Saturday, which is really powerful. Heller Financial, Inc., one of our big corporate sponsors, sends its staff for one-on-one tutoring to help the kids overcome their fear of performance in the classroom.

Parents who work during the week and haven't completed their required volunteer time teach kids survival cooking in our kitchen. Other parents teach kids sewing, quilting, and laundry skills. We tell the kids: "Bring in all your dirty clothes, and we'll teach you how to wash and iron them on Saturday."

In the process, Hawkins and the school staff work with the parents, instilling good parenting skills, such as "Ten Secrets to Kids' Self-Esteem," which emphasize bringing out the best in each child (see p. 36). For example: "Don't worry that offering too much affection is 'overprotective.' " Another important secret: "Don't be afraid to teach family and moral values, so that your children can become role models for tomorrow."

Another activity that continues after school, on Saturday, and on field trips is what Hawkins calls "pregnancy prevention":

In this 9-week course, students walk around with an egg all day, without breaking it. They go through the entire life cycle of an unborn baby—every week represents a month of the baby's life. The kids have to figure out a budget for food, child care, diapers, and other expenses. They call hospitals and find out how much it costs to have a baby in the hospital without public aid. They create scenarios for life skills, for example, for a married couple, including where they work and how much they make an hour and whether they earn enough to care for a child.

Students have to visit a clinic. They visit museums where they might take their children, and they visit bookstores and buy books they would read to them. And at the end of the course, we show them a real-life video of a woman having a baby.

The first thing the kids say (after their shocked reaction to the video, that is) goes something like this: "I can't afford to have a baby. It costs too much to have a baby for real—when they cut public aid, I wouldn't be able to buy diapers." In the six years of this program, only two teens got pregnant before they finished high school.

Successes and Challenges

Hawkins keeps track of her middle school graduates in their high school work, through information supplied by the board of education. For example, of the 15 students who completed the 8th grade at the academy in 1993 and who are scheduled to graduate from high school in June 1997, only 2 have dropped out. The 2 students who became pregnant did not drop out; they are on the honor roll. The 13 students remaining in school are in the top 25 percent of their graduating class. Four students are the number one

students in their schools—and they all go to different high schools.

The academy's program includes many components that ensure students' success, such as using recorded books and replicating them on mastering systems so that many children can listen in privacy with earphones (Momma records many stories herself; parents and volunteers record others). Classes include test-taking skills—"Every Friday afternoon"—and improved scores on the Iowa Test of Basic Skills reflect the hands-on work the children do in, say, whole numbers. Performance assessments include video, audio, and photographic assessments.

Momma Hawk mentors teachers all over the state of Illinois. What most people ask her is, "How do you do it? How do you keep going?"

Momma's Continuing Education

One way Momma Hawk prevents her own burnout is by going back to school herself—and bringing her homework into the academy.

I made one of the greatest sacrifices in my life when I returned to school, to take an accelerated administrative program at Roosevelt University in Chicago. I have learned about special education laws and important educational research from professors who have gone through what we are trying to do. In the past, I just went at this from my heart. Now I'm learning how to do it from the law. I haven't been too far off base, but now I can come back to school and implement what I have learned with a tremendous burst of energy.

Perhaps the greatest benefit of Hawkins's graduate school experience is the example she is setting for lifelong learning. Hawkins says that she has to leave school early two days a week to attend classes, and her students cheer her on and help her:

I tell the children, "You see, I'm asking for excellence out of you, and I miss school to get excellence for myself." I involve my students in helping me do my class projects. I say, "Momma's in school, and I need you to help me."

Before I leave for class, they'll say, "Momma, you got your homework done? Is everything ready? Don't be late. Momma, you know that's not excellence. You have to leave now." When it's time for my grades, they want me to put them up on the wall next to theirs. It is just so precious because it helps them to see that you're never too old to learn, and that you need to continue to go forward in life.

In the future, Hawkins wants to expand. The academy is already running out of space. She dreams of adding more grade levels, continuing through 12th grade. She wants the foundation to acquire an emergency shelter for children without homes. She fervently believes in public education and wants to expand within that setting. Hawkins wants to begin a teacher education institute—"It begins with the teacher. Educators need to realize the power they have to affect the lives of students." She has large visions—and works to make them happen.

Ten Secrets to Kids' Self-Esteem

1. Always think about how to bring out the best in your child.

2. Praise your children's achievements and efforts.

3. Create an aura of compassion in your home.

4. Listen more than you talk with your children.

5. Give your kids hugs and love every day.

6. Create warm memories around learning experiences to motivate your children.

7. Make sure your children know that you will be there for them when they need you.

8. Don't worry that offering too much affection to children is "over-protective."

9. Read to children every day, and let them read to you.

10. Don't be afraid to teach family and moral values, so that your children can become role models for tomorrow.

 Article Review Form at end of book.

What kinds of agencies are joining together with schools to provide services to low-income families/students? What does it mean to transform a school into a "one-stop shopping center"?

Teamwork for Tough Times

Schools battle to help high-risk kids

Victor Dwyer

With Jake MacDonald in Winnipeg

It may be an exercise in frustration, but Sally Sinclair is only too happy to be a part of it. Crouching with parents and youngsters in the so-called parenting room at the inner-city Dundas Public School in Toronto, Sinclair is doing her best to entice her 18-month-old son, Martin, to play with a small toy. Martin is not interested. Defiantly, he thrusts a picture book towards his mother, and holds it there until she takes a seat beside him and begins to flip through. Minutes later, sitting under a bulletin board that sports information on everything from reading and writing to nutrition and housing, Sinclair describes how the parenting centre has helped put her family on the road to academic success. "I have learned a lot about parenting, and the children have about learning," says Sinclair, who also has two sons in kindergarten. For principal Kemp Rickett, whose school also offers breakfast and lunch programs, the centre, where parents get advice and guidance on a range of literacy and parenting issues, is one part of an ambitious bid to limit the effects of difficult times. "We fill in the blanks," says Rickett. "And as more families struggle to make ends meet, there is no question there are more blanks to fill in than ever before."

As Finance Minister Paul Martin trumpeted new measures to help Canada's poorest families in last week's federal budget, educators like Rickett continue to wage their own quiet battle to help disadvantaged students. For many, that has meant transforming their schools into one-stop shopping centres, where families stretched for time and resources can get help from community and government agencies. Like Rickett, some have launched an all-out drive to lure children—and their parents—into the schoolhouse, long before it is time to enroll. Others are crafting programs designed to convince high-risk kids that hard work pays off. "Children spend a lot of their waking hours at school," says Jim Robson, principal of Kincaid Central School, in Kincaid, Sask., a farming community 200 km southwest of Regina. "It makes sense for us to be the quarterback."

And in a downsizing, high-pressure world, it is not only children from the poorest homes who are showing up at school ill-prepared to learn. Middle-income parents took home four per cent less money in 1993 than a decade earlier, according to a study released last year by the Canadian Council on Social Development. And their shrinking paycheques were mirrored by what the council calls "a poverty of family time": on average, they spent eight per cent more time at work than 10 years earlier.. "The kids in those families are eating, and not coming to school in rags," says Bauni Mackay, president of the Alberta Teachers' Association. "But as parents face underemployment, or longer hours at the jobs they have kept, the stress on families is building."

Failing to address the fallout head-on can have long-term academic consequences. Alan Pence, a professor at the School of Child and Youth Care at the University of Victoria, tracked the educational success of children from 60 families in the city over a 10-year period beginning in 1983. His conclusion: children from low-income homes, who were in poor-quality child care and whose parents had minimal education, tended to fall behind in language measures as early as age 3. What's more, those same children continued to trail their peers at age 13. Another study, released last year by the Council on Social Development, concluded that twice as many poor as non-poor teens drop out before completing high school.

Facing a tough battle, teachers increasingly see their task as a team effort. In the toughest neighborhoods, where poverty goes hand in hand with youth crime and gang violence, law enforcement agencies often play a major role. Last fall, with an annual budget of $123,000 shared by the local, provincial and federal governments, four inner-city Winnipeg schools launched a three-year pilot program called Choices for Youth. The program is aimed at 67 children in grades 6 to 8 who have been identified as "at risk," but who, in the words of probation officer Wendy Huggan, "have not yet become committed to the gang lifestyle." Along with Const. Darrall Kotchon, Huggan holds classes on conflict resolution, anger management, and the destructive aspects of life on the street. And volunteers, many of them university students, work one-on-one to improve the children's academic skills. "A lot of my friends were getting into gangs—doing break and enters, assaults, beating up old people for beer money," says Barbara Wesley, a Grade 8 student at Hugh John MacDonald School. "Now, I have someone to talk to about the violence, and I'm hooking up with other kids who don't want to be a part of it."

Other schools are working hard to connect with groups and agencies responsible for the welfare of children, encouraging them to make the schoolhouse a central dispensary. Last year, Saskatchewan launched Integrated School-Linked Services, a unique program jointly funded by the ministries of education, justice, social services and health. It helps principals like Robson develop teams of social workers, parole officers, child protection workers and others who meet with families to solve immediate and chronic problems that get in the way of learning.

As governments cut back education budgets, such partnerships can be a matter of survival. Ryerson Community School in Toronto has developed ties with 59 agencies and businesses, from a local women's shelter to the Metro Toronto Housing Authority, fast-tracking help to families who need it. "In the past, especially the '80s, teachers tried to be all things to all students," says principal Chris Bolton. "There are just not the resources for that now." Meanwhile, the school has developed its own programs, including "night gym," in which kids can spend supervised evenings off the streets. "It means nobody can call you chicken for not hanging out looking for trouble," says Grade 7 student Abdi Okash. "Now, you can just tell them you've got better things to do."

Key to many programs is getting entire families onside. In Winnipeg's Choices for Youth, that means holding separate evening classes where parents can talk with volunteer counsellors about broader issues of home life and stress reduction. The Toronto board's 34 parenting centres work with more than 7,000 families in inner-city neighborhoods. Their

twin goals are to equip preschoolers with literacy and other skills, and to engender positive attitudes to education in parents who have often had a personal history of failure at school. "We're not into this warm, fuzzy self-esteem business," says program co-ordinator Mary Gordon. "We're into hard-core self-esteem, where parents can say, 'My child knows this because I worked hard to get him learning.' "

At least some politicians appear to be recognizing the wisdom of helping all kids get an early start to learning. Although cuts of $400 million on Ontario's education budget have led some boards to eliminate junior kindergarten, other governments are placing a high priority on such programs. After off-loading half the cost of kindergarten to boards and families in 1994, Alberta resumed close to full funding last September. "It's a big relief," says Mackay, "because the very kids who needed it the most came from the homes that were least able to afford it." In Quebec, meanwhile, Education Minister Pauline Marois has announced plans to invest up to $100 million in full-time kindergarten for five-year-olds and part-time junior kindergarten for students from low-income families.

While educators are encouraged by such moves, they are clearly skeptical about depending on politicians to make a significant difference—Martin's recent announcement notwithstanding. Ryerson's Bolton notes that the Ontario government has begun to reduce permanent funding for breakfast and after-school programs, replacing it with seed money dispensed on an ad hoc basis.

And although Mackay is relieved by Alberta's decision on

kindergarten funding, she notes that the majority of other new spending has been earmarked for a $50-million drive to computerize classrooms. "We won't say no to that offer," says Mackay. "But when a child is hungry, or coming in from a family in severe financial crisis, hooking him up to the Internet isn't going to mean a heck of a lot to him." Still, at a time when one in five children continues to live in poverty, many teachers say they have little choice but to carry on with the job at hand. "It's not a perfect world— for families or schools," says Saskatchewan's Robson. "But our job is to take kids how we get them, and work with whoever will help us to give every student a fair shot at success."

 Article Review Form at end of book.

What specific services were provided to the school by business and service groups? How were volunteers used to assist the needs of the homeless?

School-Community Partnerships and the Homeless

Working together, school and community can become the extended family of homeless students, fulfilling many of the needs their own families are unable to meet

Maria Luisa Gonzalez

Maria Luisa Gonzalez is Associate Professor, New Mexico State University, Department of Educational Management and Development, Dept. 3N, Box 30001, Las Cruces, NM 88003-0001.

City Park is proof that a school can successfully serve diverse populations, including the homeless. Two years ago, I was principal of this inner-city Dallas, Texas, school, then an early childhood center for children from pre-kindergarten through 3rd grade. More than half the population were Hispanic, one-third were black, and the remaining were mainly Anglo children residing at one of the three nearby downtown shelters for the homeless. The uniting characteristic of the majority of these children was poverty.

However, it was our homeless students who became the catalyst in bringing together resources from all sectors of the community to help the children. Through the dedication of our teaching and support staff, the community had become aware that these children were willingly accepted and made part of a strong academic program (with 100 percent mastery on the state's criterion-referenced test). Then, when community members learned about the tremendous needs of these children, they responded—and a partnership was created. Today, City Park School is considered an exemplary program for homeless students— 1 of the top 15 in the nation.

Local Churches Pitch In

When students suffer the compounding effects of poverty, the school may provide the only enrichment and recreation in their lives. However, because of the fast-paced curriculum that we must adhere to daily, we had difficulty extending our efforts into enrichment and recreation. To help us, our major adopter, the First Presbyterian Church, conducted a Saturday School. Once a week, volunteers from the church provided field trips and worked with young children in arts and crafts.

The Saturday School volunteers worked closely with the City Park staff, immediately notifying us if they detected any problems. For example, when a volunteer discovered that a little girl had trouble sitting because her mother had spanked her, we were able to enroll the mother in a parenting program at our school.

The First Presbyterian Church went beyond offering Saturday classes for students. They also provided computer equipment, with hardware and software that were compatible with the school's computer lab. In addition, they were instrumental in writing a grant for $40,000 to buy much needed new playground equipment for our school. In addition, the generous scholarship fund they helped establish—for students who had attended City Park and wished to attend a college or university upon graduation from high school—helped raise the career aspirations of our boys and girls.

Another organization, the Dallas Jewish Coalition for the Homeless, also provided many resources, including volunteers who tutored in the classroom on a daily basis. Every week many of the women also ate lunch with the children to help us provide the nurturing children need. In memory of a couple who had been strong supporters of the school, the Jewish Coalition set up a library fund to provide money to replace books inadvertently lost

due to the high mobility of the population. Through this fund, we were able to strengthen our commitment to make the homeless feel "at home" while at school. And, finally, the Jewish Coalition contracted with the YWCA to arrange day-care activities after school for all our students for the year. They later set up a permanent activity center for all homeless children to attend either after school or during the weekend.

Business and Service Groups Do Their Part

Business and service organizations enhanced our efforts to serve our homeless students. During the Christmas holidays, for example, a local talk-radio station adopted City Park. For a month, the station collected toys and clothes and then organized a special program to distribute the items to our students. Appreciative parents often remarked that these were the only gifts their children would be receiving that winter.

A private law firm established a fund to provide instructional materials available through the district. From our teachers' "wish lists," the firm would then estimate the budget and issue a check for the amount required. We spent a large percentage of the money on manipulatives, as children learn better through concrete, hands-on activities.

Other groups, such as the Lion's Club, took some of our neediest children to a department store to buy new clothing every year. In a school where most children are poor, it is not easy to decide which ones are the neediest. By keeping careful records, we were able to ensure that new children were selected each year.

Individual Volunteers Lend a Hand

Other community members further enriched our daily program by offering recreational activities not available through the neighborhood or the district. For example, when the children expressed an interest in karate, ballet, soccer, and baton-twirling, several volunteers pitched in to provide lessons, including a probation officer, a young journalist, a university student, and one of our teachers.

These enriching activities helped diminish disciplinary problems by building students' self-esteem and providing a proper outlet for pent-up energies and emotions. The value of the positive role models these volunteers provided for our youngsters was immeasurable. For children who participated continuously in the recreational programs, the benefits were often dramatic. For example, Jonathan, a young boy of 9 being raised by his grandmother, chose to remain at the shelter for two years. When asked why he preferred living at the shelter, he said he stayed "because I love the teachers and all the neat

Assisting Migrant Students in Your Area

The children of migrant workers are one segment of the student population whose home status is precarious. Readers who would like to learn how to help migrant students in their locales can contact:

Francis Corrigan
Director of Migrant Education
400 Maryland Ave., SW
Washington, DC 20202
202-401-0740

He will be able to direct readers to local Migrant Education offices around the country.

things to do at City Park."

Since the school is situated in a high-crime area known as "the war zone," we believed that a close relationship with the police would give the children a sense of security. Many of the police officers willingly obliged by becoming a visible presence in the school, often stopping by to have lunch with the children in the cafeteria. They also made a concerted effort to attend PTA meetings and all special events.

The Shelters Offer Support

Support from the shelters was another integral part of our efforts to care for our homeless children. The personnel there set up a process by which the time-consuming paperwork for enrollment began at the shelters, thus giving us more time to orient parent and child to their new school. In addition, the shelters helped provide school supplies when our packages ran out. They also en-

Personal attention from a concerned adult enhances the child's experiental background and self-esteem and, in turn, facilitates the teaching-learning process.

couraged parents to meet with us on a continuous basis, and they offered parenting classes.

Another way the shelters helped was to keep us abreast of additional problems the families of our children were encountering. As soon as they notified us of a difficulty, I met with the child's nurse, counselor, and teacher to formulate a plan for how best to address the situation.

For example, with the help of the shelter, we were able to provide psychological support for a child traumatized by his mother's terminal illness and, later, reading lessons for his father. Such cooperation between school and shelter can help homeless child *and* parent alike.

An Extended Family

Coordinating a variety of programs for homeless children is not an easy task. Every school may not have access to the wealth of volunteer services available in the City Park community, and educa-

tors may have to expend great effort to recruit such resources. Another obstacle is that all people working with children traumatized by homelessness and/or poverty need training in advance. Such a time-consuming task may be exacting.

Nevertheless, the additional time and effort schools spend in gaining support from their communities is returned manyfold. Community groups furnish "extras" that go far beyond the tangible. For example, the impact that a concerned adult can have on a homeless child—through tutoring, playing after-school games, or stopping by for lunch—is immeasurable. Such personal attention enhances the child's experiential background and self-esteem and, in turn, facilitates the teaching-learning process. In this way, community support benefits not only the child but the entire school as well. Working closely with the school, the community, thus, becomes part of an extended family for the poor and the homeless.

 Article Review Form at end of book.

In what way can schools be more flexible to help effectively educate homeless students? Describe how a teacher might use a detailed manual that lists the available community resources for homeless students. What specific services for homeless students could be provided?

Homeless Students, Heroic Students

Yvonne M. Vissing, Dorothy Schroepfer, and Fred Bloise

Yvonne M. Vissing is an associate professor of sociology at Salem State College, Salem, Mass., and director of Community Organization Research Associates, Durham, N.H. Dorothy Schroepfer is an education consultant in the Early Learning Unit of the New Hampshire Department of Education, Concord. Fred Bloise is a graduate student in photography at the University of New Hampshire, Durham.

From their experience in New Hampshire, the authors have derived recommendations for concrete actions that schools can take to help homeless student.

Joe and Heidi met at a Florida high school during the fall of 1989 and quickly became serious about each other. Both students' home environments were far from ideal. Joe lived with his mother and her abusive boyfriend, and their drinking frequently led to loud—sometimes violent—arguments. Heidi lived with her mother and stepfather in a home where there was more bickering than love. Their domestic problems helped the two teens bond together in hopes of creating a loving and supportive relationship.

The desperate living conditions they were both experiencing caused Joe to call his father in New Hampshire and tell him about the problems that he and Heidi were struggling with. His father agreed to let him move north, and an uncle paid Joe's plane fare. Heidi did not move to New Hampshire immediately. She did move out of her mother's house, though, and bounced around a couple of places in Florida before moving to New York to live with her grandparents.

Heidi admits that the move to New York was a calculated one, because her mother would not have allowed her to leave home to be with Joe. Within a month after Heidi moved to New York, Joe came for her. His father and stepmother agreed she could live with them. But there was one restriction: they could not be sexually active.

Joe and Heidi agreed. For the first time, things appeared to be falling into place for them. They lived in a more stable home, in which they could finish their schooling and earn high school diplomas. But they were in love, and, within a few months, Heidi was pregnant. Heidi was told she had to move out of the house im-

mediately. A teacher at the high school, who taught classes for pregnant teens, heard about Heidi's troubles and contacted the local shelter for the homeless. "We knew the rules, and we goofed," Heidi now says. "But we never thought it would come to [our being homeless]."

Living in the shelter solved Heidi's housing difficulties, but it posed problems for her relationship with Joe. He did not want to leave the security of his home to live in a shelter, but he couldn't leave his pregnant girlfriend. "I felt torn. What should I do? Go with the woman I loved and become homeless or stay with the family I loved? What family do I go with?" Joe wondered.

Joe made his decision. He moved into the shelter with Heidi. They were married, and both the wedding and the reception were held at the shelter. With the help of the shelter providers, they continued to attend high school and received prenatal care for their baby. Heidi was an A student and earned an outstanding achievement award for her work in her law class. Joe, an average student, found that he enjoyed school much more in his new living arrangements than he did when troubles at home pushed education off his list of priorities.

Both Joe and Heidi felt far older than their peers. Though they seldom had time to be kids,' they did go to the prom. Heidi found a dress at a used clothing store for $50, and Joe bought the $20 prom tickets. Instead of going out to a restaurant for their prom dinner, they ate at the shelter. "I would have liked all the extra stuff for her," Joe stated. "Fancy restaurant, limo, and all the fun stuff that a lot of my friends are doing. But it's too expensive."

After graduation, Joe and Heidi made decisions about how best to keep their life in order. Heidi moved back to Florida to live with her mother while she awaited the arrival of their child. Joe began a five-year hitch in the Navy. He chose to enter the service because of the instant paycheck it provided his young family. "We're banking on the fact that the Navy will be the beginning of the end of our struggle," Joe said, hoping that he would be assigned to a base where Heidi could soon join him.

Both of them used to get angry with people in their school who seemed to take money for granted and with those who would characterize people on welfare as shiftless and exploitative. "There are people who don't care and who don't want to try," they admit. "But then there are people like us. We'd do anything to get out of the shelter. People should open their eyes and see that the homeless aren't just the people you see on the streets and in doorways. There are a lot of people out there with a lot of good reasons for being without a home."

Everyone who knew Joe and Heidi came to respect them. "They tried so hard and were such good kids," reported one professional who worked closely with them. "They both worked part-time and went to school. They were polite and respectful. No one could say anything bad about them. They were real good kids, and I'm sure they are gong to make it." At last report, this young family is well on the path toward success.

Homeless but Heroic

Joe and Heidi are but two of the thousands of homeless but heroic students. I borrow the term heroic from a school nurse in New Hampshire.

I think [homeless students] are heroic. How do they come through those doors in the morning? They are dealing with stuff that I hope I never have to, and I am an adult! If you can survive, the way that these kids are surviving, that has to have some kind of heroics behind it. They've got to have some kind of strength, something special. They don't give up. A New Hampshire principal agreed: I think the homeless kid is a motivated kid. These kids are resilient; there is a stick-to-itiveness about them. . . . In spite of anything going on, . . . they hold on to school. Contrary to what other people say, I would tell you this right now: these are nice kids. They're not wise guys. They're not bashing anyone down. They're not aggressive people. They're holding jobs, and they're taking care of themselves. I would put my money on a homeless kid more than other kids. A homeless kid is a kid who comes to school and really tries to make it. They have really good feelings about school, and they are motivated and try to hang on because they know it's important to them.

Homeless teenagers who decide to stay in school and make it work are special people.[1] It is not that they don't have problems, indeed, they have a great many problems. However, the ones who stay in school have made a commitment to themselves and to their education. For Joe and Heidi, the school and shelter were able to work together to ensure that they could attend classes regularly, complete their assignments, and graduate. How can schools help other heroic students? From our experience in New Hampshire, we have derived a number of recommendations for concrete actions that schools can take to help homeless students.

Flexible admissions criteria. Homeless students are often not allowed to attend school because they are unable to provide the necessary documentation.[2] We encourage schools to admit these students on a temporary basis, while the staff works with them to obtain the necessary paperwork.

We also encourage schools to work with schools in nearby districts regarding the admission of students, because homeless students move frequently in search of affordable housing. The community next door may have cheaper housing but be outside the student's school district. If the student wants to make the commitment to keep attending his or her former school, the educational and social continuity should outweigh the administrative benefits of restricting admission.

Flexible attendance policies. Because homeless students seldom have control over the environment in which they spend each night, often hold jobs with odd hours, and have unreliable transportation arrangements, it is not uncommon for them to arrive at school late. Penalizing them for lateness encourages them to skip school altogether, because then they can be excused as sick without penalty. Hence tardiness policies frequently create the absenteeism they are intended to curb.

Homeless parents and children confront a host of bureaucratic problems that undermine schools' efforts to ensure regular attendance. Thus estimates of school attendance rates for homeless children range widely, from as low as 43% to 57% to as high as 70%.[3] Attendance rates decline for all students as grade levels increase.[4] This is because the older the student gets, the more likely it is that he or she will be employed. Holding a job and going to school simultaneously are often incompatible. As one principal reported:

Homeless students are not arriving late because they are blowing off school. These kids are busy fighting for survival. So long as they are coming to school—even late, even infrequently— I haven't lost them. I still have a chance to educate them, to help them. They still have faith if they come to school. They haven't given up and dropped out. Should I let a bunch of policies that were written for a different type of student get in the way of doing what is right for these kids?

Flexible course offerings. Required courses that are offered at designated hours or only during certain times of the year make it difficult for homeless students to graduate. Given their transience, homeless students may enter school missing some classes and having completed only parts of others. This causes homeless students to graduate behind schedule.[5] Offering courses at different times of the day can be helpful for students who work.

Courses that run only for a full year or a full semester may be difficult for homeless students to complete. However, miniclasses and courses that are divided into segments make it possible for students to obtain partial credit hours. A crediting system that allows a student who leaves before the end of the term to take away some credits can also help.

Flexible class assignments. Homeless students are at a disadvantage when it comes to produc-

ing high-quality work. The job schedules of older students may interfere with homework or studying. Older students may also have significant child-care responsibilities. Just finding a quiet place to do homework may be impossible. In addition, homeless students do not have home libraries and may not be able to get to the public library. It is common to find homework "unacceptably" messy or torn because it was written on the dashboard of a car that also serves as the kitchen table for those living in the car. Homework assignments are geared for a more stable, middle-class population of students and require either technical or conceptual resources that are unavailable to homeless students.

Schools must be sensitive to the fact that many children do not live in situations in which it is possible to do certain types of homework. Alternatives, without penalties attached, need to be available for these students. When assignments are given, homeless students often need a longer time to complete them than students in stable home environments. Schools and libraries that open earlier and close later also create greater opportunities for students to get their homework done.

Special education services. Because homeless students may exhibit the accumulated effects of chronic medical conditions, developmental problems, and the stressors and disruptions of moving often, they almost inevitably require some type of special education. Of homeless students who took the Metropolitan Achievement Test in math, only 28% scored at or above grade level, compared with 57% of the nonhomeless students.[6] These results are consistent with those of David Shaffer and Carol Canton,

who found that more than half of their sample of homeless 10- to 17-year-olds were more than one standard deviation below grade level on their reading achievement tests.[7]

The aid that homeless students often need to help them catch up could be provided through tutoring, after-school meetings with the teacher, or various kinds of peer instruction. Yet such services are not always available. Asking one's teacher or peers for special help is embarrassing and stigmatizing. In addition, many schools will provide special education services only to students who have been officially "coded." This coding is difficult for homeless students to obtain, because school systems are reluctant to code transient students for special education services when the district will be responsible for paying for those services even if students move out of the district. The result is that homeless students move from place to place without ever receiving the needed help.

If homeless students are to succeed in school, the schools must acknowledge that these students will need help in their classes until they catch up. Where, when, and by whom the help is provided is less important than seeing to it that help is available for these students.

Transportation. Depending on where homeless students live, it may be difficult for them to secure the appropriate transportation to get to school. Students may not be able to come up with bus fare. In poorer, rural areas, no bus service may exist where the student "lives," and the distance to school can easily be farther than Abe Lincoln would have walked. If a student has to depend on others for transportation, then he or she is at the mercy of other people's schedules. In cases where students are having transportation difficulties, it is important for schools to work to create a voucher system for the use of buses or taxis. School-sponsored carpools may be useful as well.

Emotional support. School is one of the few sources of consistency in the lives of homeless students. It is where they get information on how to help themselves. Homeless students are embarrassed about their lack of housing and money. Studies indicate that many of these children suffer from low self-esteem and feel isolated.[8] School personnel may be the only ones who can provide counseling and support for students in crisis.

Homelessness is associated with a variety of physical, social, emotional, and educational problems. Adolescents prefer to hide their homelessness rather than bring attention to their lack of housing. When they decide to seek help, they will do so only from those they trust. Students do not routinely know where to go for help, so they seek the assistance of a trusted teacher, secretary, school nurse, or counselor. Children in crisis need help immediately and cannot wait weeks—or even days—for aid. It takes a great deal of courage for them to ask for help, so, when they do, help needs to be delivered in a prompt and sensitive manner. As one counselor reported:

One day a student I did not know knocked on my door. She asked to speak with me privately and told me how her father had kicked her out and thrown all of her possessions on the front lawn and set them on fire. This shy, quiet girl was given clothes by different friends, who traded off giving her places to sleep. No one had thought to give her underwear, and she was too embarrassed to ask them. Knowing no one else who could help her, she turned to me, a

total stranger, because she heard the school counselor was "okay."

School personnel need to listen to students who cry for help, even if their cries are in the form of whispers or nonverbal signals. But providing a listening ear is not enough; they must find a way to bring the needs of individual students to the attention of those who know how to gain access to existing community resources.

Development of community resources. Being sympathetic won't put food in hungry stomachs or coats on shivering backs. One must know how to help students get the services that are essential for their survival. While the school is not a social service agency, it cannot fulfill its mission unless it helps students to be receptive learners. And this can require assistance from a variety of school personnel and other community service providers. Schools could help each student to find the basic necessities for survival. This means nutritious food at regular intervals; safe and clean places to sleep; access to personal hygiene facilities; appropriate clothing, from underclothes to shoes to coats; and access to routine health care. School social workers, counselors, and nurses must find out where to refer students for help, so they can avoid the experience of one counselor who "called every agency I could think of one Friday afternoon and found after 32 calls that not one was able to help this girl to avoid being on the streets for the weekend."

We recommend that every school district develop a detailed manual that lists the available community resources for homeless students. Then, when students need help, school personnel would know what services exist and how to make use of them. All schools should be able to help students secure housing, food,

clothes, counseling, mental health support, vocational training, and employment assistance.

Community partnerships must be formed so that everyone in the community knows who provides what services to adolescents at risk. This type of communication would allow gaps in the system to be identified and filled. The development of an interagency partnership on behalf of homeless and at-risk youths requires an ongoing commitment from the entire community. The school may have to be the one to take the lead in developing the partnership. Together, a community can do more than any school or other agency can do alone.[9]

Equal treatment of all students. Like it or not, schools cannot fulfill their mission to educate students unless they also address the social, physical, and emotional needs of all students—including the homeless. What is fair for one student must be made fair for all, and schools should always keep in mind the student who has the fewest resources.[10] One principal described the situation that schools face today.

We run our schools as if education is the number-one priority for all students. The fact is, for many it is not. The fact is, for many kids school shouldn't be their top priority. If they live in homes of chaos and violence, when they don't know what they are going to eat or where they are going to sleep, if they are pregnant or using drugs or in trouble with their peers—these are their priorities. For the schools to play ostrich and ignore the fact that these kids live complicated lives and have adult problems is just plain stupid. Schools must adapt and bend their policies to help the kids, or we are going to lose greater and greater numbers of them. That is the fact.

Schools play a more central role in securing the health and well-being of children than ever before.

Homeless adolescents count on the school to be an extension of their families. They rely on the school and its personnel to help them, to guide them, and to care about them. For children who have been let down by every other institution, the school has a special responsibility to help them succeed. In their efforts to manage adversity, homeless students are truly heroic—but even heroes fall when no one cares.

1. Nationally, it is estimated that there are approximately 300,000 adolescents living on the streets who receive no supervision, nurturance, or regular assistance from a parent or responsible adult. See American Nightmare: A Decade of Homelessness in the United States (Washington, D.C.: National Coalition for the Homeless, 1989).

2. Jonathan Kozol, Rachel and Her Children: Homeless Families in America (New York: Crown, 1988); and Yvonne Rafferty and Norma Rollins, Learning in Limbo: The Educational Deprivation of Homeless Children (New York: Advocates for Children of New York, Inc., September 1989).

3. The 43% figure comes from American Nightmare; the 57% figure comes from Penelope L. Maza and Judy A. Hall, Homeless Children and Their Families: A Preliminary Study (Washington, D.C.: Child Welfare League of America, 1988); and the 70% figure comes from "Double Jeopardy: Homeless and Illiterate," Adult Literacy: Programs, Planning, Issues: A Newsletter for the Business Community, U.S. Department of Education, Washington, D.C., October 1988.

4. Yvonne Rafferty, "Developmental and Educational Consequences of Homelessness on Children, and Youth," in Julee Kryder-Coe, Lester Salamm, and Janice Molnar, eds., Homeless Children and Youth (New Brunswick N.J.: Transaction, 1991), pp. 105–14.

5. Ellen L. Bassuk and L. Rosenberg, "Why Does Family Homelessness Occur? A Case-Control Study," American Journal of Public Health, vol. 14, 1988, pp. 125–36; and David Shaffer and Carol L. M. Caton, Runaway and Homeless Youth in New York City (New York: Division of Child Psychiatry, New York State Psychiatric Institute, and Columbia University College of Physicians and Surgeons, 1984), pp. 80–82.

6. Rafferty and Rollins, op. cit.

7. Shaffer and Caton, op. cit.

8. Bassuk and Rosenberg, op. cit.; and Rafferty and Rollins, op. cit.

9. Atelia Melaville, What It Takes: Structuring Interagency Partnerships to Connect Children and Families with Comprehensive Services (Washington, D.C.: William T. Grant Foundation, 1993).

10. Benjamin Barber, An Aristocracy of Everyone: The Politics of Education and the Future of America (New York: Ballantine, 1992).

Article Review Form at end of book.

WiseGuide Wrap-Up

- Poor and homeless students confront a variety of challenges that hinder their success in school, including social, physical, and emotional issues.

- Flexible classroom and school policies can assist poor/homeless students in their learning performance and school attendance.

- Teachers may perform a broad variety of activities to assure greater success for poor and homeless students.

- Partnerships between schools and public/private agencies can provide needed resources for addressing the needs of the poor and homeless.

R.E.A.L. Sites

This list provides a print preview of typical **coursewise** R.E.A.L. sites. (There are over 100 such sites at the **courselinks**™ site.) The danger in printing URLs is that Web sites can change overnight. As we went to press, these sites were functional using the URLs provided. If you come across one that isn't, please let us know via email to: webmaster@coursewise.com. Use your Passport to access the most current list of R.E.A.L. sites at the **courselinks**™ site.

Site name: National Coalition for the Homeless

URL: http://nch.ari.net/

Why is it R.E.A.L.? A national advocacy network of homeless persons, activists, service providers, and others committed to ending homelessness. The site features legislation and policy alerts, library directories, resources, and events calendar.

Key topics: homeless, educational policy

Activity: Skim "Facts about Homelessness" to learn more about specific causes, issues, populations, and conditions of homelessness.

Site name: School Programs and Practices for Homeless Students

URL: http://eric-web.tc.columbia.edu/digests/dig105.html

Why is it R.E.A.L.? This ERIC digest comprehensively reviews approaches to educating homeless students. It includes practices, policies, research, links to other articles, and a reference list.

Key topics: homeless, poverty, educational policy, partnership

Activity: Review the ancillary services described in the website that enhance learning opportunities for homeless students.

Site name: Making the Grade: Successes and Challenges in Educating Homeless Children and Youth

URL: http://nch.ari.net/education/

Why is it R.E.A.L.? The 1996 Position Document of the National Association of State Coordinators for the Education of Homeless Children and Youth. The website includes an executive summary, history review, directory information, and state profiles.

Key topics: homeless, educational policy

Activity: Review the purpose, history, and effects of the McKinney Homeless Assistance Act.

section 6

Blending Colors: Multiracial and Bicultural Learners

Learning Objectives

- Identify the issues and challenges faced by multiracial students and their interracial families.

- Describe the historic events that led to racial and ethnic classification efforts.

- Compare and contrast the political influences for and against including a "multiracial" category on the U.S. Census.

- Detail current interracial marriage trends by race/ethnicity.

- Identify and describe proactive steps that will assist interracial families and their multiracial children with healthy identity development.

 **WiseGuide Intro**

Thirty years ago, sixteen states in America still had laws restricting interracial marriage. But both before and after that date, multiracial American children were being born to interracial couples. These children have faced historic discrimination and prejudicial policies that overshadow the experiences of other single-minority cultures. In addition to clear discrimination and prejudice, they have faced difficult issues of acceptance by their respective cultural groups, and have been forced to "officially" identify with a single cultural classification, effectively denying their other cultural heritage(s).

This negative historical experience is just beginning to change as public recognition, national policies, increasing numbers, and multiracial activism have surfaced. From kindergarten enrollment forms to college entrance applications and U.S. Census surveys, these multiracial individuals are flexing their collective muscle. And the changing face of America is beginning to acknowledge mixed-heritage Americans.

The articles in Section 6 highlight the issues facing multiracial children and the challenges and opportunities for educators in addressing their unique needs. "Freedom from Choice: Being Biracial has Meant Denying Half My Identity" details the experience faced by multiracial individuals in the pursuit of their identity within the context of the society in which they live. The historical context of that society is detailed in "The One-Drop-of-Blood Rule," where political forces are revealed to be in conflict with biologists and anthropologists as America continues its obsession with racial and ethnic classification. While exploring additional historical imperatives, "The Hard Question: Race for the Cure" presents alternative suggestions based on the purpose of classification. Recognizing and addressing the rich heritage of multiracial students, educators can better implement specific strategies, as detailed in "Children of Mixed Parentage: How Can Professionals Respond?" The section concludes with a recent American hero who represents eloquently the plight and delight of multiracial America— Tiger Woods. The article, "I'm Just Who I Am: Mixed Race Americans," envisions the future, using statistical data and individual experiences, as America moves into the twenty-first century.

Questions

Reading 27. What pressures for acceptance by members of their respective ethnic/racial groups are placed on biracial individuals? Why does the American obsession with labeling present a problem for biracial individuals?

Reading 28. What was the "one-drop-of-blood" rule? Why do powerful political interests want to preserve the status quo on racial classifications?

Reading 29. Any race and ethnicity questions on the U.S. Census should provide accurate data for what purpose? When and why did race become a factor in the U.S. Census?

Reading 30. Why is the issue of identity important for children of mixed heritage? What specific steps might educators take to work effectively with multiracial children?

Reading 31. What kinds of programs are administered on the basis of racial tallies? What is meant by the "browning of America"?

What pressures for acceptance by members of their respective ethnic/racial groups are placed on biracial individuals? Why does the American obsession with labeling present a problem for biracial individuals?

Freedom from Choice

Being biracial has meant denying half my identity

Brian A. Courtney

As my friend Denise and I trudged across the University of Tennessee campus to our 9:05 a.m. class, we delivered countless head nods, "Heys" and "How ya'doin's" to other African-Americans we passed along the way. We spoke to people we knew as well as people we didn't know because it's an unwritten rule that black people speak to one another when they pass. But when I stopped to greet and hug one of my female friends, who happens to be white, Denise seemed a little bothered. We continued our walk to class, and Denise expressed concern that I might be coming down with a "fever." "I don't feel sick," I told her. As it turns out, she was referring to "jungle fever," the condition where a black man or woman is attracted to someone of the opposite race.

This encounter has not been an uncommon experience for me. That's why the first 21 years of my life have felt like a never-ending tug of war. And quite honestly, I'm not looking forward to being

dragged through the mud for the rest of my life. My white friends want me to act one way—white. My African-American friends want me to act another—black. Pleasing them both is nearly impossible and leaves little room to be just me.

The politically correct term for someone with my racial background is "biracial" or "multiracial." My mother is fair-skinned with blond hair and blue eyes. My father is dark-complexioned with prominent African-American features and a bead of woolly hair. When you combine the genetic makeup of the two, you get me—golden-brown skin, semi-coarse hair and a whole mess of freckles.

Someone once told me I was lucky to be biracial because I have the best of both worlds. In some ways this is true. I have a huge family that's filled with diversity and is as colorful as a box of Crayolas. My family is more open to whomever I choose to date, whether that person is black, white, biracial, Asian or whatever. But looking at the big picture, American society makes being

biracial feel less like a blessing than a curse.

One reason is the American obsession with labeling. We feel the need to label everyone and everything and group them into neatly defined categories. Are you a Republican, a Democrat or an Independent? Are you pro-life or pro-choice? Are you African-American, Caucasian or Native American? Not everyone fits into such classifications. This presents a problem for me and the many biracial people living in the United States. The rest of the population seems more comfortable when we choose to identify with one group. And it pressures us to do so, forcing us to deny half of who we are.

Growing up in the small, predominantly white town of Maryville, Tenn., I attended William Blount High School. I was one of a handful of minority students—a raisin in a box of cornflakes, so to speak. Almost all of my peers, many of whom I've known since grade school, were white. Over the years, they've commented on how different I am from other black people they know. The implication was that I'm better because I'm only half black. Acceptance into their world has meant talking as they talk, dressing as they dress and appreciating the same music. To reduce tension and make everyone feel comfortable, I've reacted by ignoring half of my identity and downplaying my ethnicity.

My experience at UT has been very similar. This time it's my African-American peers exerting pressure to choose. Some African-Americans on campus say I "talk too white." I dress like the boys in white fraternities. I have too many white friends. In other words, I'm not black enough. I'm a white "wanna-be." The other day, an African-American acquaintance told me I dress "bourgie." This means I dress very white—a pastel-colored polo, a pair of navy chinos and hiking boots. Before I came to terms with this kind of remark, a comment like this would have angered me, and I must admit that I was a little offended. But instead of showing my frustration, I let it ride, and I simply said, "Thank you." Surprised by this response, she said in disbelief, "You mean you agree?"

On more occasions than I dare count, black friends have made sweeping derogatory statements about the white race in general. "White people do this, or white people do that." Every time I hear them, I cringe. These comments refer not just to my white friends but to my mother and maternal grandmother as well. Why should I have to shun or hide my white heritage to enhance my ethnicity? Doesn't the fact that I have suffered the same prejudices as every other African-American— and then some—count for something.

I do not blame my African-American or white friends for the problems faced by biracial people in America. I blame society for not acknowledging us as a separate race. I am speaking not only for people like myself, who are half black and half white, but also for those who are half white and half Asian, half white and half Hispanic, or half white and half whatever. Until American society recognizes us as a distinct group, we will continue to be pressured to choose one side of our heritage over the other.

Job applications, survey forms, college-entrance exams and the like ask individuals to check only one box for race. For most of my life, I have marked BLACK because my skin color is the first thing people notice. However, I could just as honestly have marked WHITE. Somehow when I fill out these forms, I think the employers, administrators, researchers, teachers or whoever sees them will have a problem looking at my face and then accepting a big x by the word WHITE. In any case, checking BLACK or WHITE does not truly represent me. Only in recent years have some private universities added the category of BIRACIAL or MULTIRACIAL to their applications. I've heard that a few states now include these categories on government forms.

One of the greatest things parents of biracial children can do is expose them to both of their cultures. But what good does this do when in the end society makes us choose? Having a separate category marked BIRACIAL will not magically put an end to the pressure to choose, but it will help people to stop judging us as just black or just white and see us for what we really are—both.

 Article Review
Form at end of book.

What was the "one-drop-of-blood" rule? Why do powerful political interests want to preserve the status quo on racial classifications?

The One-Drop-of-Blood Rule

Dinesh D'Souza

Susan Graham is a white woman married to a black man. When she received her form from the U.S. census a few years ago, she realized there was no descriptive category for her children. She called the Census Bureau and was told that her children should take the race of their mother. They were white. At her son's school, however, the teacher was asked to classify the child based upon observation of his features. The verdict: black. "White on the U.S. census, black at school and multiracial at home," marvels Graham.

The Census Bureau and other federal and state agencies categorize American citizens into six groups: white, black, Hispanic, Asian/Pacific islander, American Indian, other. Congress and several federal agencies are holding hearings on proposals to add a new "multiracial" category, or perhaps to eliminate race-based classification altogether.

For more than a decade scholars have pointed out that the existing racial boxes make no sense. Hispanic and Asian are not racial but rather cultural and continental categories. Hispanic is, more precisely, a linguistic classification whose heritage includes white, black and native Indian.

The category "black" is equally dubious. Biologists and anthropologists tell us that the overwhelming majority of African-Americans have both black and white heritage. So why are people like Whitney Houston and Jesse Jackson, despite their mixed ancestry, automatically classified as black?

The answer will not please the people who favor this kind of classification. The system can be traced to a U.S. peculiarity called the "one-drop rule," according to which a single drop of black blood is sufficient to assure membership in the black race.

The one-drop rule was invented by southern slaveowners. It guaranteed that the illegitimate offspring of a white slavemaster and his black concubine remained a slave. In adopting the one-drop rule and tracing racial descent through the mother, the Census Bureau is strictly following antebellum precedent.

Intermarriage is growing by leaps and bounds. Only about 5% of African-Americans marry whites, but each year the number increases. One-fourth of Hispanics now marry outside their group, and one-third of Asians living in the U.S. are married to non-Asians. There will soon be millions of chil-

dren like my own 22-month-old daughter Danielle who are literally beyond racial classification.

It makes eminent sense to get rid of these historically and scientifically absurd classifications, but powerful political interests have mobilized to preserve the status quo. They want to protect the racial privileges that the current system provides, while others seek to amend their racial titles in order to expand their race-based entitlements.

Testifying at the hearings, civil rights activists condemned proposals to eliminate racial classification. They seemed unconscious of the irony that they were perpetuating the racial lexicon of their oppressors and rejecting the colorblind principal for which generations of black leaders from Frederick Douglass to Martin Luther King Jr. had labored.

The motives of these activists were entirely pragmatic. They pointed out, correctly, that if the government stops counting its citizens by race, this could mean the end of college admissions, faculty recruitment, scholarships, hiring, promotion, government contracts, race-based set-asides and voting districts based on race.

The chicanery that emerged at the hearings was even a little comic. The National Council of La Raza astonished scholars by asserting that Hispanics were not a cultural group but rather a distinct brown-skinned "race." The Arab-American Institute insisted that Americans of Middle Eastern descent, heretofore counted as white, should be given a separate affirmative action category. Hawaiian groups demanded to be moved from the Asian/Pacific islander box to the American Indian box, thus making them eligible for gambling concessions currently available to Indians but not to Asians.

These displays show racial preferences for what they really are: Pure political pork—or rent-seeking, to use the term economists use.

Consistent with Martin Luther King's vision, the government should stop color-coding its citizens. A new generation of Americans, like Susan Graham's children and mine, should be able to think of themselves as Americans, and not have to go through life checking racial boxes that force them into artificial categories.

 Article Review Form at end of book.

Any race and ethnicity questions on the U.S. Census should provide accurate data for what purpose? When and why did race become a factor in the U.S. Census?

The Hard Questions

Race for the cure

Nathan Glazer

Over the past several years, people of mixed race have been pushing for the addition of a "multiracial" category to the Census. One can only be sympathetic to the desire of increasing numbers of people whose parents are of different races to escape from a forced choice between "black," "white" or a dazzling array of Asian and Pacific Islander groups, all of which are considered separate "races" on our confusing Census forms.

Black and Hispanic groups, for their part, worry that a multiracial box would reduce their numbers. Though their fears are not altogether imaginary, they are, according to the most recent government studies, at least exaggerated. Only about 1.5 percent of Americans would select the new "multiracial" designation (that is, about 4 million people). Still, many black and Hispanic organizations resist the designation.

This burgeoning controversy has raised an important question. Why has the Census gotten so deeply into this business of trying to make ever more refined racial and ethnic classifications at all? Race first becomes a factor in the Census because the government needed to count slaves to fulfill its constitutional duty of apportioning representatives to the states. Five slaves were deemed equal to three whites, and this served to reduce the number of members of Congress from the slave states.

The Census also counted free blacks. From this modest beginning, a few other ethnic and racial categories were added over time as a result of immigration. But it is only in the last few decades that the number of categories has exploded. The Census short form, which must be filled out for every American, is now an astonishing document, more than two-fifths of it devoted to racial and ethnic questions. The question that asks the person's race is followed by various boxes to check, from white and black to Samoan and Guamanian. The Census considers every Asian group a separate "race." Native Americans are also considered a separate race. Then the government asks: "Is this person Hispanic?" with follow-up prodding to determine just what kind of Hispanic the person is, including a list of helpful options such as Argentinean, Dominican, Nicaraguan, Salvadoran and, surprisingly, Spaniard. Finally, there is a question on "ancestry," with more helpful hints. (Among them: You cannot answer "Jewish." That is "religion," a strict no-no on the Census.)

But how many Americans can properly distinguish between "race," "ancestry" and "Hispanic origin"? When the "multiracial" alternative was tested by the Bureau of Labor Statistics, a good number of people answered, "yes, I am multiracial," but on follow-up explained they were of mixed Irish and Italian descent—which of course is not what the advocates of the multiracial category were after at all.

The relatively new question on "ancestry" is there to please various ethnic-group advocates who want to determine their numbers. Previously the Census had asked whether a person was foreign-born, and in which country, and whether that person's parents were foreign-born, and in which country. So, while it was possible to determine the numbers of first- and second-generation Irish, or Italians, or Poles, the third generation disappeared into the general, undifferentiated category of native-born Americans.

In the 1970s, with the revival of ethnic identities as points of pride rather than something to be gotten over, the "ancestry" question was added. Then we had an estimate of all Americans of Italian or Irish descent, not only those of the first or second generation. But strange things happened. It turned out that answers varied greatly depending on the prompts. Many respondents wanted to be just Americans, and nothing more, and many were of such varied ancestries that the effort to make any sense of the results was daunting. Were there really 40 million Americans of Irish ancestry? (There are only 5 million in Ireland, north and south.)

Rather than add yet another category and increase the confusion, I have a radical solution (though it's probably a long shot): reduce the number of categories—race, ancestry, Hispanic group—to those that people can answer with some degree of reliability and that are important for public policy. The tremendous rise in the amount of intermarriage among the various groups, racial and ethnic, is reason enough to drop the ancestry question. In every European-origin group well over half marry outside the group. As this pattern continues, the ethnicity of the children becomes ever more vestigial and symbolic, and

their answer to the ancestry question ever less meaningful. The race question, insofar as it deals with Asians, is increasingly irrelevant. Marriage outside that group runs 30 percent or more in the second generation. For Hispanics, outmarriage is just as high. Much has been made of Census estimates that by the year 2050 fewer than half of all Americans will be, as that inelegant Census formulation has it, "non-Hispanic white." But long before that date the distinction will have lost the portentous meaning it now carries. The differences between Asians, Hispanics and whites, except for immigrants and their children, will simply not mean much.

There remains one exception to this pattern of mingling and merging of races: blacks. Despite recent increases in intermarriage between blacks and others, the number of such marriages is of a completely different order of magnitude from the one-third to one-quarter outmarriage rates we see among Asians and Hispanics. This is despite the fact that so many Asians and Hispanics are recent immigrants and could be expected to be more insular.

Race in America means blacks, as a result of our long, sad, history, and it is of course blacks

for whom the numbers are important, to rate our progress, or lack of it, in achieving equality. That is the only race that counts. There is no reason to count Asian groups to the nth generation. In any case, intermarriage will make the effort futile in a few decades. There is no need to count American Indians, either. The figures have been inflated wildly in the last two counts as people with only a fraction of Indian ancestry call themselves American Indians. And there is no need to record "Hispanicity," as if it were an indelible mark impervious to American assimilation.

Ideally, the Census should ask only two or three questions about race or ethnicity: Are you black? Where were you born? Where were your parents born? That would tell us all we really need to know or can know with any degree of accuracy. Politically, though, this sensible solution is quite impossible, and so all Americans will have to struggle with the lengthy and basically pointless interrogation on their race and ethnicity.

 Article Review Form at end of book.

Why is the issue of identity important for children of mixed heritage? What specific steps might educators take to work effectively with multiracial children?

Children of Mixed Parentage
How can professionals respond?

Francis Wardle

Francis Wardle, Ph.D., is Director, Adams County Head Start, Commerce City, Colorado.

In order to work effectively with children and their families, people in the helping professions must be sensitive to a wide variety of issues and factors that contribute to a child's behavior and well-being. Does the child live with one or both parents . . . with a stepparent . . . with a foster family? Is he or she adopted . . . a member of a minority group? Does the child have a disability or handicap?

Children of mixed racial or ethnic parentage also have unique needs—but often the professionals who work with these children in day care centers, schools, or social service or health care settings lack the training or awareness to provide the best possible services, support, and encouragement to these children and their families.

While the most obvious example of children of mixed heritage are those with one white parent and one black parent, these children also include Amerasians,

black/Native Americans, Hispanic/white, black/Hispanic—any combination of two racial or ethnic groups. Under certain circumstances it also includes Native Americans who have married across tribal lines. Children of mixed natural parents who are in foster or adoptive families are also part of this population.

The latest census figures report 632,000 interracial marriages in the United States, of which 125,000 are black/white marriages. This is a conservative figure that does not include non-legal relationships. There are no statistics on the number of children of mixed heritage because the Census Bureau does not recognize this as a category. However, any casual observer can see that their numbers are increasing in schools, child care and Head Start centers and other programs serving children.

Identity

Historically, children of mixed parentage were identified with the parent of color—if one parent

was black, then the child was considered black. If both parents were of color, one being Native American, then the child was Native American (if the percentage of Native American heritage met federal standards). Of course, if the child of any mixed marriage looked white, he or she might try to "pass" as white.

Today, parents assume one of three positions as to the identity of their interracial children. Some insist that their child is "human above all else" and that race or ethnicity is irrelevant, while others choose to raise their children with the identity of the parent of color.[1] Another growing group of parents is insisting that the child has the ethnic, racial, cultural and genetic heritage of both parents. More and more extended family members (particularly proud grandparents) are also insisting on this inclusive identity.[2]

Since healthy identity development is crucial to the formation of a normal personality, the issue of identity of children of mixed heritage is critical. However, ex-

From Francis Wardle, "Children of Mixed Parentage" in *Children Today,* 18 (4), 1989, U. S. Department of Health & Human Services.
1. J. Ladner. "Providing a Healthy Environment for Interracial Children," *Interracial Books for Children Bulletin,* June 1984.
2. P. Baptiste and S. Cambell. "The Contemporary Interracial Child," *Communique,* April 1985.

perts do not agree as to what that identity should be. Some believe an interracial child should have the identity of the parent of color because historically that has been the case, and also because society "sees" these children as having the identity of the parent of color.[3] Others have argued that the identity of any child is based on an accurate presentation of his or her true background—a child should know, for example, that his "white" mother has a Scottish heritage while his "black" father claims African, Native American and Asian roots.

Because of the history of racial discrimination in this country, the issue of the identity of mixed children often becomes an extremely emotional one. Some experts believe that because of this history, these children are not viewed as a rich combination of their full heritage.

Among the various names used to describe children of mixed heritage are biracial, multi-racial, interracial, mixed, brown and rainbow. While there are some specific names, such as Amerasian, K. Shackford suggests the term interracial, which includes families from a variety of backgrounds.[4]

Working with Interracial Children and Families

While most young families are under considerable stress, interracial families often have the additional stress of dealing with negative racial comments or downright harassment from other children and adults, or, in some cases, overcoming the loss of economic and emotional support from disapproving family members. Professionals who are not sensitive to the unique needs of these children and their families can also add to this stress.

Professionals who work with interracial children and families should receive specific training, including an orientation to the rich American history of intermarriage (couples of mixed religious, ethnic, linguistic, economic and national backgrounds), and the legal and social taboos against marriages between people of color (at least up to 1967). Such training should explore the myths about people who marry across racial lines—for sexual conquest or economic advancement, for example—and show the normalcy of interracial families.

Professionals should also be encouraged to examine their own views on interracial families and children. To work effectively with these families they need to understand that people of different racial and ethnic backgrounds have a right to marry and have children, and that these parents can choose to raise their children with a rich interracial identity. These parents are often very conscientious because they don't want their children to suffer for being interracial.

Specifically, there are several things that professionals can do to work effectively with interracial children and families. He or she should:

- support the parents' right to be part of a mixed marriage. Help them understand their responsibility to raise healthy children, and provide advice, support, counseling and referral based on the individual needs of the family or child.

- not automatically assume that an interracial child has the identity only of the parent of color. Talk to the parents about how they are raising their children. Many interracial parents are still searching for a true identity for their children, and a caring professional can give them an opportunity to examine their options by giving them reading material, lists of interracial support groups, and a community resource person who is part of an interracial family. Most importantly, the professional can let parents know they can choose an interracial identity for their child. Parents should be advised that their child, at about age four, will be concerned about his or her identity; if they choose to define their child's identity as that of the parent of color, the child will be confused about the white parent.

- provide parents with suggestions for exposing their children to the richness of their heritage—through festivals, books, art, music and drama, for example—and encourage them to enroll their children in school and recreational programs that serve an integrated population.

- encourage parents and children to openly discuss all aspects of a mixed heritage, including skin and eye color, national origin, language and difficulties with other children stemming from prejudice.

- provide parents and children with tools—the right words—to defend and protect themselves from others who don't appreciate differences, and help families to feel proud of their mixed heritage.

- be fully aware of the vast individual differences within racial and ethnic groups,

3. J. Washington. *Marriage in Black and White,* Boston, Beacon Press, 1974, and Ladner, op.cit.
4. K. Shackford. "Interracial Children: Growing Up Healthy in an Unhealthy Society," *Interracial Books for Children Bulletin,* June 1984.

including class, culture, religion, political affiliation and education.

- avoid labeling an interracial child with the stereotypes of the parent of color—don't assume that a child's dark curly hair comes from the parent of color, for example. Each interracial child should be treated as a unique individual with gifts, interests, abilities and preferences of his or her own.

- not automatically attribute a child's problems to his or her mixed heritage.[5] Children have many developmental tasks to accomplish, including developing a healthy self-concept, and any of these can cause problems for the child. Explore causes that are not related to identity first.

- encourage interracial families, and programs serving such families, to provide a variety of books, music, dolls, art materials and other materials that reflect a rich variety of the family backgrounds. For instance, preschool classrooms should have black, white, *and* biracial dolls, and posters that don't divide the world into only white, black, Hispanic and Native American people. Several shades of brown crayons should be available, and children can be shown how to mix paints to get their flesh color.

Professionals who work with foster and adoptive parents of interracial children should make a special effort to help these families provide the children with information about that part of their heritage that may not be represented in the child's current situation. This includes teaching them hair care skills, helping them choose clothing that compliments their skin tone, exposing them to children and adults of the same background, and introducing them to books with multiracial characters. One of the best ways to accomplish this is to live in an integrated neighborhood and have the child attend school with children from many different backgrounds and cultures.

However, interracial children in foster, adoptive and single parent homes should not be made to feel guilty about the white side of their heritage. Not only is this bad for the child's sense of self, but it can destroy the bond between the child and his or her parent or other caretaker.

Conclusion

All parents—whether they be biological, foster or adoptive parents—face a variety of daily challenges in raising interracial children in a society that is, at best, ambivalent and, at worst, openly hostile toward these children. Children of mixed heritage also have their own daily struggles with other children, adults and even some professionals. Thus, it is vital that teachers, social workers, health care professionals and others who come into contact with multiracial families understand their unique needs and provide support for their full growth and development.

 Article Review Form at end of book.

5. J. R. Brandell. "Treatment of the Biracial Child: Theoretical and Clinical Issues," *Journal of Multicultural Counseling and Development,* Oct. 1988.

What kinds of programs are administered on the basis of racial tallies? What is meant by the "browning of America"?

'I'm Just Who I Am'

Mixed race Americans

Jack E. White

His nickname notwithstanding, professional golfer Frank ("Fuzzy") Zoeller saw Tiger Woods quite clearly. He gazed upon the new king of professional golf, through whose veins runs the blood of four continents, and beheld neither a one-man melting pot nor even a golfing prodigy but a fried-chicken-and-collard-greens-eating Sambo. Zoeller saw Woods, in short, as just another stereotype, condemned by his blackness to the perpetual status of "little boy."

Zoeller soon paid a price for saying openly what many others were thinking secretly. K Mart, the discount chain with a big African-American clientele, unceremoniously dumped him as the sponsor of a line of golf clothing and equipment, and he abjectly withdrew from the Greater Greensboro Open tournament. "People who know me know I'm a jokester. I just didn't deliver the line well," Zoeller tearfully explained. But his real crime was not, as he and his defenders seem to think, merely a distasteful breach of racial etiquette or an inept attempt at humor. The real crime was falling behind the times. The old black-white stereotypes are out of date, and Zoeller is just the

latest casualty of America's failure to come to grips with the perplexing and rapidly evolving significance of racial identity in what is fast becoming the most polyglot society in history.

If current demographic trends persist, midway through the 21st century whites will no longer make up a majority of the U.S. population. Blacks will have been overtaken as the largest minority group by Hispanics. Asians and Pacific Islanders will more than double their number of 9.3 million in 1995 to 19.6 million by 2020. An explosion of interracial, interethnic and interreligious marriages will swell the ranks of children whose mere existence makes a mockery of age-old racial categories and attitudes. Since 1970, the number of multiracial children has quadrupled to more than 2 million, according to the Bureau of the Census. The color line once drawn between blacks and whites—or more precisely between whites and nonwhites—is breaking into a polygon of dueling ethnicities, each fighting for its place in the sun.

For many citizens the "browning of America" means a disorienting plunge into an uncharted sea of identity. Zoeller is far from alone in being confused about the complex tangle of geno-

types and phenotypes and cultures that now undercut centuries-old verities about race and race relations in the U.S. Like many others, he hasn't got a clue about what to call the growing ranks of people like Woods who inconveniently refuse to be pigeonholed into one of the neat, oversimplified racial classifications used by government agencies—and, let's face it, most people. Are they people of color? Mixed race? Biracial? Whatever they like?

And if we don't know what to call them, how are we supposed to cope with them? Are they a new and distinct category of "real" Americans, due the same respectful recognition—and governmental protections—as more familiar groups? Or should they be lumped into the demeaning catchall category of "minorities" or "other"? How we eventually answer these questions will affect everything from the first Census forms of the 21st century, which will be issued a mere three years from now, to university admissions policies to the way civil rights laws are enforced. Even more important, it may ultimately transform the way Americans identify themselves and the tribe or tribes they belong to. In one grandiose vision, shared by conservative analyst Douglas Besharov of the American Enterprise

Institute and communitarian sociologist Amitai Etzioni of American University, the ambiguous racial identity of mixed-race children may be "the best hope for the future of American race relations," as Besharov puts it. Letting people define themselves as multiracial, Etzioni argues, "has the potential to soften the racial lines that now divide America by rendering them more like economic differences and less like harsh, almost immutable, caste lines." Those who blend many streams of ethnicity within their own bodies, the argument goes, will render race a meaningless concept, providing a biological solution to the problem of racial justice. This idea reflects a deeply pessimistic view of human nature. It suggests that people can get along with each other only if they are all the same, instead of learning to accept and respect differences.

In any event, the way Americans think and talk about race will have to catch up with the new reality. Just how anachronistic our racial vocabulary has become was made clear by Woods in an appearance last week on The Oprah Winfrey Show. When asked if it bothered him, the only child of a black American father and a Thai mother, to be called an African American, he replied, "It does. Growing up, I came up with this name: I'm 'Cablinasian,' " which he explained is a self-crafted acronym that reflects his one-eighth Caucasian, one-fourth black, one-eighth American Indian, one-fourth Thai and one-fourth Chinese roots with a precision that a racial-classifications expert under South African apartheid would admire. He said that when he was asked to check a box for racial background, he couldn't settle on just one. "I checked off 'African American'

and 'Asian.' Those are the two I was raised under, and the only two I know."

Kerboom! a min-racial fire storm erupted. Woods' remarks infuriated many African Americans who hailed his record-setting triumph at the Masters as a symbol of racial progress but see him as a traitor. To them Woods appeared to be running away from being African-American—a condition, they were quick to point out, that he himself had emphasized when he paid tribute to black golf pioneers Teddy Rhoades, Charlie Sifford and Lee Elder in his graceful victory speech. In a mirror image of Zoeller's constricted views, some blacks saw Woods' assertion of a multiracial identity as a sellout that could touch off an epidemic of "passing." Arthur Fletcher, a black member of the U.S. Commission on Civil Rights, testified at a 1993 congressional hearing devoted to whether a new, "multiracial" category should be added to U.S. Census forms that "I can see a whole host of light-skinned black Americans running for the door the minute they have another choice. All of a sudden they have a way of saying, 'In this discriminatory culture of ours, I am something other than black.' "

In their rush to judgment, the fearful apparently never stopped to consider that Woods was not turning his back on any part of his identity but instead was embracing every aspect of it. As he put it, "I'm just who I am, whoever you see in front of you"—and that includes his Asian side. "The influence of Tiger's mother Kultida in his life is very important," declares a family friend. "He goes to the temple with her occasionally. She's a devout Buddhist. He wears a family heirloom Buddha around his

neck. He's a hybrid of a lot of things, and that's how he sees himself. He honestly sees himself as a somewhat separate person from the norm—not in terms of talent but in terms of his makeup."

Woods grew up in a suburb of Los Angeles with mostly white friends. But over the years he has made four visits to Thailand, where locals like to say he's "Asian from the eyes up," and he has also embraced the role model of his father Earl, who was the first black to play baseball in the Big Eight (for Kansas State). Now Tiger seems to be saying that if acknowledging the totality of his genetic and cultural makeup is difficult for many Americans, they will just have to try harder.

If history is any guide, a lot of them won't try at all. "It's very hard for other folks to embrace our philosophy without thinking we are being racist or trying to create a new race," says Nancy G. Brown, who is a past president of the 10-year-old advocacy group Multiracial Americans in Southern California. "It's hard for people to believe we are just looking for equality and that we are able to live with the concept of duality. Constantly calling Tiger Woods black is a good example of what we are talking about."

Groups like Brown's have lobbied for a multiracial category on government forms, but they also point out that recognizing multiracialism is more than just a matter of "psychic comfort." There are important health issues, for example, such as bone-marrow matching and how such race-specific syndromes as Tay-Sachs manifest themselves and get treated in biracial individuals. And most multiracial Americans have had the experience of being arbitrarily assigned an ethnic identity by a school principal, a caseworker or an employer that may differ from other family members'—or from one form to the next.

The noxious practice of pigeonholing people in narrow racial classifications is a deeply ingrained American habit that predates independence. It began with a desire to enforce firm distinctions between free citizens and slaves. In 1661, for example, Virginia decreed that the legal status of the mother would determine whether a black child was a slave or free. Three years later, Maryland went a step further, declaring that if either of a child's parents was a slave, the child would also be. The purpose of this law, its authors said, was to deter "divers freeborn English women" from marrying black slaves. But it did nothing to deter white male slave owners from trying to expand their human holdings by impregnating black female slaves.

Eventually, these pioneering efforts at codifying racial distinctions hardened into so-called miscegenation laws, which aimed to preserve the "purity" of the white race by making interracial sex a crime. Though upholding such laws required ever more tortured legal definitions of who was black and who wasn't, 16 states continued to ban interracial marriages until 1967, when the U.S. Supreme Court struck down such laws. In what was perhaps the most ridiculous example of racial pigeonholing, Louisiana ordained that anyone with a "trace" of black ancestry would be classified as black. Then, in an ostensibly "humane" 1970 reform, it enacted the "one thirty-second rule," by which anyone with a single black great-great-great-great-grandparent and 31 white great-great-great-great-grandparents was legally black.

That regulation went unchallenged until Susie Guillory Phipps, the wife of a wealthy seafood importer who had always considered herself white, got a look at her birth certificate when applying for a passport and discovered that according to the state, she was black. In 1982 she sued the state, which hired a genealogist to delve into Phipps' ancestry. He dug up, among other ancestors, Phipps' great-great-great-great-grandmother—the black mistress of an Alabama plantation owner back in 1760—and concluded the Phipps was precisely three thirty-seconds black. The preposterous law stayed on the books until 1983.

For many decades, people on all sides of the color line chafed at these legal restraints on their ability to love and procreate. Even where black-white marriages were legal, these couples had to seek refuge in more tolerant black neighborhoods and raise their children as African Americans. But in the past 20 years, as the number of mixed-race marriages has increased dramatically, to more than 3 million by some estimates, attitudes among all racial groups have evolved. Tracey Mandell, 26, is an English instructor at Loyola Marymount University. Her partner Michael Bartley is a black man from Jamaica, and their son Noah is coming up on his first birthday. Mandell remembers last March, when she and members of her family were taking a get-acquainted tour of the maternity ward at Santa Monica Hospital. "There were about 50 couples on the tour," she says. "At least half of them were multiracial. My cousin, who lives in Minnesota, pointed it out to me. I hadn't even noticed. I think in L.A. there are so many multiracial people you don't even pay atten-

tion. But it's different when you leave Los Angeles."

It is precisely because they feel under attack and in need of solidarity that many American minorities fear the blurring of racial lines. Congressional black leaders argue that adding a multiracial category to Census forms, which the Office of Management and Budget will be considering through June of this year, would make it much harder to detect and combat racial discrimination. For example, according to a recent article in Emerge, the black newsmagazine, in 1991 some 35,000 people chose "other" on Home Mortgage Disclosure Act papers meant to track bias in lending. Allowing people to opt out of traditional race categories, says Congressional Black Caucus chairwoman Maxine Waters, a California Democrat, "just blurs everything. [People pushing for a multiracial category] want to be seen for all they are, but I don't think they're making the connection about how it could affect how they're represented, or who's being an advocate for them when they get mistreated." Among the many programs administered on the basis of racial tallies: minority employment on government contracts, court-ordered school desegregation plans and protection of minority voting rights. All would have to be retooled, at great cost, if the categories change.

In the end, however, the impact of multiracialism will be decided not by the content of a Census form but in the hearts of Americans. Tiger Woods can proclaim his personal diversity, but if more people, like Zoeller, just see a "boy," it won't make much difference. Multiracial Americans will not get the right to define themselves as they choose without a fight.

Melding Pot

Percentage of African Americans Marrying Whites

	Women	Men
1970	0.7	1.9
1993	3.9	8.9

"You Can't Be a Fairy"

When Sheba Howerton auditioned for a sixth-grade performance of Sleeping Beauty, two white girls in the play told her to forget it. "You're black," they said. "You can't be a fairy." But when she tried to mix with a group of African Americans in high school, she got another challenge. "Why is your skin so light?" one demanded. Says Howerton, 15, whose father is of African, Cherokee and Irish descent and whose mother comes from a family of German Jews: "I can't pass for white, and I can't pass for black. But I definitely feel there is a lot of pressure to align myself with one group or another."

Instead Howerton has tried to find a middle ground, choosing friends of all races and switching between ethnic cliques at De Anza High School in Richmond, California. "I flow back and forth," she says. To combat further their alienation, Sheba and her 12-year-old sister Shira have joined Generation Pride, a group of a dozen teenagers of interracial background in the San Francisco Bay Area. The group holds social gatherings and discussions about interracial issues, offering a rare space free from racial pigeonholing. The group is an offshoot of an adult group, Interracial/Intercultural Pride, whose members are of mixed races or in mixed couples. Doug Howerton, Sheba's father, is I-Pride's vice president. "Those that are biracial and multiracial have a unique look" at things, he says. "They see from both sides, and they try to be more just."

Who Would "See the Asian in Me"?

Fay Yarbrough, 21, can still feel the tug of ethnic loyalties from her Korean mother. "In high school," recalls the daughter of an African-American serviceman, "after I cut my hair, my mother looked at me with this really sad expression on her face. She said people would not be able to see the Asian in me, and that was hard for her. I didn't feel I was making some kind of statement, but my mother took it as a rejection of that cultural side of me."

When she was a freshman at Rice University in Texas, she recalls, she walked to a meeting of the Korean Student Association and stunned a fellow student by talking to her in Korean. The schoolmate had just said, " 'Oh, no, we couldn't possibly be going to the same place. I am eating with the Korean Student Association.' The other students looked at me the same way, even though I was one of a handful who could speak Korean and who ever had lived in Korea."

Yarbrough now leans toward her black heritage, finding African Americans more receptive. "Blacks come in all shapes and colors," she says. "Koreans are very homogenous. Someone like me is a much bigger issue for them." She is dating a black man. "Asian men don't date women who look like me."

A Mother's Cry: "My Son is Three Races"

Melissa Meyer and Thallieus Massey don't simply want to check off a box marked "multiracial" for their eight-year-old son Jordan. With light brown skin, golden, wavy hair and light brown eyes, Jordan Massey is clearly the product of several races. Yet when his mother enrolled him in second grade at Coconut Grove Elementary in Dade County, Florida, the school registrar gave her a form that asked her to pick just one of the following: black, white, Hispanic, American Indian/Alaskan Native, or Asian/Pacific Islander. Meyer, 31, who is white and whose husband's ancestors included both African and Native Americans, refused to select a box. "My son is three races," she said. "Can I choose all three?"

When the school said no, Meyer contacted the American Civil Liberties Union, and after a lot of wrangling, Dade County public schools agreed in 1995 to add a multiracial option on school-registration forms. But Meyer and Massey are not satisfied, because their son still cannot choose all three races. "We're not saying one race is better than the other," she says. "But he is our child, and we want him to understand exactly who he is." Sitting in his Boy Scout uniform, Jordan proclaims, "I'm African American, European, American Indian."

Article Review Form at end of book.

WiseGuide Wrap-Up

- In the past, multiracial children (and their parents) have been forced to select an individual cultural identity because of formal and informal pressures.

- Multiracial students face a host of peer pressures from their respective cultural groups for singular cultural identification.

- Educators can assist multiracial students and families by supporting the richness of their heritage through resources (books, art, music, drama), services (counseling, discussion groups, networking), and acceptance of their individual uniqueness.

- Multiracial individuals should be viewed as a rich combination of their full heritage in order to develop a healthy identity.

- Racial and ethnic questions on the U.S. Census should serve the development of public policy, not political agendas.

R.E.A.L. Sites

This list provides a print preview of typical **coursewise** R.E.A.L. sites. (There are over 100 such sites at the **courselinks**™ site.) The danger in printing URLs is that Web sites can change overnight. As we went to press, these sites were functional using the URLs provided. If you come across one that isn't, please let us know via email to: webmaster@coursewise.com. Use you Passport to access the most current list of R.E.A.L. sites at the **courselinks**™ site.

Site name: Interracial Voice

URL: http://www.webcom.com/~intvoice/

Why is it R.E.A.L.? An independent, information-oriented, networking news journal serving the mixed-race/interracial community in cyberspace. This electronic publication advocates universal recognition of mixed-race individuals as constituting a separate "racial" entity and supports the initiative to establish a multiracial category on the 2000 Census. Includes excellent links to articles, essays, and resources.

Key topics: race, multiracial, U. S. Census

Activity: Review collection of current news articles on multiracial issues from all over the country. What theme appears to be surfacing in the current news?

Site name: Association of MultiEthnic Americans

URL: http://www.ameasite.org/index.html

Why is it R.E.A.L.? This comprehensive website includes census information, legislation, course links, an extensive bibliography, including children's books, health and education resources, and race classification information.

Key topics: multiracial, U.S. Census, race, interracial marriage

Activity: Review the Loving Decision of 1967, in which the Supreme Court overturned all anti-interracial marriage laws in the United States.

Site name: The Multiracial Activist

URL: http://www.geocities.com/CapitolHill/Lobby/5006/

Why is it R.E.A.L.? This site is dedicated to the struggle for governmental and social recognition of multiracial individuals. An information center and news outlet for those interested in adding a multiracial category with or without racial subidentifiers to the census and other government forms that collect racial data. Includes editorials and essays related to multiracial issues.

Key Topics: multiracial, U. S. Census, interracial marriage, race

Activity: Review the essays and editorials arguing for a "multiracial" category on the U.S. Census. Of particular interest are those articles written by parents of multiracial children.

section 7

Future Perspectives: Society's Conscience

 **WiseGuide Intro**

"Be afraid to die until you've won some small victory for mankind." (Horace Mann)

Equity, understanding, unity, acceptance, and quality education are the challenges educators address as the new millennium becomes a reality. Assuring quality education for all students is a promise educators must keep. As schools face an increasingly diverse student population—with differences of gender, special needs, race/culture, linguistics, economics, and bi-raciality—educators face the special task of finding solutions in an atmosphere filled with competing public opinion and political posturing.

It will be the role of educators and schools to affirm and educate our diverse learners. This challenge can only be undertaken when policies and practices are grounded in research and the goal is building student capacity toward academic success. Assuring each student's academic future will contribute to the quality of the community, the country, and our world. Educators are enlisting the help of a variety of individuals and organizations toward that end.

This section examines the future of education for diverse learners and the impact that aggressive, proactive programs and measures can have when implemented in local schools. We begin with the importance of parents as children's first teachers in "Challenges to Family Involvement." Parents' contributions and impact on the lives of their children are further examined in developing learning environments free of bias and prejudice in "Involving Parents in Creating Anti-Bias Classrooms." The sometimes whispered debate concerning nature vs. nurture is considered in "Ability and Biology: Within Every Race, There Are Genetic Differences Among Individuals and Families." And just when we begin to believe that we now have a thorough understanding of the complexities of our diverse population, we must address those who cross borders in "Scholars Explore Blurred Lines of Race, Gender, and Ethnicity." In taking responsibility and advocating for the educational needs of our diverse learners, we find that no single solution exists. Instead we must embrace the concept that educating diverse populations means embracing diverse solutions as presented in "Diverse Learners and the Tyranny of Time: Don't Fix Blame, Fix the Leaky Roof." Finally, we look at our diverse learners as part of the larger world population, with all the accompanying needs, issues, and complexities. And to better serve our students as they truly become "world citizens," as no previous generation has been required to do, we look toward "Global Education's Promise: Reinvigorating Classroom Life in a Changing, Interconnected World".

? Questions ?

Reading 32. What are two basic challenges that family involvement efforts face? What are the factors that create discontinuity between schools and families?

Reading 33. What is an anti-bias curriculum? How can teachers involve parents in creating anti-bias classrooms?

Reading 34. What did Edward Banfield's study of urban life reveal? Describe the relationship between mathematical and musical ability. Why have these abilities translated into different performance by black Americans?

Reading 35. What do some scholars believe are the benefits of crossing the boundaries of gender, race, or ethnicity? Give examples of individuals who have challenged boundaries by "crossing over," and describe the advantages or disadvantages they experienced.

Reading 36. Describe the six pedagogical principles for developing literacy programs for diverse learners. Describe why multiple perspectives are important in addressing the needs of diverse learners.

Reading 37. What is the rationale for supporting global education? What are "essential questions" and why are they important in global education?

What are two basic challenges that family involvement efforts face? What are the factors that create discontinuity between schools and families?

Challenges to Family Involvement

Mick Coleman and Susan Churchill

Mick Coleman is Associate Professor and Susan Churchill is a doctoral student in the Department of Child and Family Development, University of Georgia, Athens.

The percentage of 3- and 4-year-olds enrolled in early childhood education programs has risen more than threefold since the mid-1960s (U.S. General Accounting Office, 1990). Public schools increasingly provide child care, preschool education and before- and after-school care for young children. Such school-based early childhood programs reflect a growing interest in early educational enrichment experiences for children in general, as well as an expansion of compensatory education programs for children who are judged to be at risk for school failure because of poverty, lack of proper health care, inadequate home-learning environments and a lack of adult protection (Swick & Graves, 1993, pp. 26, 93).

Recognizing the mutuality of families' and schools' concerns about children's growth and development, educators are seeking new ways to involve families in their children's education (Boyer, 1991; Silvern, 1988; U.S. Department of Education, 1991). While family involvement is a concept that has wide appeal, only limited institutional support exists (Epstein & Dauber, 1991; Greenberg, 1989; Swick & McKnight, 1989).

Challenges to Family Involvement

No conclusive evidence exists that family involvement programs are uniformly effective (White, Taylor & Moss, 1992), despite the many positive ways families can affect their children's academic efforts (see, for review, Henderson, 1988; Hess & Holloway, 1984; Peters, 1988; Rutter, 1985; White et al., 1992), and the many positive ways quality early childhood programs can affect families (see Pence, 1988; Powell, 1989; Schorr & Schorr, 1988). Family involvement efforts face two challenges aside from the difficulties associated with the diverse methodologies used in family involvement studies (White et al., 1992).

* Ambiguous definitions of family involvement. It is hard to find consensus on the meaning of family involvement (Haseloff, 1990; White et al., 1992). Family involvement may include the following elements, among others: providing parents with facts about their child's development, teaching parents to become effective change agents for their child, providing parents with emotional support, training parents to guide and teach their child, exchanging information about a child between parents and teachers, hosting joint parent/teacher activities like childhood assessments or program planning, and helping parents get access to community services (McConachie, 1986; Peterson & Cooper, 1989).

Ambiguous definitions of family involvement can result in programs that are merely a series of disconnected activities with little relevance to family or classroom environments. To be effective, family involvement planners must address the ambiguous boundaries that exist between home and school (Johnston, 1990), and the resulting sense of intrusion and power imbalance that can occur when parents and teachers attempt to coordinate their interactions with children (Haseloff, 1990).

(*) Themes for guiding family involvement philosophies

In practice, family involvement planning must include the formulation of a family involvement philosophy and supportive goals. In the course of conducting in service workshops on family involvement, the authors have discovered that sufficient attention is not always paid to this conceptual process. Subsequent discussions about the meaning and purpose of family involvement, however, often uncover a common set of philosophical themes (see Table 1). Teachers can use the themes in Table 1 as an aid to beginning the reflective process. Teachers should delete from, or add to, the list so that it meets their schools' particular concerns and interests.

The list of themes is used as a planning device so that teachers can prioritize their family involvement goals while thinking about past family involvement experiences. In most cases, teachers can select one theme that best reflects their family involvement goal for the upcoming year. They can then develop specific family involvement objectives that reflect their school's diverse family-school environments.

*Diversity of family-school environments. The call for greater collaboration between families and schools is admirable in that it recognizes the different contexts in which children learn. Nevertheless, the discontinuities between a young child's home and school lives can pose numerous challenges (Hess & Holloway, 1984; Peters,1988; Silvern, 1988). A school's customs, schedules, spaces, resources, expectations, experiences, languages and values, for example, may not be reflected in the same way or to the same degree at home. This may be especially true for children from racial and cultural minority families, as well as those from lower socioeconomic families.

In particular, school environments may fit better with the family environments of children from middle-class families because public schools are often staffed with middle-class administrators and teachers. Middle-class families subsequently may be more responsive to school policies and family involvement programs than lower socioeconomic families.

Parent education and family socioeconomic status are two factors that may create discontinuity between schools and families. Although it is true that parents with higher levels of education and from higher socioeconomic backgrounds show greater family involvement, this trend does not necessarily indicate differential interest in family involvement (Epstein & Dauber, 1991; Stevenson & Baker, 1987). In fact, parents from low-income families are as supportive of the family involvement concept as parents with higher incomes (Chavkin & Williams, 1989).

One way parents from lower and higher income families may differ is where they are willing or able to be involved in their children's education. Researchers have found a positive relationship between socioeconomic status and school-based family involvement activities such as parent conferences and volunteering, as well as teacher perceptions of parent support; socioeconomic status, however, has not been associated with home-based activities like tutoring (Hoover-Dempsey, Bassler & Brissie, 1987). This finding may reflect the difficulty or hesitancy parents from lower socioeconomic backgrounds may experience when directly interacting with schools. Some parents may have conflicting work and family demands. Others may limit their involvement with schools because of their own negative school experiences and feelings of academic inadequacy.

Table 1 Themes for Guiding Family Involvement Philosophies

Theme	Goal
Empowerment	To provide families with the information and support they need to actively participate in school-related discussions regarding their children's education
Parenting	To support parents in nurturing and guiding their children
Family Strengths	To assist families in identifying and developing strengths and coping mechanisms as a means of managing family life stressors
Child-Siblings	To prepare school-age children and their younger siblings for schooling
Community Resources	To provide parents with the information, support and skills necessary to identify and manage community services
Educational Modeling	To involve parents in identifying education objectives and providing supportive in-home learning opportunities for their children
Family-Teacher Relations	To improve the quality of interpersonal relations between teachers and children's families

* The purpose of the themes is to help structure ideas about family involvement and their implications for planning practical family involvement strategies. Some overlap is expected.

Parents with higher levels of education tend to be more involved in school activities, and their children are more likely to be doing well in school (Stevenson & Baker, 1987). These findings may reflect parental attitudes, work schedules and lifestyle priorities that are congruent with those found in schools. Parents with more education may have more positive attitudes toward school, resulting in more frequent and positive interactions with teachers and more reinforcement of classroom activities in the home. Parents with higher levels of education also may have more flexible work schedules, allowing them to assist with homework projects and attend school functions. Also, these families' adult-child interactions and childhood behavioral expectations may resemble more closely those found in the school.

To develop strategies that link the early learning experiences in home and school settings, planners must address the discontinuities between those environments.

The authors have summarized in Table 2 some of the themes that they have found useful in helping family-school coordinators and teachers link family and school environments.

Teachers can use Table 2's themes to further expand their family involvement philosophies. Using the guides, for example, can facilitate the planning and implementation of enrollment interviews, home visits, parent-teacher meetings and classroom activities. Some teachers use the themes to formulate questions and possible explanations about family-school disagreements (e.g., home-school differences in behavior management and self-help expectations). Or, the themes can be used to structure classroom activities that build upon children's home experiences (e.g., childhood interests, home routines, family relationships). The themes in Table 2, like those in Table 1, are only a beginning point. Teachers can add themes that reflect their school's individual concerns.

Working with Family Professionals

Stamp and Groves (1994) suggested that family involvement be viewed as a "third institution" whose primary purpose is to strengthen family-school linkages. As we already have noted, the diversity of family structures and lifestyles can present barriers to creating such a "third institution."

On the other hand, a conclusion that families and schools cannot be linked would be based on too narrow an interpretation of family and school goals regarding early childhood education. The traditionally stated goals of child care (protection, nurturing and socialization) and school (education and socialization) always have been interdependent (Caldwell, 1990). Today, more than ever, academic education (learning to read and write) and life-skills education (learning self-help and social responsibilities) are mutually supportive endeavors that occur across family and school settings. Likewise, parents and teachers, although sometimes depicted as adversarial, have similar educational goals (Epstein, 1991) and philosophies (Stipek, Milburn, Clements & Daniels, 1992).

Thus, creating a "third institution" of family involvement is not impossible, although greater attention must be given to devising practical strategies for linking families and schools (Sexton, Aldridge & Snyder, 1994). The authors will now examine some ways in which three types of family professionals can work with schools to develop practical strategies for strengthening family involvement.

* Teacher training: Family life educators. Teachers whose training in family relations is limited

Table 2 Themes for Guiding Family-School Interactions

Theme	Example
Home Routines	Child's typical daily schedule and activities
Child's Interests	Child's favorite toys, television programs, foods, games, books, etc.
Behavior Management	Types of encouragement, reinforcements, limits and consequences used by parents to guide child's behavior
Communication	Verbal and nonverbal strategies used by parents to instruct, deliver explanations and make requests of child
Child's Fears	Objects, events and situations feared by a child
Community Involvement	Community events, activities and institutions that families attend (e.g., church, library, recreational, cultural)
Relationships	Child's most important interpersonal relationships within and outside the home setting
Self-Help Expectations	Self-help skills relating to personal hygiene and home chores that parents expect child to perform
Instructional Strategies	Strategies used by parents to teach a child (e.g., instruction, demonstrations, play)

have only their own family experiences to guide them when developing a family involvement program. Family life educators can help address teachers' questions about potential barriers to family involvement. During inservice training, teachers should brainstorm questions. Some common questions regarding family involvement follow:

- What are the challenges that confront families from different socioeconomic backgrounds, and how do they influence families?

- What concerns do families from different ethnic, religious, racial and sexual orientation backgrounds have regarding how their families are depicted in school?

- What are the potential stressors associated with divorce, death and remarriage in relation to child-teacher and parent-teacher relations?

- What strategies can be used to acknowledge the roles of foster parents, grandparents and other extended family guardians?

Barriers to family involvement go beyond school-based issues. Family life educators can help coordinate and facilitate the following professional learning experiences:

- Selected teachers might receive release time for social service internships in order to better understand the diversity of family life within a community context.

- Teachers might be asked to develop a family involvement program that is tied to a youth program, or that is based at a work site, community center or church.

- Inservice training can be provided to highlight the different roles that parents can play in supporting their children's development and education within and outside school and home settings.

One of the most popular topics in education today is diversity (Jacob & Jordan, 1993; McCracken, 1993; Neugebauer, 1992). Teachers need opportunities to explore their own respective cultures, as well as those of others, in relation to curriculum issues. They should be careful, however, not to overgeneralize or stereotype, since all families are unique regarding their rates of cultural assimilation or their racial, ethnic, religious, socioeconomic and sexual orientation backgrounds. Family life educators can facilitate the following:

- Keep personal journals related to positive and negative family-school interactions to encourage reflective thought on teaching practices involving children from different family backgrounds.

- Discuss the meaning of "family diversity" and its implications for classroom practices to facilitate group creativity and problem-solving. The authors have found it useful to ask teachers to reflect upon their own meaning of "family" as a beginning reference point.

- Ask teachers to develop parent workshops on topics of their choosing that take into account the different family backgrounds represented in their respective classrooms.

- Community education: Family life advocates. Early childhood advocates warn that educators must not promise more than early childhood programs can deliver, since legislators tend to view early childhood programs as a means by which to achieve sweeping education and social reforms (Morado, 1986). Family life advocates can work with teachers to ensure that family involvement expectations are kept realistic.

- Form task forces to identify barriers and recommend strategies for strengthening family-school-community linkages. School-community linkages may be needed, for example, to ensure the efficient delivery of social services to families who are recent immigrants and/or who have limited means of transportation or income.

- Encourage school administrators to make family life education an integral part of the curriculum. The concept of "families" rather than "family" should be stressed in order to reflect the diversity of family structures and lifestyles in contemporary society.

- Provide training to expand parents' child advocacy efforts. Such training might include establishing parent advisory boards, arranging co-teaching experiences and informing parents of child advocacy efforts in the community.

- Family involvement research: Family researchers. Although the effectiveness of family involvement programs has not been adequately documented, parents and teachers continue to search for meaningful ways to support each other. Teachers can work with family and education researchers to clarify the importance of family involvement through examination of the following questions:

- Are parents better able to understand and implement information regarding child guidance and education when it is presented in parent-led support groups as opposed to teacher-led educational groups? A study about strategies for coordinating family-school expectations and practices regarding children's guidance and education would be useful.

- Do children from certain family backgrounds (e.g., well-established versus recently immigrated; different socioeconomic levels) perform better in the classroom when classroom activities include materials found in their homes, rather than standard classroom materials? Teachers could benefit from learning how to use home materials to support and expand the classroom curriculum.

- Are community-based programs that link families with human services agencies more effective than similar school-based programs? This question could be answered by comparing the joint efforts of teachers and family service workers with those of schools and human service agencies.

- In what ways does family involvement serve as a mediating variable in children's short- and long-term academic and social adjustment? Educators could benefit from studies about family involvement programs' timing, structure and content.

- What are the secondary effects of family involvement programs? Research is needed, for example, on how family involvement programs may benefit younger siblings still at home and the ability of parents to advocate for their children across community settings.

Conclusion

Understanding family lives is central to building a meaningful family involvement program. Family professionals can work with school administrators and teachers to meet the challenges associated with family involvement by helping to develop a family involvement plan that is both practical and relevant to community needs.

References

Boyer, E. L. (1991). *Ready to learn: A mandate for the nation.* Lawrenceville, NJ: Princeton University Press.

Caldwell, B. M. (1990). Educare: A new professional identity. *Dimensions, 18,* 3–6.

Chavkin, N. F., & Williams, D. L. (1989). Low-income parents' attitudes toward parent involvement in education. *Journal of Sociology and Social Welfare, 16,* 17–28.

Epstein, J. L. (1991). Paths to partnership: What we can learn from federal, state, district, and school initiatives. *Phi Delta Kappan, 72,* 344–349.

Epstein, J. L., & Dauber, S. L. (1991). School programs and teacher practices of parent involvement in inner-city elementary and middle schools. *The Elementary School Journal, 91,* 289–305.

Greenberg, P. (1989). Parents as partners in young children's development and education: A new American fad? Why does it matter? *Young Children, 44,* 61–75.

Haseloff, W. (1990). The efficacy of the parent-teacher partnership of the 1990s. *Early Child Development and Care, 58,* 51–55.

Henderson, A. T. (1988). Parents are a school's best friends. *Phi Delta Kappan, 70,* 148–153.

Hess, R. D., & Holloway, S. D. (1984). Family and school as educational institutions. In R. D. Parke, R. N. Emde, H. P. McAdoo, & G. P. Sackett (Eds.), *Review of child development research: The family* (Vol. 7) (pp. 179–222). Chicago: University of Chicago Press.

Hoover-Dempsey, K. V., Bassler, O. C., & Brissie, J. S. (1987). Parent involvement: Contributions of teacher efficacy, school socioeconomic status, and other school characteristics. *American Educational Research Journal, 24,* 417–435.

Jacob, E., & Jordon, C. (1993). *Minority education: Anthropological perspectives.* Norwood, NJ: Ablex.

Johnston, J. H. (1990). *The new American family and the school.* Columbus, OH: National Middle School Association.

McConachie, H. (1986). *Parents and young mentally handicapped children: A review of research issues.* Cambridge, MA: Brookline.

McCracken, J. B. (1993). *Valuing diversity: The primary years.* Washington, DC: National Association for the Education of Young.

Morado, C. (1986). Prekindergarten programs for 4-year-olds: Some key issues. *Young Children, 41,* 61–63.

Neugebauer, B. (1992). *Alike and different: Exploring our humanity with young children.* Washington, DC: National Association for the Education of Young Children.

Pence, A. (1988). *Ecological research with children and families.* New York: Teachers College Press.

Peters, D. L. (1988). Head Start's influence on parental and child competence. In S. K. Steinmetz (Ed.), *Family and support systems across the life span* (pp. 73–97). New York: Plenum.

Peterson, N. L., & Cooper, C. S. (1989). Parent education and involvement in early intervention programs for handicapped children. In M. J. Fine (Ed.), *The second handbook on parent education: Contemporary perspectives* (pp. 197–233). New York: Academic.

Powell, D. (1989). *Families and early childhood programs.* Washington, DC: National Association for the Education of Young.

Rutter, M. (1985). Family and school influences on cognitive development. *Journal of Child Psychology and Psychiatry, 26.*

Schorr, D., & Schorr, L. (1988). *Within our reach: Breaking the cycle of disadvantage.* New York: Doubleday.

Sexton, D., Aldridge, J., & Snyder, P. (1994). Family-driven early intervention. *Dimensions, 22,* 14–18.

Silvern, S. (1988). Continuity/discontinuity between home and early childhood education environments. *The Elementary School Journal, 89,* 147–159.

Stamp, L. N., & Groves, M. M. (1994). Strengthening the ethic of care: Planning and supporting family involvement. *Dimensions of Early Childhood, 22,* 5–9.

Stevenson, D. L. & Baker, D. P. (1987). The family-school relation and the child's school performance. *Child Development, 58.*

Stipek, D., Milburn, S., Clements, D., & Daniels, D. H. (1992). Parents' beliefs about appropriate education for young children. *Journal of Applied Developmental Psychology, 13,* 293–310.

Swick, K., & Graves, S. B. (1993). *Empowering at-risk families during the early childhood years.* Washington, DC: National Education Association.

Swick, K., & McKnight, S. (1989). Characteristics of kindergarten teachers who promote parent involvement. *Early Childhood Research Quarterly, 4,* 19–29.

U.S. Department of Education. (1991). *Preparing young children for success: Guideposts for achieving our first national educational goal.* Washington, DC: Author.

U.S. General Accounting Office. (1990). *Early childhood education: What are the costs of high-quality programs?* (GAO/HRD-90-43BR). Washington, DC: Author.

White, K. R., Taylor, M. J., & Moss, V. D. (1992). Does research support claims about the benefits of involving parents in early intervention programs? *Review of Educational Research, 62,* 91–125.

 Article Review Form at end of book.

What is anti-bias curriculum? How can teachers involve parents in creating anti-bias classrooms?

Involving Parents in Creating Anti-Bias Classrooms

Jim Barta and Teresa Winn

Jim Barta, Ph.D., is a professor in the Department of Early Childhood and Reading at Georgia Southern University in Statesboro, Georgia. He has traveled extensively teaching children in Alaska, Colorado, Georgia, and Oregon, as well as in Norway and England in grades K–12. His areas of specialization include multicultural/anti-bias education, preservice teacher training, and curriculum design. He sits on Georgia Southern University's Diversity Council and is dedicated to improving educational opportunities for all students.

Teresa Winn is a graduate student in the Guidance and Counseling Program at Georgia Southern University, where she earned her Bachelor's Degree in Early Childhood Education.

Children begin to develop biases and prejudices long before they reach our classrooms. Research (Alejandro-Wright, 1885, Baratz A Baratz, 1970, Katz, 1982) shows that children as young as two years of age begin to develop discriminatory perceptions of bias and prejudice which, if unchallenged, may later develop into overtly racist or other discriminatory behaviors. In a society where racism, bias, prejudice, and discrimination continue to exist, it should be no surprise that children reach our classrooms carrying these harmful attitudes and behaviors. Who is to blame: society at large, schools, teachers, parents? We are all responsible for the problem as well as its solution.

Solutions are being proposed and implemented. In classrooms around the country, students are learning more about themselves and the multiple races, ethnic groups, and cultures making up America through multicultural education. Anti-bias curriculum (Derman-Sparks, 1989) is extending this learning by focusing more specifically on the reactions people have to racial and cultural variations. Phillips (1989) insists that the problem is not the differences between people, rather, it is how people value and respond to these differences. Cultural bias leads to prejudicial attitudes which result in discriminatory behavior. Anti-bias curriculum in classrooms educates children to diffuse the bias which precedes prejudice and discrimination.

Teachers cannot do it alone. If our efforts in schools to develop children tolerant of racial, ethnic, and cultural differences are to be effective and lasting, then it is imperative that teachers more closely examine the role parents can and do play in determining the attitudes and behaviors of their children. In order to create an anti-bias classroom environment support of the parents is needed. Berger contends that our students are not "individuals isolated and unaffected by their environments, but rather they are the product of their own biology, deeply influenced by their parents and extended family (1991, pg. 101).

Parents, after all, are our students' first teachers. Some parents are aware of the necessity of cultural validation and raise their children congruent with this belief. In other homes, however, opposing perspectives expressed by parents model long held bias and prejudices, which are passed on to a new generation. Since family (Locke, 1992) is the building block of culture, children are instilled with their parents' attitudes, either positively or negatively. Howard (1993) searched the role that parental attitudes play, particularly those of the European-American, -in affecting the relationships of their children with others. He found that there exists a significant influence of parental attitudes on those of their children. When parents perceive their race and cultural identity superior to that of others, children tend to feel superior too. Parents who are culturally isolated, with little or no professional or social interaction with those of different cultures, tend to further embed their

From Jim Barta and Teresa Winn, "Involving Parents in Creating Anti-Bias Classrooms" in *Chidren Today,* 24 (1). Summer-Fall 1996. U. S. Department of Health & Human Services.

negative stereotypes. When parents involve themselves and their children with people of other races, ethnicities, or cultural traditions, positive attitudes develop as misperceptions are replaced with human understanding and acceptance.

Many positive outcomes result when parents become involved with their child, education at all levels. So, how can teachers involve their parents in creating anti-bias classrooms? Here are a few suggestions.

A "curriculum partnership" is recommended by Keenan, Willett, and Solsken (1993). Parents are invited to participate in the development of the classroom curriculum. Meetings are held to explain to parents what anti-bias curriculum is, the need for it, and the benefits their children will reap. Together, teachers and parents chart the direction of their efforts congruent with the cultural influences of the particular school. These meetings, if held regularly, provide the foundation for further trust and stimulate open communication between teachers and parents. Parents who feel their insights and opinions matter are more likely to be supportive and take a greater interest in their child's education. Parents recently immigrating to the United States may be surprised to be asked for their participation. Explaining to them the instructional techniques used in the classroom and the rationale for them can provide proactive collaboration. As all additional benefit, teachers gain greater insight and understanding as they allow the parents to explain their cultural characteristics and beliefs.

Knowledgeable and informed parents can do a great deal in helping children develop non-biased attitudes. Abt-Perkins and Gomez (1993) discuss the critical need for self-awareness. They state that only after one's personal cultural identity is examined can one then look at the cultural identity of others meaningfully.

Basic awareness of what one is modeling for children can, at least, prompt parents to reflect on their attitudinal and behavioral orientation toward people from different cultures (Swick, 1986, pg. 75). Parents need to be made aware of the cultural influences they have on their children. Educating parents about the role they can play in helping their children develop positive perceptions of culturally diverse people can have lasting results.

A parental committee can be established to design a monthly educational newsletter reflecting culturally relevant content and comment. Parents can be encouraged to submit essays, poems, comments, or drawings which address growing awareness concerning cultural diversity and human responses to it. For example, mannerisms and gestures which are culturally appropriate in one culture may be insulting to another. In Southeast Asian culture for instance, children are taught it is disrespectful to stare into the eyes of an adult and a teacher's pat on the head is perceived as offensive rather than kindly. Teachers and parents can use this newsletter to include timely articles to further inform and educate parents. A student authored section can be an ideal addition to this collaborative effort.

Schedules of multicultural events which include notices of upcoming cultural experiences in the school or in the community can be published and distributed to parents. Television, press, and radio do not always present cultural diversity effectively. Those who learn of others only through the media do so vicariously. Often stereotypic images and bias result from minimal interaction with those perceived as different. Direct experience presents a much clearer and more accurate portrayal of other cultures and encourages parents to interact as they construct their own ideas and opinions.

Teachers and their classrooms can sponsor special cultural programs highlighting the diversity present in their classroom, school, or community. Programs that promote a sense of pride in the diversity of children and involve parents in sharing their culture affect attitudes positively. Rather than sponsoring ethnic or cultural awareness days or weeks, which tend to pay tribute one or two times during the year, teachers can produce "Grandmother's Day," for instance, where grandmothers from various cultures come to share their culturally significant traditions, stories and practices. Students learn that we all have grandmothers. Some may speak a different language or dialect, prepare different foods, etc., but they all care for us and share their love. Students learn the important lesson that it is only in the ways in which we express our similarities that we are different. Keenan (1993) highlights the merits of actively involving heritage with students. Parental participation in the education of their child must be seen as vital. Students not only gain an increased understanding of culture, but also learn to develop an attitude which respects and celebrates cultural differences.

There is no one script all teachers can use to develop anti-bias classrooms. The preceding suggestions are presented as possible techniques for getting parents involved in this vital effort.

Successful parental involvement in creating anti-bias classrooms results from culturally literate teachers who are able to convey their knowledge of diverse cultures to parents who may be willing to learn. It requires teachers who are dedicated to empowering all children and who comprehend the significance of parental involvement. Teachers must help parents realize the important role they play in determining their children's attitudes and behaviors. Parents must be made aware that without their participation, the teacher cannot be as effective. Teachers who invest the time and energy necessary to involve parents in helping them create anti-bias classrooms will realize the long-term benefits for themselves and their students.

References

Abt-Perkins, D. & Gomez, M. (1993, March). A good place to begin—examining our personal perspectives. *Language Arts,* 193–202.

Alejandro-Wright, M. (1985). "The child's conception of racial classification." In M. B. Spencer, G. K. Brookins & W. R. Allens (Eds.). *Beginnings: The social and affective development of black children* (pp. 185–200). Hillsdale, NJ: Erlbaum.

Baratz, S. & Baratz, J. (1970). Early childhood intervention: The social science base of institutional racism. *Harvard Educational Review 40*(1). 29–50.

Berger, E. (1991). *Parents as Partners in education.* New York, NY: MacMillan Publishing Company.

Derman-Sparks, L. (1989). *Anti-bias Curriculum: Tools for Educating Young Children.* Washington, DC.: National Association for the Education of Young Children.

Diaz, C. F. (1992). "Resistance to multicultural education and education." In C. F. Diaz (Ed.), *Multicultural education for the 21st century* (pp. 193–203). Washington, DC.: National Education Association of the United States.

Gloves, D. (1987). *A Multicultural early childhood Resource Guide* (Report No. UD 025 425). Albany, NY: New York State Education Department, Albany Division of civil rights and intercultural Relations. (ERIC Document Reproduction Service No. ED 280 924).

Howard, G. R. (1993, September). Whites in Multicultural education. *Phi Delta Kappan,* 36–41.

Katz, P. (1982). "Development of children's racial awareness and intergroup attitudes." In L. G. Katz (ed.). *Current Topics in Early Childhood Education, 4,* 17–54. Norwood, NJ: Ablex.

Keenan, J. W., Willett, J., & Solsken, J. (1993, March). Focus on research: Constructing an urban village: School/home collaboration in a multicultural classroom. *Language Arts* 204–214.

Locke, D. C. (1992). "A model of multicultural understanding." In *Increasing multicultural understanding* (pp. 1–14). Newbury Park, CA: SAGE publications.

McCracken, J. B. (1992). "Tossed salad is terrific: Values of multicultural programs for children and families." In B. Neugebaur (Ed.) *Alike and different* (2nd ed., pp. 92–97). Washington, D.C.: National Association for the Education of Young Children.

Olmstead, P. P. (1991). Parent involvement in elementary education: Findings and suggestions for the follow through programs. *The Elementary School Journal, 91,* 221–231.

Phillips, B. C. (1988, January). Nurturing diversity for today's children and tomorrow's leaders. *Young Children.*

Swick, K. (1986). Parents as models in children's cultural development. Clearing House, 60, (2), 72–75.

 Article Review Form at end of book.

What did Edward Banfield's study of urban life reveal? Describe the relationship between mathematical and musical ability. Why have these abilities translated into different performance by black Americans?

Ability and Biology

Within every race, there are genetic differences among individuals and families

Thomas Sowell

Sowell is a senior fellow at The Hoover Institution.

Mathematical ability and musical ability may not seem on the surface to be connected, but people who have researched the subject—and studied the brain—say that they are. Research for my book "Late-Talking Children" drove home the point to me. Three quarters of the bright but speech-delayed children in the group I studied had a close relative who was an engineer, mathematician or scientist—and four fifths had a close relative who played a musical instrument. The children themselves usually took readily to math and other analytical subjects—and to music.

Black, white and Asian children in this group show the same patterns. However, looking at the larger world around us, it is clear that blacks have been greatly overrepresented in the development of American popular music and greatly underrepresented in

such fields as mathematics, science and engineering.

If the abilities required in analytical fields and in music are so closely related, how can there be this great disparity? One reason is that the development of mathematical and other such abilities requires years of formal schooling, while certain musical talents can be developed with little or no formal training, as has happened with a number of well-known black musicians.

It is precisely in those kinds of music where one can acquire great skill without formal training that blacks have excelled—popular music rather than classical music, piano rather than violin, blues rather than opera. This is readily understandable, given that most blacks, for most of American history, have not had either the money or the leisure for long years of formal study in music.

Blacks have not merely held their own in American popular music. They have played a dispro-

portionately large role in the development of jazz, both traditional and modern. A strong string of names comes to mind—Duke Ellington, Scott Joplin, W. C. Handy, Louis Armstrong, Charlie Parker . . . and on and on.

None of this presupposes any special innate ability of blacks in music. On the contrary, it is perfectly consistent with blacks' having no more such inborn ability than anyone else, but being limited to being able to express such ability in narrower channels than others who have had the money, the time and the formal education to spread out over a wider range of music, as well as into mathematics, science and engineering.

There is no way of knowing whether Duke Ellington would have become a mathematician or scientist under other circumstances. What is clearer is that most blacks have not had such alternatives available until very recently, as history is measured. Moreover, now that cultural traditions have been established, even those blacks who have such alternatives available today, and who have the inborn abilities to pursue them, may nevertheless continue for some time to follow well-worn paths.

In these supersensitive times, merely suggesting that there is such a thing as inborn ability is taboo. Yet the evidence is overwhelming that mental abilities run in families, even when the families are broken up when the children are young and siblings are raised separately and in complete isolation from one another.

When it comes to the role of heredity and environment, a key sentence written all in italics has nevertheless been one of the most ignored sentences in one of the most widely discussed books of our time: *That a trait is genetically transmitted in individuals does not mean that group differences in that trait are also genetic in origin.* This sentence is from "The Bell Curve," a book routinely accused of being racist, especially by those who have not read it.

What this italicized sentence is saying, in effect, is that environmental differences between two groups may be much greater than environmental differences between two individuals chosen at random from the general population. Since tests measure devel-

oped capabilities, rather than inborn potential, you would expect groups from very different environments to differ in particular capabilities, even if most differences among individuals are due to heredity.

That makes sense when you stop and think about it. What is remarkable is how few people have stopped to think about it before going ballistic. Mention genetics and it will be taken as a code word for race. But, within every race, there are genetic differences among individuals and families.

There are important biological differences that are not genetic. Recent research has indicated that the brain's physical development is promoted by an environment in which there is much interaction with a baby during the brain's early formative years.

If even half of what has been said about the old-fashioned "Jewish mother" is true, then her busy, talkative attentiveness to her children may have given major lifelong advantages to the very children who later complained about how smothered they felt.

Contrast that with other cultural groups and social classes who pay little attention to small children, replying to their questions with impatient short an-

swers or even telling them to shut up. More than a quarter of a century ago, Edward Banfield's classic study of urban life, "The Unheavenly City," said that this unresponsive reaction to children's questions and comments was characteristic of a lower-class lifestyle and pointed out how stunted the development of such children might be. Now brain research backs him up.

Those who argue that there is no innate difference in the mental abilities of different racial and ethnic groups often conclude that different social results must therefore reflect discrimination by "society." But equal innate potential at the moment of conception does not necessarily mean equal mental capacity even at the moment of birth, given the many prenatal influences at work, such as the mother's use of alcohol or drugs.

Add differences in child-rearing practices and the culture of the home and the street, and there can be very large differences among children from different backgrounds before they ever reach the first employer or otherwise encounter the larger society.

 Article Review Form at end of book.

What do some scholars believe are the benefits of crossing the boundaries of gender, race, or ethnicity? Give examples of individuals who have challenged boundaries by "crossing over" and describe the advantages or disadvantages they experienced.

Scholars Explore Blurred Lines of Race, Gender, and Ethnicity

Recent research examines how people move from one category to another or blend them

Karen J. Winkler

In the early 20th century, a Jewish boy named Asa Yoelson donned blackface and built a successful music and acting career as Al Jolson. In 1993, the actor Ted Danson sparked a storm of protest when he wore blackface to a Friars Club roast. Is that progress?

In Charles W. Chesnutt's 1899 novel *The Conjure Woman*, a slaveholder dreamed of becoming black. Did that vision help the white character—and readers—better understand the plight of slaves?

The jazz musician Billy Tipton married at least five times and was the father of three adopted children; only at his death did family and fans learn that he was a she. The masquerade opened professional doors for Tipton, but was it demeaning?

Elizabeth Stern, the illegitimate daughter of a Welsh Baptist and a German Lutheran, used the persona of the daughter of an Eastern European rabbi when she wrote *I Am a Woman—and a Jew,* a best-selling novel of immigrant life. The 1926 book is still taught in college classes on women and Judaism. Has it fostered stereotypes of Jews?

A burgeoning scholarly literature is raising those questions today. Scholars who study culture are fascinated with crossing the boundaries of race, gender, or ethnicity. They are talking about transvestism, about impersonation, about "passing," about racial mixtures—all complications to the notion of stable identity. For many scholars, discussions of crossing hold out a hope of moving beyond some of today's most contentious issues about race and gender.

Check out recent scholarly titles: From Marjorie Garber's 1992 *Vested Interests: Cross-Dressing & Cultural Anxiety* to Susan Gubar's just-published *Racechanges: White Skin, Black Face in American Culture,* crossing boundaries is big. Look at papers given at the most recent meeting of the American Studies Association: "The Whiteness of the Jew in Blackface," "Crooners and Gangsters: Love and Violence in Black/Italian Crossover," "Masculinities in Motion: Transvestism and Migration."

Last fall, graduate students at Columbia University sponsored a much-discussed conference called "Pass*ing"—more evidence, scholars say, of the many dissertations on the subject now in progress.

"I'm still surprised by the changed climate for this kind of work," says Werner Sollors, a professor of English and Afro-American studies at Harvard University. His new book, *Neither Black Nor White Yet Both: Thematic Explorations of Interracial Literature,* spans texts from ancient times to the present that have explored mixed identity. It calls attention to a long tradition of books that do not fit neatly into such categories as African-American literature or white culture.

Dr. Sollors remembers a literacy conference a number of years ago, when a speaker read aloud the description of a fictional mixed-race character. "Almost everyone in the audience laughed," he says. "When I asked what was so funny, there was a moment of embarrassed silence. That wouldn't happen today."

Indeed, scholarly interest in crossing is the product of converging trends. On one level, crossovers are ubiquitous in contemporary culture, crying out for study. White suburban youths imitate ghetto dress and music; Dennis Rodman preens in a wedding dress; Robert Colescott plays on race to transform well-known works of art—for example, turning a picture of George Washington crossing the Delaware into one of George Washington Carver. A 1993 cover of *Time* shows faces from various racial and ethnic groups morphing into a composite "New Face of America."

Many Americans are also increasingly unwilling to accept society's definition of their identity. In a 1993 piece published in *Transition*, the performance artist and Wellesley College professor of philosophy Adrian M.S. Piper described the conflicting emotions and caustic comments she has endured as a light-skinned, white-looking woman who identifies herself as black. Growing up, she was rejected by black children; in graduate school, a white professor accused her of trying to cash in on affirmative action.

"So no matter what I do or do not do about my racial identity, someone is bound to feel uncomfortable," she concluded. "But I have resolved that it is no longer going to be me."

Elaine K. Ginsberg, a professor of English at West Virginia University, chose to end the collection of essays that she edited, *Passing and the Fictions of Identity* (1996), with Dr. Piper's piece. "More and more people want to be able to say, This is who I am—I don't fit into your categories," says Dr. Ginsberg. "Scholarship has picked up on that."

The new work on crossing also grows out of 20 years of trends in the humanities. By challenging traditional gender identities, feminist research and "queer studies" have opened the door to the exploration of crossovers. Many of today's scholars working on posing, passing, and impostors credit Judith Butler's argument about gender and "performativity" (from her 1990 book, *Gender Trouble*) with stimulating their own research.

In like fashion, African-American studies has highlighted the issue of racial identity. For years, black writers and scholars, from W.E.B. Du Bois to Toni Morrison, have urged Americans to consider how an awareness of black people has helped shape white identity. Now some scholars are taking that admonition into studies of "whiteness," while others examine black influences on white culture.

Still others are looking at impersonation. Dr. Gubar's *Racechanges,* for example, takes up the myriad ways that whites have imitated and impersonated blacks in the 20th century. A professor of English at Indiana University, she has been in England this summer. She says her mother recently called to say that bookstores in New York are selling her book in their sections on African-American studies. "At first I thought, Hey, my book is about white people," Dr. Gubar says. "But then I realized that it fits, because my work is so indebted to African-American studies."

In another sense, however, recent work on crossing and mixing identities also attempts to go beyond African-American and gender studies—and beyond the identity politics that an increasing number of scholars say has run its course.

A reviewer in *The Nation* noted that Dr. Gubar's "exuberant, full-contact absorption in the details and lore of transracial adventure in literature, art, and the movies is tonic for nerves battered by Galloping Otherness."

"For a long time," Dr. Gubar says, "people were afraid to talk about crossing. They had been taught by right-minded academics to speak only as a member of a correct and authentic category."

"But the history of cross-racial and cross-gender impostors suggests that identity politics may be a fiction—we're all hybrids. People are ready to hear that today."

"A number of us are looking for a middle ground in culture," agrees Dr. Sollors.

That's the optimistic interpretation. Ann duCille, the author of *Skin Trade*—on how America peddles racial and gender stereotypes, from Barbie dolls to breakfast foods—is more pessimistic. "Scholars like Susan Gubar have done important work, with wonderful close readings of texts," says Dr. duCille, a professor of American and African-American literature at the University of California at San Diego. "But black writers have been talking about crossing the boundaries of identity for a long time."

"It's taken the interest of white scholars to make the issue important in the academic world," she says.

"There's a basic naivete at work here," says Bell Hooks, a professor of English at City University of New York City College. "So many scholars seem to have a fantasy that we can solve racism or sexism simply by emphasizing mixing and crossing. Race and gender aren't as fluid as they think."

That is the crux of debate about crossing: Is it transformative? Transgressive? Appropriate? Denigrating?

The manufacturer of the best-selling Barbie doll has brought out a variety of "ethnically correct" versions, but in fact just a few stereotypical features have been added to the white version, notes Dr. duCille. "The new Barbies represent a way of denying that race matters," Dr. duCille says. They are less a sign of a new multicultural society than evidence that white society can deal with race only in superficial ways, she argues.

Laura Browder, a professor of English at Virginia Commonwealth University, has looked at what she calls "ethnic impostors"—people such as Elizabeth Stern, who pretended in her fictional autobiography to be an immigrant Jew.

In a book due out next year, Dr. Browder argues that posing fulfills complex psychological needs for the poser: Stern had been sexually abused by a Jewish foster father and, like many other victims, took the identity of her oppressor.

Ethnic impostors play a role in society as well. "They appear in clusters, at times when American identity is up for grabs—like the period of massive immigration—and people are nervous," Dr. Browder says. "By their very nature, impostors succeed by acting within an accepted tradition and reaffirming stereotypes."

"It's a question of at whose expense mimicry comes," says Michael Rogin, a professor of political science at the University of California at Berkeley. "And who profits."

In last years *Blackface, White Noise: Jewish Immigrants in the Hollywood Melting Pot*, Dr. Rogin argued that Jewish immigrants in the early 20th century put on blackface in the movies as a way of becoming American. Calling the American heritage of slavery their own, they defined themselves as white by being able to put on—and take off—blackface. And they made money doing so, while black actors were shut out of the early cinema, Dr. Rogin noted.

Other scholars are not quite so critical of crossing. Its cultural uses have changed over time, Dr. Gubar says. When blackface first showed up on-screen, she notes, it often served to discredit blacks. In *Birth of a Nation* (1915), white actors blacked up to pose as sexual predators and criminals. Al Jolson's *The Jazz Singer* (1927) demeaned blacks as boyish Uncle Toms.

But today, Dr. Gubar continues, there are signs of change. Painters such as Robert Colescott mock racial stereotypes. Performance artists such as Anna Deveare Smith take on the personas of Hasidic Jews, Korean shopkeepers, blacks, and still others.

"That kind of thing holds out hope that racial divisions are mutable, that we can move toward a post-racist culture," says Dr. Gubar.

Other scholars say it would be a mistake to forget how much fun impersonations can be. Diane Wood Middlebrook, a professor of English at Stanford University, is writing a book on Billy Tipton, the jazz musician, that is due out next spring. She calls Tipton an "opportunist" who masqueraded as a man to gain entry into the man's world of jazz.

But more was at stake than career success. Dr. Middlebrook places Tipton in the context of lesbian culture and speculates that she thoroughly enjoyed playing the role of a man. "The people I talked to who had been fooled by Billy said she had given them so much pleasure, they wished she had gotten away with it."

Scholars are asking a host of other questions about crossing. If you write about someone such as Billy Tipton, who kept her identity a secret, are you violating her privacy? "The dead are fair game," Dr. Middlebrook says, but some scholars worry about "outing," even posthumously. When the literary critic Henry Louis Gates, Jr., recently revealed in *The New Yorker* that the late cultural critic Anatole Broyard was black, some people said Broyard had been entitled to present himself as he wished.

If you emphasize the ease of crossing identities, are you homogenizing cultures—as many critics say the *Time* composite face of the "New American" did?

Moreover, is there a fundamental asymmetry in crossing? Is it different for blacks than for whites? John Howard Griffin, whose 1961 book *Black Like Me* described traveling the South while posing as a black man, wasn't trying to convince black people that he was black. He was trying to tell white people about black life. But novels such as Nella Larsen's 1929 *Passing*, featuring black people passing as white, stress the anxiety of being found out—and the guilt of denying one's race.

In 1993, Eric Lott, a professor of English at the University of Virginia, wrote an acclaimed book, *Blackface Minstrelsy and the American Working Class*. It argued that

19th-century minstrel shows were racist—allowing vulnerable white workers to feel superior to black people—as well as transgressive, filled with white envy of and identification with black sexuality.

Subsequent scholarship left Dr. Lott with doubts. "When all the books came out saying that crossing is part of what a culture lets you do safely, without threatening established norms, I began to worry that I had been wrong to talk about transgression," he says. "Now Susan Gubar's book makes me more willing to stick to my guns."

His ambivalence marks most of the current scholarship on the subject. "Crossing," he says, "is a complex issue that is by no means settled."

A Selection of Recent and Forthcoming Books on "Crossing"

Laura Browder, *Ethnic Performance and American Identities*, University of North Carolina Press, 1998.

Ann duCille, *Skin Trade*, Harvard University Press, 1996.

Lesley Ferris, ed., *Crossing the Stage: Controversies on Cross-Dressing*, Routledge, 1993.

Marjorie Garber, *Vested Interests: Cross-Dressing & Cultural Anxiety*, Routledge, 1992.

Elaine K. Ginsberg, ed., *Passing and the Fictions of Identity*, Duke University Press, 1996.

Susan Gubar, *Racechanges: White Skin, Black Face in American Culture*, Oxford University Press, 1997.

Saidiya Hartman, *Scenes of Subjection: Terror, Slavery, and Self-Making in 19th Century America*, Oxford University Press, 1997.

Diane Wood Middlebrook, A biography of Billy Tipton (no title yet), Houghton Mifflin, 1998.

Stephen Orgel, *Impersonations: The Performance of Gender in Shakespeare's England*, Cambridge University Press, 1996.

Michael Rogin, *Blackface, White Noise: Jewish Immigrants in the Hollywood Melting Pot*, University of California Press, 1996.

Werner Sollors, *Neither Black Nor White Yet Both: Thematic Explorations of Interracial Literature*, Oxford University Press, 1997.

 Article Review Form at end of book.

Describe the six pedagogical principles for developing literacy programs for diverse learners. Describe why multiple perspectives are important in addressing the needs of diverse learners.

Diverse Learners and the Tyranny of Time

Don't fix blame; fix the leaky roof

Edward J. Kameenui

Kameenui is Associate Dean of the College of Education and Associate Director of the National Center to Improve the Tools of Educators at the University of Oregon, Eugene, Oregon. His research and writing have focused on instructional approaches for special education students and other diverse learners.

In this commentary, I argue against a single "right" method or approach to literacy instruction. I assert that such a search for the "right" approach to literacy instruction is misguided and takes its greatest toll on students who have diverse learning and curricular needs. Instead, I suggest that diverse learners face on a daily basis the tyranny of time, in which the educational clock is ticking while they remain at risk

This article is based on a Visiting Minority Scholar lecture at the University of Wisconsin-Madison, March 19, 1992. The preparation of this paper was supported in part by the National Center to Improve the Tools of Educators (NCITE), Grant H180M10006 from the U.S. Department of Education, Office of Special Education Programs.

of falling further and further behind in their schooling. I maintain that we should not spend any more time and effort determining or assigning fault for why diverse youngsters are failing, or which approach is the "right" approach to literacy instruction. Rather, we ought to move forward by designing, implementing, and validating instructional programs and interventions for children with diverse learning and curricular needs. These programs and interventions should not be wedded to any single, "right" instructional method, but instead simply work. To achieve this end, I offer six general pedagogical principles that provide a conceptual framework for guiding educators in the development of literacy programs for diverse learners.

The Right Method Myth

As reading professionals, we have imposed upon ourselves an untenable standard of always searching for the single right best

method, process, or approach to literacy development and instruction, especially for children in the formative years of schooling. The search for "rightness" is not unique to reading, nor is it unique to reading educators. It seems to be a peculiar and persistent artifact of human beings, no matter what craft we profess or practice. According to literary folklore, Mark Twain once observed, "The difference between the almost right word and the right word is really a large matter—'tis the difference between the lightning bug and the lightning." In another attempt to discern the rightness of something, the noted physicist Wolfgang Pauli responded to a highly speculative proposal in physics by stating, "It's not even wrong" (Flanagan, 1988, p. 226).

Discerning what is *right*, what is *almost right*, and what's *not even wrong* is an especially troublesome task these days for educators, reading researchers, administrators, publishers, and the international reading community in general. The difficulty rests in part in responding to the unique and diverse needs of learners in the classroom. Evidence of this difficulty can be found in the current debates and discussions about definitions of literacy (Calfee, 1991; Goodman, 1990; McGill-Franzen & Allington, 1991; Rush, Moe, & Storlie, 1986; Venezky, 1990, 1992; Venezky, Wagner, & Ciliberti, 1990), literacy instruction (Fisher & Hiebert, 1990; Yatvin, 1991), whole language and direct instruction (Chall, 1992; Goodman, 1992; Kameenui, 1988; Liberman & Liberman, 1990; Mather, 1992), beginning reading (Adams, 1990, 1991; Bower, 1992; Chaney, 1991), and diverse learners (Garcia, Pearson, & Jimenez, 1990; Stein, Leinhardt, & Bickel, 1989).

Although such debates are intellectually stimulating, they are often based upon the premise that there is a right approach, philosophy, or method of literacy instruction, something that is unlikely to be empirically established anytime soon, and even less likely to be accepted by reading professionals who hold multiple perspectives and epistemologies. Further, the identification of children as diverse learners itself suggests that *multiple* perspectives and approaches will be necessary to accommodate the needs of children who possess differences in abilities and learning histories, and who will be schooled in various instructional contexts.

The Realities of Diversity

While many of these debates and discussions about the right approach to literacy development and instruction take place within the professional community of reading educators, they are often distant from the realities of the world outside the reading community.

Some of these realities were made stark in a recent article by Hodgkinson (1991) entitled "Reform Versus Reality":

- Since 1987, one-fourth of all preschool children in the U.S. have been in poverty.

- Every year, about 350,000 children are born to mothers who are addicted to cocaine during pregnancy. Those who survive birth become children with strikingly short attention spans, poor coordination, and much worse. Of course, the schools will have to teach these children, and getting such children ready for kindergarten costs around $40,000 each— about the same as for children with fetal alcohol syndrome.

- On any given night, between 50,000 and 200,000 children have no home.

- The "Norman Rockwell" family—a working father, a housewife mother, and two children of school age— constitutes only 6% of U.S. households.

- About one-third of preschool children are destined for school failure because of poverty, neglect, sickness, handicapping conditions, and lack of adult protection and nurturance.
(Hodgkinson, 1991, p. 10)

These facts, according to Hodgkinson, are indicative of education's "leaky roof," a metaphor he uses "for the spectacular changes that have occurred in the nature of the children who come to school" (p. 10).

Hodgkinson's (1991) demographic analysis is reinforced by additional reports in the popular press documenting the plight of diverse learners. For example:

The child poverty rate rose by more than 11% during the 1980s, reaching 17.9% in 1989. Black children were the most likely to fall into this group. In 1989, a black child had a 39.8% chance of living in poverty, a Native American child a 38.8% chance and a Hispanic child a 32.2% chance. The figure for Asian children was 17.1% and for white children 12.5%. ("Poverty Rates Rise," 1992)

Similarly, an advertisement for the Children's Defense Fund reads:

Approximately 2.5 million American children were reported abused or neglected last year. . . . Fourteen nations boast smarter 13-year-olds than the United States. ("Children's Defense Fund," 1992)

Hodgkinson (1991) concludes his analysis by offering a poignant soliloquy on the current slings and arrows of education's outrageous fortunes:

There is no point in trying to teach hungry or sick children. From this we can deduce one of the most important points in our attempts to deal with education: *educators can't fix the roof all by themselves.* It will require the efforts of many people and organizations— health and social welfare agencies, parents, business and political leaders—to even begin to repair this leaky roof. There is no time to waste in fixing blame; we need to act to fix the roof. And unless we start, the house will continue to deteriorate,

> The identification of children as diverse learners itself suggests that *multiple* perspectives and approaches will be necessary to accommodate the needs of children who possess differences in abilities and learning histories, and who will be schooled in various instructional contexts.

and all Americans will pay the price. (p. 10)

The Tyranny of Time

Hodgkinson's assertion that *"there is no time to waste in fixing blame; we need to act to fix the roof"* is of particular significance to students who reside in the basement of the house with the leaky roof— children identified as poor readers, reading disabled, at-risk, low performers, mildly disabled, language delayed, and culturally disadvantaged, all of whom have diverse learning and curricular needs. Like literacy, the face of diversity is complex, and at this point, it defies a definition comprised of only the right words (Garcia et al., 1990).

Despite the differences that these children bring to school, what is profoundly and unequivocally the same about them is that they are behind in reading and language development. Moreover, they constantly face the tyranny of time in trying to catch up with their peers, who continue to advance in their literacy development. Simply keeping pace with their peers amounts to losing more and more ground for students who are behind. This predicament has been referred to as the "Matthew effect," a concept resurrected and insightfully applied to reading by Stanovich (1986). According to the Matthew effect, the literacy-rich get richer, and the literacy-poor get poorer in reading opportunities, vocabulary development, written language, general knowledge, and so on.

The pedagogical clock for students who are behind in reading and literacy development continues to tick mercilessly, and the opportunities for these students to advance or catch up diminish over time. Benjamin Bloom (1964)

concurred with this general phenomenon almost 30 years ago when he observed that *"growth and development are not in equal units per unit of time"* (p. 204, emphasis added). In other words, not all human characteristics (e.g., height, intelligence, vocabulary) grow at the same rate over time; there are periods of rapid growth and periods of relatively slow growth. Bloom noted what we have now come to accept as a developmental and pedagogical truism: "Although it is not invariably true, the period of most rapid growth is likely to be in the early years and this is then followed by periods of less and less rapid growth" (p. 204).

Evidence of the critical importance of what Bloom (1964) referred to as "the early environment and experience" (p. 214) now appears overwhelming:

- According to a study by Juel (1988), the probability that a child who is a poor reader at the end of Grade 1 will remain a poor reader at the end of Grade 4 is .88. There is a near 90% chance of remaining a poor reader after 3 years of schooling. Juel noted, "Children who did not develop good word recognition skills in first grade began to dislike reading and read considerably less than good readers both in and out of school" (p. 27).

- Allington's program of research (1980, 1983, 1984) on the opportunities children have to read reveals that the average skilled reader reads almost

three times more words than the average less-skilled reader (Stanovich, 1986). Similarly, students identified as mildly handicapped appear to "spend significantly less time engaged in writing and silent reading, and more time passively attending, than do their nonhandicapped peers" (O'Sullivan, Ysseldyke, Christenson, & Thurlow, 1990, p. 143).

- Phonemic awareness and knowledge of letter names that prereaders have upon entering school appear to influence reading acquisition (Adams, 1990; Griffith & Olson, 1992; Stahl, 1992; Williams, 1984). As Adams (1990) states, "In the end, the great value of research on prereaders may lie in the clues it gives us toward determining what the less prepared prereaders need most to learn. For these children, we have not a classroom moment to waste. The evidence strongly suggests that we must help them develop their awareness of the phonemic composition of words" (p. 90).

- The amount of reading that children do outside of school appears to strongly influence reading proficiency (Anderson, Wilson, & Fielding, 1988). However, many children come from homes in which there is very little, if any, preschool language and literacy support (Heath, cited in Adams, 1990).

- Children in Grades 2 and 3 who lack decoding skills and a

> Hodgkinson's assertion that *"there is no time to waste in fixing blame; we need to act to fix the roof "* is of particular significance to students who reside in the basement of the house with the leaky roof.

reasonable base of sight words "may be condemned to school careers marred by increasing distance between them and other children unless successful remediation occurs" (Byrne, Freebody, & Gates, 1992, p. 150).

- Matching classroom instruction with reading abilities appears to be difficult for teachers in general education kindergarten classrooms (Durkin, 1990). Durkin notes, "Use of whole class instruction was the practice even when differences in children's abilities were so great as to be obvious to anyone willing to take but a few minutes to observe. Such differences meant that some children kept hearing what they already knew; for others, the observed lesson was too difficult and proceeded too quickly" (p. 24).

Teacher Uncertainty and Experimentation in the Face of Diversity

When this evidence is considered in the context of education's leaky roof, it carries the potential for creating at least two serious problems for reading educators. The first is pedagogical paralysis, which is in part reflected in a teacher's lack of personal teaching efficacy (e.g., "What can I possibly do as one teacher to make a difference?") in the face of a "concentration of low-achieving students" in the classroom (Smylie, 1988, p. 23). In a study of teachers' teaching efficacy, Smylie observed, "The lower the achievement level of students in the class, the less likely teachers seem to be to believe that they can affect student learning, despite the level of confidence they may have in their

knowledge and skills related to teaching" (p. 23.) The characteristics of the classroom (e.g., class size) and heterogeneity of learners appear to affect teachers' beliefs about their ability to influence student learning (Chard & Kameenui, 1992).

Equally problematic, however, is the tendency for educators to engage in fashionable experimentation—experimentation that often draws on fad and fashion (Kameenui, 1991; Slavin, 1989)—rather than well-established and documented practice. This kind of experimentation often occurs when teachers are unsure of what to do with children who are behind. As a result, they experiment with practices that leave some children at risk of falling even further behind in their reading and language development. The experimentation reflects teachers' genuine desire to do the best for their children who, they believe, despite their diverse learning and curricular needs, should benefit from the same "literacy events" and reading activities provided more able readers. However, children who are behind because of language, learning, or reading problems *do* require substantially different kinds of *reading experiences*—ones that go beyond those typically provided more able readers (Mather, 1992).

Some have argued that the current emphasis on "whole language" approaches to beginning reading exacts its harshest consequence on students with learning and language difficulties (Liberman & Liberman, 1990; Mather, 1992). Others have called for striking a reasonable balance between whole language and direct instruction (Chall, 1992; Cunningham, 1991). Still others have argued for whole language only

(Edelsky, 1990; Goodman, 1992). While the debates about how best to teach beginning reading are age-old, reaching back more than 100 years to the "beginning of pedagogy" (Bower, 1992, p. 138), the current context of education's leaky roof requires that we consider the purpose and consequences of these debates.

Although educators alone cannot fix education's leaky roof, the plight of today's children in society (Garcia et al., 1990; Hodgkinson, 1991) places an unusual burden on schools, teachers, and even professional organizations such as the International Reading Association to get their houses in order. The water from the leaky roof is rising in the basement, and its cost is greatest to students with diverse curricular, learning, and literacy needs. There is not time to waste in fixing blame; we need to act *now* to fix the roof.

Principles for Guiding Action

The realities that poor readers remain poor readers, that insufficient opportunities to read seriously deter reading progress, and that particular instructional arrangements (e.g., whole-class instruction) fail to promote adequate reading growth set the stage for the reading community to reconsider the needs of students who face pedagogy's ticking clock. The reading experiences required for these students can be derived and constructed from at least six general pedagogical principles (Dixon, Carnine, & Kameenui, 1992). These principles do not prescribe a single method and by no means represent an exhaustive list. Rather, they offer a conceptual framework for informing our decisions about how to develop the early reading and literacy experiences of these students:

1. *Instructional time is a precious commodity; do not lose it.* If a reading strategy, concept, or problem solving analysis can be taught two different ways and one is more efficient, use the more efficient way.

2. *Intervene and remediate early, strategically, and frequently.* The magnitude of growth in the early years for students who are behind is influenced substantially by what we teach and how we teach. As Stanovich (1986) argues, "Educational interventions that represent a *more of the same* approach will probably not be successful. . . . The remedy for the problem must be more of a *surgical strike*" (p. 393). The following applications should be considered:

- Provide children with more frequent opportunities to read.

- Promote instructional arrangements that allow children to actively participate in literacy activities, for example, small group story reading instead of one-to-one or whole-class instruction (Morrow & Smith, 1990).

- Help children develop phonemic awareness and knowledge of letter names early.

3. *Teach less more thoroughly.* The conventional wisdom in working with students who have diverse learning and curricular needs is to teach more in less time (Kameenui, 1990; Kameenui & Simmons, 1990). While the logic of this advice seems reasonable (i.e., children who are behind in conceptual knowledge and skills must be taught more in a shorter period of time in order to catch up), the actual practice of trying to teach more in less time simply ignores the constraints of teaching. Instead, by selecting and teaching only those objectives that are essential, and by focusing instruction on the most important and most generalizable concepts or strategies (i.e., "big ideas," Calfee, Chambliss, & Beretz, 1991; Carnine & Kameenui, 1992), more can be learned more thoroughly in the limited time available.

4. *Communicate reading strategies in a clear and explicit manner, especially during initial phases of instruction.* For many students with learning problems, new concepts and strategies should be explained in clear, concise, and comprehensible language. Explicit instruction is still most effective for teaching concepts, principles, and strategies to at-risk students.

Children will not automatically bloom by being immersed in a literacy hothouse rich with literary events and activities.

5. *Guide student learning through a strategic sequence of teacher-directed and student-centered activities.* Teacher-directed instruction is necessary if students are to catch up and advance with their able-reading peers. Children will not automatically bloom by being immersed in a literacy hothouse rich with literacy events and activities. While these activities enrich students' literacy development, they are not sufficient for children who are behind. Teacher-directed instruction need not preempt, minimize, or supplant child-directed activities to develop literacy (Yatvin, 1991). Both sets of activities have their place; however, reading instruction guided by an efficacious teacher is essential. The goal of reading and literacy instruction is to move from teacher-directed to student-centered activities.

6. *Examine the effectiveness of instruction and educational tools by formatively evaluating student progress.* In testimony given on March 18, 1992, to the Select Committee on Education, Kenneth Komoski, Director of the Education Products Information Exchange, noted educational materials (e.g., print materials, computer software) are used during more than 90% of the 30 billion hours in which America's 40 million students are in school. In many cases, the efficacy of these materials is questionable, despite state laws (e.g., Florida statute 233.25) that require a learner verification and revision process to substantiate their "instructional effectiveness." Teachers must formatively evaluate the effectiveness of their instructional approaches and materials in order to adapt instruction to meet the needs of learners. As a guideline, current research suggests that measuring student performance twice per week provides an adequate basis for instructional decision making (Deno & Fuchs, 1987).

Conclusion

Human beings, like the words they use, are peculiar creatures, idiosyncratically possessive of their thoughts and words (Bryson, 1990). Even under ideal circumstances, finding the *right* words is indeed difficult. Unless you are part of Wolfgang Pauli's professional community of physics, selecting the right word in the Twain tradition is risky business. Paradoxically, it seems as though words have gotten in the way of our real goal. The standard of always searching for the single right best method for literacy development may be misguided. The search instead should be for multiple perspectives of rightness guided by the diverse needs of learners and sound instructional principles, practices, and craft knowledge.

Hodgkinson (1991) concludes his analysis of the realities in educational reform by posing two "high-priority" questions— "What can educators do to reduce the number of children 'at risk' in America and to get them achieving well in school settings? And how can educators collaborate more closely with other service providers so that we can all work together toward the urgent goal of providing services to the same client?" (p. 16). Before reading educators can begin to collaborate with "other service providers," they must first collaborate with one another. Our charge is clear, and because the rain won't cease, there is no time to waste; we need to fix education's leaky roof. These are the right words; anything less is not even wrong.

References

Adams, M. (1990). *Beginning to read: Thinking and learning about print*. Cambridge, MA: MIT Press.

Adams, M. (1991). Beginning to read: A critique by literacy professionals. *The Reading Teacher, 44*, 371–372.

Allington, R. L. (1980). Poor readers don't get to read much in reading groups. *Language Arts, 57*, 872–876.

Allington, R. L. (1983). The reading instruction provided readers of differing reading abilities. *The Elementary School Journal, 83*, 548–559.

Allington, R. L. (1984). Content coverage and contextual reading in reading groups. *Journal of Reading Behavior, 16*, 85–96.

Anderson, R. C., Wilson, P. T., and Fielding, L. G. (1988). Growth in reading and how children spend their time outside of school. *Reading Research Quarterly, 23*, 285–303.

Bloom, B. S. (1964). *Stability and change in human characteristics*. New York: Wiley.

Bower, B. (1992). Reading the code, reading the whole: Researchers wrangle over the nature and teaching of reading. *Science News, 141*(9), 138–141.

Bryson, B. (1990). *The mother tongue: English and how it got that way*. New York: Morrow.

Byrne, B., Freebody, P., & Gates, A. (1992). Longitudinal data on the relations of word-reading strategies to comprehension, reading time, and phonemic awareness. *Reading Research Quarterly, 27*, 141–151.

Calfee, R. (1991). What schools can do to improve literacy instruction. In B. Means, C. Chelemer, & M. S. Knapp (Eds.), *Teaching advanced skills to at-risk students* (pp. 176–203). San Francisco: Jossey-Bass.

Calfee, R. C., Chambliss, M. J., & Beretz, M. M. (1991). Organizing for comprehension and composition. In W. Ellis (Eds.), *All language and the creation of literacy*. Baltimore, MD: Orton Dyslexia Society, Inc.

Carnine, D., & Kameenui, E. J. (1992). *Higher order thinking: Designing curriculum for mainstreamed students*. Austin, TX: Pro-Ed.

Chall, J. (1992, May). *Whole language and direct instruction models: Implications for teaching reading in the schools*. Paper presented at the meeting of the International Reading Association, Orlando, FL.

Chaney, J. H. (1991). Beginning to read: A critique by literacy professionals. *The Reading Teacher, 44*, 374–375.

Chard, D. J., & Kameenui, E. J. (1992). *Instructional efficacy: Toward a specification of efficacy research*. Monograph Number 3, Project PREPARE. Eugene, OR: University of Oregon.

Children's Defense Fund. (1992, July). *SV Entertainment*, p. 13.

Cunningham, P. (1991). *What kind of phonics instruction will we have?* Paper presented at the National Reading Conference, Palm Springs, CA.

Deno, S., & Fuchs, L. (1987). Developing curriculum-based measurement systems for data-based special education problem solving. *Focus on Exceptional Children, 19*(8), 1–16.

Dixon, R., Carnine, D. W., & Kameenui, E. J. (1992). *Curriculum guidelines for diverse learners*. Monograph for National Center to Improve the Tools of Educators. Eugene, OR: University of Oregon.

Durkin, D. (1990). Matching classroom instruction with reading abilities: An unmet need. *Remedial and Special Education, 11*(3), 23–28.

Edelsky, C. (1990). Whose agenda is this anyway? A response to McKenna, Robinson, and Miller. *Educational Researcher, 19*(8), 7–11.

Fisher, C. W., & Hiebert, E. H. (1990). Characteristics of tasks in two approaches to literacy instruction. *The Elementary School Journal, 91*, 3–18.

Flanagan, D. (1988). *Flanagan's version: A spectator's guide to science on the eve of the 21st century*. New York: Vintage.

Garcia, G. E., Pearson, P. D., & Jimenez, R. T. (1990). *The at risk dilemma: A synthesis of reading research*. Champaign, IL: University of Illinois, Reading Research and Education Center.

Goodman, K. (May, 1992). *Whole language and direct instruction models: Implications for teaching reading in the schools*. Paper presented at the meeting of the International Reading Association, Orlando, FL.

Goodman, Y. M. (Ed.). (1990). *How children construct literacy*. Newark, DE: International Reading Association.

Griffith, P. L., & Olson, M. W. (1992). Phonemic awareness helps beginning readers break the code. *The Reading Teacher, 45*, 516–523.

Hodgkinson, H. (1991). Reform versus reality. *Phi Delta Kappan, 73*, 9–16.

Juel, C. (1988, April). *Learning to read and write: A longitudinal study of fifty-four children from first through fourth grade*. Paper presented at the annual meeting of the American Educational Research Association, New Orleans, LA.

Kameenui, E. J. (1988). Direct instruction and the Great Twitch: Why DI or di is not the issue. In J. R. Readence & S. Baldwin (Eds.), *Dialogues in literacy research: Thirty-seventh yearbook of the National Reading Conference* (pp. 39–45). Chicago, IL: National Reading Conference.

Kameenui, E. J. (1990). The language of the REI—Why it's hard to put into words: A response to Durkin and Miller. *Remedial and Special Education, 11*(3), 57–59.

Kameenui, E. J. (1991). Guarding against the false and fashionable. In J. F. Baumann & D. D. Johnson (Eds.), *Writing for publication in reading and language arts* (pp. 17–28). Newark, DE: International Reading Association.

Kameenui, E. J., & Simmons, D. C. (1990). *Designing instructional strategies: The prevention of academic learning problems.* Columbus, OH: Merrill.

Liberman, A., & Liberman, I. (1990). Whole language vs. code emphasis: Underlying assumptions and their implications for reading instruction. *Annals of Dyslexia, 40,* 52–76.

Mather, N. (1992). Whole language reading instruction for students with learning disabilities: Caught in the cross fire. *Learning Disabilities Research & Practice, 7,* 87–95.

McGill-Franzen, A., & Allington, R. L. (1991). Every child's right: Literacy. *The Reading Teacher, 45,* 86–90.

Morrow, L. M., & Smith, J. K. (1990). The effect of group size on interactive storybook reading. *Reading Research Quarterly, 25,* 213–231.

O'Sullivan, P. J., Ysseldyke, J. E., Christenson, S. L., & Thurlow, M. L. (1990). Mildly handicapped elementary students' opportunity to learn during reading instruction in mainstream and special education settings. *Reading Research Quarterly, 25,* 131–146.

Poverty rates rise. (1992, July). *Time,* p. 15.

Rush, R. T., Moe, A. J., & Storlie, R. L. (1986). *Occupational literacy education.* Newark, DE: International Reading Association.

Slavin, R. (1989). PET and the pendulum: Faddism in education and how to stop it. *Phi Delta Kappan, 90,* 750–758.

Smylie, M. A. (1988). The enhancement function of staff development: Organizational and psychological antecedents to individual teacher change. *American Educational Research Journal, 25,* 1–30.

Stahl, S. A. (1992). Saying the "p" word: Nine guidelines for exemplary phonics instruction. *The Reading Teacher, 45,* 618–625.

Stanovich, K. E. (1986). Matthew effects in reading: Some consequences of individual differences in the acquisition of literacy. *Reading Research Quarterly, 21,* 360–407.

Stein, M. K., Leinhardt, G., & Bickel, W. (1989). Instructional issues for teaching students at risk. In R. E. Slavin, N. L. Kesweit, & N. A. Madden (Eds.), *Effective programs for students at risk* (pp. 145–194). Boston: Allyn & Bacon.

Venezky, R. L. (1990). Definitions of literacy. In R. L. Venezky, D. A. Wagner, & B. S. Ciliberti (Eds.), *Toward defining literacy* (pp. 2–16). Newark, DE: International Reading Association.

Venezky, R. L. (1992, Summer). Matching literacy testing with social policy: What are the alternatives? *Connections.* Philadelphia, PA: National Center on Adult Literacy, University of Pennsylvania.

Venezky, R. L., Wagner, D. A., & Ciliberti, B. S. (Eds.). (1990). *Toward defining literacy.* Newark, DE: International Reading Association.

Williams, J. P. (1984). Phonemic analysis and how it relates to reading. *Journal of Learning Disabilities, 17,* 240–245.

Yatvin, J. (1991). *Developing a whole language program for a whole school.* Richmond, VA: Virginia State Reading Association.

Article Review Form at end of book.

What is the rationale for supporting global education? What are "essential questions" and why are they important in global education?

Global Education's Promise

Reinvigorating classroom life in a changing, interconnected world

Ronald S. Byrnes

Ronald S. Byrnes is assistant professor of education at Guilford College, Greensboro, NC.

Ideally, education equips one to participate widely in the human conversation. The human conversation is a metaphor for what humans feel, think, do and express. However, both the participation and the conversation tend to be narrow if what one brings to them and takes from them embraces no more than one's own experience with a necessarily small sample of what the whole of humankind feels, thinks, does and expresses. (Goodlad, 1986, p. 424)

Signs of global education's importance abound. Increasingly, schools are introducing globally oriented content. Numerous global education centers such as the Stanford Program on International and Cross-Cultural Education (S.P.I.C.E.) and the American Forum for Global Education produce and disseminate materials, conduct teacher workshops, and provide support for teachers and schools committed to global education. Several study commissions have recommended intensive national efforts to improve and expand global education (Becker, 1990; Kniep, 1985; National Governors' Association, 1989).

States increasingly emphasize its importance as well. Furthermore, a significant body of literature has evolved and convincing rationales for global education have been clearly developed and articulated. The rationales emphasize that we live in a rapidly changing, interconnected world, and that education must equip students to cope with the new demands placed upon them by these conditions (Anderson, 1982, 1990; Case, 1993; Kniep, 1985, 1986a, 1986b). Yet, despite global education's increasing importance, little is known about teachers' efforts to implement global education.[1] As a result, little is known about promising practices in global education.

This article focuses on three promising practices in global education—the tendency of global educators to emphasize interdisciplinary concepts, model inquisitive- ness and skepticism, and stress participatory learning. The promising practices are examined in the context of classroom life at the Shoreline Foreign Language/ International Studies magnet school.[2] Located along the California coast, 550 students attend Shoreline F.L./I.S. magnet school, a school-within-a-school that opened in 1988 to help stem the comprehensive school's declining enrollment. In addition to studying one of seven languages each semester, the only "international studies" requirement that sets the magnet students apart from their comprehensive school counterparts is a one semester, tenth-grade world geography course.

I have been interested and involved in global education since 1985 when the social studies department at the California high

Byrnes, R. S. (1996). Global Education's Promise: Reinvigorating Classroom Life in a Changing Interconnected World. *Theory Into Practice*, 36, 95–101. (Theme issue of "Exploring the Margins: Lessons From Alternative Schools"). Copyright 1997, College of Education, The Ohio State University. Reprinted with permission.

1. Merry Merryfield is one researcher examining teachers' efforts to implement global education (1993b, 1994).
2. The school's name and the subsequent teachers' names are pseudonyms.

school where I was student teaching was selected by the Danforth Foundation to receive special training. In 1993, as a doctoral student, I decided to write my dissertation on what takes place within globally oriented classrooms. The Shoreline F.L./I.S. magnet school program director and faculty agreed to let me explore their work and tell their story (Byrnes, 1993). Before turning to a few of the insights gained from that examination, I address global education's diffuse nature and its importance. I conclude by discussing the educational significance of the practices for schools more generally.

What is Global Education?

Merryfield (1993a) has suggested that global education is "one of the more ambiguous innovations in education today" (p. 28). Merryfield's point is well taken given the range of educational activities that pass as global education. Anderson (1990) explains:

The people involved in global education are trying to globalize American education in a variety of ways. Some of the movement's participants focus on expanding and improving the study of world history, world geography, world economics, world politics, or world ecology. Others seek to expand students' understanding of cultural diversity through the cross-cultural study of literature, art, music, dance, religion, and social customs. Many seek to expand and improve the study of foreign languages, including rarely studied languages that are of growing importance to the United States, such as Japanese, Chinese, Russian, and Arabic. Many global educators devote their energies to improving instruction about often-slighted regions of the world: Asia, Africa, the Middle East, and Latin America. Still others focus on improving education about world problems such as the maintenance of national security, the control of warfare, the reduction of world poverty, the promotion of human rights, and the preservation of ecological well-being. (pp. 13–14)

Anderson's examples illustrate that some global educators teach traditional subjects in global contexts and that others favor interdisciplinary teaching. The examples highlight area studies and global issues as focuses in global education as well. Within this varied context, Tye and Tye (1992) define global education by highlighting what it most often involves:

Global education involves 1. the study of problems and issues that cut across national boundaries, and the interconnectedness of the systems involved—economic, environmental, cultural, political, and technological; 2. the cultivation of cross-cultural understanding, which includes development of the skill of perspective-taking—that is being able to see life from someone else's point of view. Global perspectives are important at every grade level, in every curricular subject area, and for all children and adults. (p. 6)

The Tyes' definition is too succinct to adequately address what Begler (1993) identifies as a continual problem in the field of global education. "Generally," Begler argues, global education theoreticians "mix and muddle the substance of what we (global educators) want students to learn and the perspectives and attitudes we would like them to develop" (p. 14). Nevertheless, in singling out a few themes and skills that weave through most global education initiatives—transnational issues, global linkages, cross cultural understanding, and perspective-taking—the Tyes' definition provides an acceptable reference point for our inquiry.

Global education's importance is tied to the realization that education must equip students to cope with the new demands placed upon them by the rapidly changing, interconnected world we live in (Anderson, 1982, 1990; Case, 1993; Kniep, 1985, 1986a, 1986b). Global education can help students discover ways their lives might be enriched by people throughout the world as well. "If we fail to provide opportunities for students to participate more widely in the human conversation," Goodlad (1986) cautions, "students might conclude that a broader perspective is not worth the effort . . . and, perhaps, that everything 'out there' is inferior or even wrong" (p. 424).

Additionally, global education provides an improved context for learning. As Goodlad (1986) has pointed out, "The possibilities for providing a better context for learning to read, write and spell by studying an enticing world extending far beyond one's immediate experience appear endless" (p. 433). Finally, due to the accelerating growth of global interdependence—evident in spiraling economic, political, cultural, technological, and ecological linkages that increasingly characterize the international order—it is likely that global education will continue to gain importance (Anderson, 1990; B. Tye, 1990).

Emphasizing Interdisciplinary Concepts

When observing interns, student teachers, and experienced teachers at work in their schools, I occasionally recall Sizer's (1984) succinct description of what takes place in many classrooms: "The facts tumble forth" (p. 95). When designing a learning activity, a course, or a curriculum, Sizer suggests that "less is more" (1984, p. 226). Despite this catchphrase, many teachers continue to emphasize isolated facts and breadth of curriculum coverage. Consequently, the first promising practice in global education, the tendency of teachers in global education to emphasize interdisciplinary concepts, is of particular importance.

In *The Process of Education* (1960), Bruner writes that an idea is "fundamental" if it has "wide as well as powerful applicability" (p. 12). Bruner advocates focusing on fundamental ideas for several reasons, among them, to make subject matter more comprehensible. Bruner's references to subject matter are discipline specific. He explains, for example, that commutative, distributive, and associative laws facilitate learning about algebra (pp. 7–8). Global education, however, is interdisciplinary in nature; consequently, fundamental ideas in global education—global interdependence, contending worldviews, and multicultural understanding, for example—accentuate interdisciplinary connections and are broader in scope than fundamental ideas within specific disciplines. Interdisciplinary concepts in global education help teachers plan learning activities, design instructional units, and organize courses more effectively.

Global educators tend to emphasize interdisciplinary concepts for several reasons. First, whether teaching a "global issues" course or a more conventional course in a global context, the potential content within globally oriented courses is so great, emphasizing interdisciplinary concepts is essential. Second, in emphasizing interdisciplinary concepts, global educators help students apply what they have learned from one context to another. For example, by stressing concepts rather than isolated facts, the teachers at the Shoreline F.L./I.S. magnet school helped students make connections between historical events and more contemporary phenomenon.

In a globally oriented "ancient civilizations" class, students speculated on why there were only three great pyramids. Rather than focusing on the names and dates of different dynasties, the teacher focused on two concepts— overexpansion and overspending. These concepts were then used to connect historical processes in ancient Egypt with historical processes during the Napoleonic era and in Nazi Germany. Eventually, students applied the concepts to United States history. "The Vietnam war weakened the United States," a student pointed out. Capitalizing on this, the teacher drew parallels between ancient Egypt's overspending and the United States's overexpansion.

In the end, the teacher and students pieced together a conceptual framework that facilitated thinking about other historical events and periods. In emphasizing interdisciplinary concepts and making knowledge useful, global educators also heighten student engagement and slow the memory loss with which teachers who emphasize isolated facts and breadth of curriculum coverage are so familiar.

Interdisciplinary concepts are abstract; consequently, teaching them is difficult. Global educators teach them most effectively when they draw upon their students' experiences and organize their instruction around intermediary concepts that elucidate the interdisciplinary concepts. One teacher I observed, in a unit on global interdependence within his sophomore world geography course, focused one of the initial lessons on migration, defined for students as the movement of people, goods, and ideas from one place to another. After narrowing the focus to the movement of people, he grouped the factors commonly involved in a person's decision to migrate into "push" and "pull" factors. Before introducing the subject of Vietnamese migration and plant migration and food interdependence, however, he asked his students to think and write about the push and pull factors that led them to apply to the foreign language/international studies magnet school. The activity not only engaged the students, it prepared them to think more deeply about global interdependence.

Throughout the unit, the teacher had the interdisciplinary concept of global interdependence in mind. However, he taught toward it through two intermediary concepts—migration and push and pull factors—and beyond that, through the students' personal experiences.

Instead of focusing on isolated facts and breadth of curriculum coverage, global educators tend to stress interdisciplinary concepts such as global interdependence. Emphasizing interdisciplinary concepts not only helps global educators organize their instruction, it also helps students apply what they have learned from one context to another and makes learning more interesting and memorable. As the migration lesson suggests, global educators teach interdisciplinary concepts most effectively when they draw upon their students' experiences and organize their instruction around intermediary concepts.

Modeling Inquisitiveness and Skepticism

Implementing global education has proven contentious (Schukar, 1993). Werner (1991) explains, "Everyone wants schools to help prepare students for an interdependent world, but not everyone holds the same assumptions about how and why this should be done" (p. 11). The views of global education advocates reflect the political spectrum; nevertheless, most everyone agrees that global education should require students to learn more than new information. Increasingly, global educators acknowledge what Rosenau (1983) observed several years ago—higher levels of factual information do not necessarily contribute to good citizenship:

For recognition and comprehension of the proliferating complex processes in which all of us have become participants is not simply a matter of knowing the facts. It is rather a matter of possessing the analytic skills with which to trace the innumerable links in the causal chains that entwine our lives. Information and knowledge are inadequate guides to action. Students need the tools with which to process information, give it coherence and meaning, both as to its empirical implications and its ethical imperatives. (p. 33)

The second promising practice in global education, the tendency of teachers in global education to model inquisitiveness and skepticism inspires students to ask questions and to think critically. It also teaches them to appreciate complexity, to evaluate issues effectively, to participate responsibly in future decision making, and in the end to be thoughtful citizens. Ultimately, modeling inquisitiveness and skepticism is important because it fosters a thoughtful citizenry.

To promote inquisitiveness and skepticism among students, teachers must be inquisitive and skeptical themselves. Andrew Avery, the aforementioned "ancient civilizations" teacher, consistently modeled inquisitiveness by continually posing essential questions. In the course of one lesson he asked:

Would ancient Egypt or the world have been a better place without the pyramids? Is it part of human nature to aspire to greatness and not just physical survival? Should there be a balance, or is one greater than the other? Do you think the ruler that came after the three that built the great pyramids wanted his own?

Essential questions are open-ended questions that require students to consider historical events and the human condition simultaneously. Often, students do not respond well to these types of questions. Avery reflected:

Students want ready-made answers. My own impression is that high school students are very conservative in their thinking. They like absolutes because they're safe and secure. Students need to break those intellectually conservative tendencies and play with either-ors and, especially, both-ands.

Avery's own skepticism helped break those patterns. One day, for example, he started class with a finding from his reading: "I read in a book, *but I don't know if it is a fact,* that if the stones from the three largest pyramids were cut into one foot squares and laid out side by side, they would stretch over 1,000 miles." The qualifier—but I don't know if it is a fact—implied that one must read historical texts critically and that historical accuracy must be actively interpreted. In concluding the pyramid lesson, he utilized a similar qualifier: "If the Old Kingdom is the rubber band, what caused it to snap? Overspending? On what? The pyramids! So that which gave the greatest glory to the rulers of ancient Egypt *could have* led to the eventual collapse of that dynasty." Equally subtle, this qualifier—could have—suggested that this is a complex historical dilemma and that any conclusion should be tentatively expressed. This qualifier also implied that additional research may change his mind.

In being skeptical himself, Avery also demystified the past. During the pyramid lesson he explained that individual governors declared themselves pharaohs as they grew increasingly wealthy. In light of what one student had read in her textbook, this revelation seemed impossible. "But aren't you [the pharaoh] supposed to be a god?" she asked. "Oh come on, everybody knows that's just a game," he replied. "Look, if the pharaoh can become a god, what can you become? You can declare yourself a god." The implicit message: read critically.

Avery's inquisitiveness encouraged students to relate ancient history to contemporary life as well. During the same pyramid lesson, he asked a series of essential questions that related Egyptian pyramid building to efforts in the Dominican Republic to commemorate the Columbus quincentennial by constructing a 70 million dollar lighthouse. "Was it right to build this when the people are impoverished?" he inquired. Next, he speculated on whether the United States would "be a better place without the monuments in Washington, D.C." Later, he asked, "Should the U.S. send people to the moon? Is it worth it?" In and of itself, modeling is not a panacea. It does not guarantee that students will become inquisitive and skeptical.

Clearly though, modeling inquisitiveness and skepticism provides an improved context for learning—a context where acquiring these attributes is more likely.

Stressing Participatory Learning

When implemented most effectively, global education involves multiple subject areas. In some schools, however, it is social studies based. In the late 1970s, three scholars summarized a study of social studies education (Shaver, Davis, & Helburn, 1979). While the scholars acknowledged "instances of innovation and change," they concluded: "Despite being perplexed by student apathy, teachers generally do not make the possible connection between the lack of motivation on their students' part and their own reliance on textbook/content based, teacher dominated instruction" (p. 152). In a similar vein, Cuban (1991) identified several enduring themes in his review of research on social studies teaching. He wrote:

The most common pattern, employed by the vast majority of social studies teachers, is that of teacher-centered instruction. This pattern includes activities using the textbook and teacher as sources of information for assignments, recitation (now commonly called *discussion*), tests, and individual seatwork. Talking by the teacher . . . now exceeds talking by students . . . whose responses are generally confined to answering the teacher's questions. (p. 204)

In the end, Cuban's review points to "constancy in a narrow band of teaching practices and students' complaints about that teaching" (p. 205). The third promising practice in global education, the tendency of teachers in global education to stress participatory learning, is particularly important in this context.

Global educators foster participatory learning by using instructional activities that require them to relinquish the teacher's traditional role at the front of the classroom. In one memorable lesson, Irwin Olsen, one of Avery's colleagues, promoted participatory learning through a simulation loosely based on the partitioning of Bosnia-Herzegovenia. Through the simulation, Olsen converted his twelfth-grade international relations classroom into an international negotiations center. During the lesson, Olsen assumed several instructional roles including organizer, facilitator, encourager, and discussion leader. In alternating among instructional roles, global educators help students begin to develop the analytic and interpersonal skills needed to evaluate issues effectively and to see life from other people's perspectives.

When global educators relinquish the teacher's traditional role at the front of the classroom, new patterns of communication emerge in their classrooms, especially forms of student to student interaction. During the same simulation, for example, one student instructed another as she compared "how your hair sometimes gets wrapped around the posts of your earrings" with "what happens to propellers in a swamp." To encourage fruitful forms of student-to-student interaction, teachers have to be disciplined listeners and talk far less than they are accustomed. A turning point occurred during the simulation when a student complained to Olsen about his group's negotiations. "They don't want to compromise. They're being greedy." Olsen purposely ignored his plea. The student and his classmates resolved it themselves—a process that entailed even more vigorous interaction.

Participatory learning introduces a level of ambiguity and complexity often missing in cooperative learning. Consequently, participatory learning helps students develop analytic and interpersonal skills in ways that cooperative learning typically does not. Frequently, in cooperative learning activities, the traditional objective of transmitting and recalling information remains intact. Even though students transmit the information to one another, learning outcomes remain predictable. In contrast, in participatory learning activities, learning outcomes are unpredictable. Global educators use participatory learning activities such as simulations because they infuse their classrooms with complexity, unpredictability, and realism.

Heightened student engagement often accompanies participatory learning as well. Following the simulation lesson, students continued to negotiate as they left Olsen's room. Heightened student engagement is particularly important where students' self-motivation is not a given. If classrooms are not engaging places, disinterested students often compromise interested students' ability to learn and increase the difficulty of teachers' classroom management. In such environments, teachers cannot foster students' desires to learn about self, others, and the world.

Global educators foster participatory learning through simulations and other student-centered learning activities. These activities compel global educators to forego the teacher's traditional role in the front of the classroom in favor of alternating among instructional roles. Alternating these roles helps students develop important analytic and interpersonal skills, promotes new patterns of classroom communication, and heightens student engagement.

Conclusion and Implications

The global educators discussed in this article prepare students for the new demands placed upon them by the rapidly changing, interconnected world we live in by emphasizing interdisciplinary concepts, modeling inquisitiveness and skepticism, and stressing participatory learning. These practices enable them to provide an improved context for learning. More generally, they enable global educators to help students think conceptually, apply knowledge from one context to another, promote retention, and engage students in learning about self, others, and the world. These practices hold promise for teachers and students in conventional schools as well.

As noted earlier, the potential content within globally oriented courses is so great, emphasizing interdisciplinary concepts is essential. In actuality, teachers in all fields are faced with expanding content; consequently, teachers need to work together at identifying and ordering the important concepts and fundamental ideas in their fields. Once identified and ordered, teachers should use the concepts and fundamental ideas, in lieu of textbook outlines, for example, to frame their courses. The global educators in this article drew upon their students' personal experiences to make the interdisciplinary concepts in their courses more accessible. Teachers interested in doing similarly may need to supplement what they know about their students.

To promote inquisitiveness and skepticism, teachers need to maintain their intellectual vitality. We cannot expect students to pose questions, develop a healthy skepticism, and be engaged with classroom activities if teachers are not actively engaged in their subject matter. In some settings, aspects of the school culture—such as heavy workloads, misguided inservice initiatives, and professional isolation—impede teachers' efforts to remain intellectually alive. Nevertheless, there are steps teachers can take to foster inquisitiveness and skepticism while efforts to improve school culture continue.

When students pose questions, teachers should encourage further questioning by listening carefully to the questions and by providing ample time for responses. Teachers should also strive to design learning activities that help students learn how to read print materials and view electronic materials critically and ask and encourage essential questions that invite multiple answers. Similarly, teachers interested in promoting these sensibilities should introduce problems and issues that encourage conflicting interpretations.

Finally, teachers need to develop broad pedagogical expertise to foster participatory learning. To develop such expertise, teachers should look beyond their textbooks when planning individual learning activities and instructional units. More teachers should create their own materials. Simultaneously, teachers should search for the most substantive and engaging student-centered learning activities in their fields. Most important, when teachers forego their traditional role at the front of the classroom and begin introduc-ing student-centered learning activities, they should strive to listen more and talk less to foster student to student interaction, heightened engagement, and more active involvement in the human conversation.

References

Anderson, L. F. (1982). Why should American education be globalized? It's a nonsensical question. *Theory into Practice, 21*, 155–161.

Anderson, L. F. (1990). A rationale for global education. In K. A. Tye (Ed.), *Global education: From thought to action* (pp. 13–34). Alexandria, VA: Association for Supervision and Curriculum Development.

Becker, J. M. (1990). Curriculum considerations in global studies. In K. A. Tye (Ed.), *Global education: From thought to action* (pp. 67–85). Alexandria, VA: Association for Supervision and Curriculum Development.

Begler, E. (1993). Spinning wheels and straw: Balancing content, process, and context in global teacher education programs. *Theory into Practice, 32*, 14–20.

Bruner, J. S. (1960). *The process of education*. Cambridge, MA: Harvard University Press.

Byrnes, R. S. (1993). *Classroom life and the practitioner's plight: A qualitative inquiry into a global education magnet school*. Unpublished doctoral dissertation. The University of Denver.

Case, R. (1993). Key elements of a global perspective. *Social Education, 57*, 318–325.

Cuban, L. (1991). History of teaching in social studies. In J. A. Shaver (Ed.), The *handbook of research on social studies teaching and learning* (pp. 197–209). Washington, DC: National Council for the Social Studies.

Goodlad, J. I. (1986). The learner at the world's center. *Social Education, 50*, 424–436.

Kniep, W. M. (1985). *A critical review of the short history of global education: Preparing for new opportunities*. New York: The American Forum for Global Education.

Kniep, W. M. (1986a). Defining a global education by its content. *Social Education, 50*, 437–446.

Kniep, W. M. (1986b). Social studies within a global education. *Social Education, 50,* 536–542.

Merryfield, M. M. (1993a). Reflective practice in global education: Strategies for teacher educators. *Theory into Practice, 32,* 27–32.

Merryfield, M. M. (1993b). Responding to the Gulf War: A case study of instructional decision making. *Social Education, 57,* 33–41.

Merryfield, M. M. (1994). Shaping the curriculum in global education: The influence of student characteristics on teacher decision making. *Journal of Curriculum and Supervision, 9,* 233–249.

National Governors' Association. (1989). *America in transition: The international frontier.* (Special Issue). Washington, DC: National Governor's Association.

Rosenau, J. N. (1983). Teaching and learning in a transnational world. *Educational Research Quarterly, 8,* 29–35.

Schukar, R. (1993). Controversy in global education: Lessons for teacher educators. *Theory Into Practice, 32,* 52–57.

Shaver, J. P., Davis, Jr., O. L., & Helburn, S. W. (1979). The status of social studies education: Impressions from three NSF studies. *Social Education, 43,* 150–153.

Sizer, T. R. (1984). *Horace's compromise.* Boston: Houghton Mifflin.

Tye, B. B. (1990). Schooling in America today: Potential for global studies. In K. A. Tye (Ed.), *Global education: From thought to action* (pp. 35–48). Alexandria, VA: Association for Supervision and Curriculum Development.

Tye, K. A., & Tye, B. B. (1992). *Global education: A study of school change.* Albany: State University of New York.

Werner, W. (1991). *Contradictions in global education.* Paper presented at the annual meeting of the American Forum for Global Education, Hartford, CT.

 Article Review Form at end of book.

WiseGuide Wrap-Up

- Educators can implement activities and programs that effectively influence parental involvement to enhance the instructional and social development of children.

- The categories of race, gender, and ethnicity are fluid and changing as individuals self-identify and/or cross previously established boundaries.

- Diverse learners require and deserve diverse, multiple educational solutions to learning challenges.

- Global education assists students in addressing many educational, societal, and global issues.

R.E.A.L. Sites

This list provides a print preview of typical **coursewise** R.E.A.L. sites. (There are over 100 sites at the **courselinks**™ site.) The danger in printing URLs is that Web sites can change overnight. As we went to press, these sites were functioning using the URLs provided. If you come across one that isn't, please let us know via email to: webmaster@coursewise.com. Use your Passport to access the most current list of R.E.A.L. sites at the **courselinks**™ site.

Site name: Global Schoolhouse

URL: http://www.gsh.org/

Why is it R.E.A.L.? A varied and comprehensive website of technology resources for educators. Includes resources for the classroom, for professional development, and for community learning. Emphasizes interconnectedness and provides forums, contacts, and other school websites.

Key topics: global, diversity

Activity: Review the information provided in "Resources for Educators," to link with classrooms around the world or visit one of the forums to communicate with educators in other countries.

Site name: Teaching Tolerance

URL: http://www.splcenter.org/teachingtolerance.html

Why is it R.E.A.L.? Southern Poverty Law Center began the Teaching Tolerance project in response to the increase in hate crime among youth. The website includes legal, informational, and educational resources for educators.

Key topics: equity, poverty, race, culture, bias, prejudice

Activity: Review current articles in the online "Teaching Tolerance Magazine" for use in reports/term papers or classroom applications.

Site name: National Coalition for Parent Involvement in Education

URL: http://www.ncpie.org/start.shtml

Why is it R.E.A.L.? Advocates for the involvement of parents and families in their children's education and fosters relationships between home, school, and community that can enhance the education of all young people. Includes special activities, guidelines for schools and parents, resources, and an information fair.

Key topics: parental involvement, partnership

Activity: Review "Guidelines for Schools" and write up an analysis of their application in your school/community.

Index

Note: Entries in boldface type indicate Reading's authors and pages on which their pieces appear. Page numbers in italics indicate illustrations; page numbers followed by *n* indicate footnotes; page numbers followed by *t* indicate tables.

P

Pacific-American students, representation in gifted programs, 45
Paley, V. G., 72, 74, 75
Palmer, L., 11
Palombaro, M. M., 28, 30, 32, 34
Paratore, J. R., 35
Parenting centers, 107, 108
Parent involvement. *See* Family involvement
Parents
  activism for gifted children, 43
  assistance for parents in interracial marriages, 128-129
  backlash against bilingual education, 93-94
  denial of parental rights, 89
  education related to involvement, 139
  preferences in bilingual education, 89-90
  problems finding programs for gifted children, 40-43
  role in creating anti-bias classrooms, 143-145, 144
  socioeconomic status related to involvement, 138
  student attendance related to involvement, 103-104
Park, Ann, 5
Parker, Walter C., 72-75, 74*n*
Participatory learning, in global education, 163-164
Passing and the Fictions of Identity (Ginsberg), 149, 151
Passing (Larsen), 150
Pauli, Wolfgang, 156
Pearce, Mary, 23-26
Pearson, P. D., 153, 154, 155, 157
Pedagogical principles for literacy instruction, 155-156
Peer pressure on multiracial students, 122
Peer tutoring, in inclusion, 24
Pence, A., 107, 137, 141
Perrin, J., 61, 62
Perrone & Aleman, 45
Peters, D. L., 137, 138, 141
Peterson, N. L., 137, 141
Petrigala, M., 28, 30, 32, 34
Phillips, B. C., 143, 145
Phipps, Susie Guillory, 132
Pho, L., 35
Piaget, J., 45, 49
Pinnell, G. S., 35, 37, 38-39
Piper, Adrian M. S., 149
Piper, T., 35
Plato, 72

Pluralism, multicultural education and, 60
Pluralistic goals of bilingual education, 80, 81, 82
Pollina, Ann, 14-15
Pool, Carolyn R., 103-106
Pork-barrel politics, racial classification and, 123-124
Porter, Rosalie Pedalino, 90
Poverty. *See* Disadvantaged students
"Poverty Rates Rise" (*Time* magazine), 153, 158
Powell, D., 137, 141
Power, F. C., 74, 75
Pregnancy prevention program, 105
Prevention of Learning Disabilities program, 38
Price, G. E., 62
Principals Task Force, 20
Proactive strategies to help homeless students, 100
The Process of Education (Bruner), 161
Proctor, W. A., 36, 38
Program models
  for bilingual education, 79-83
  for content-centered language learning, 85
  ecological model of anti-bias curricula, 68, *68*
  Learning Styles Model, 61
  researching for gifted programs, 48
  traditional model of anti-bias curricula, *66,* 66-67
Pyle, Amy, 40-43

Q

Quellette, J., 35
Quinlan, Sheryl, 13
Quinn, P., 61, 62
Quinn, R., 61, 62
Quint, S., 101

R

Racechanges: White Skin, Black Face in American Culture (Gubar), 148, 149, 151
Race/ethnicity. *See also* African Americans; Hispanics; Interracial families; Multiracial and bicultural learners
  crossing boundaries of, 148-151
  in multicultural education, 69
Racial classification
  African Americans and, 126
  health issues in, 131
  one-drop-of-blood rule, 123-124

problems with, 121-122
  of U.S. Census, 123, 125-126, 128, 130, 132
Radencich, M. C., 73
Rafferty, Yvonne, 117*n*
Rainforth, B., 28, 30, 32, 34
Ramey, C. T., 38
Ramirez, G., 66, 67, 71
Ramirez, J. L., 66, 67, 71
Ramirez, M., III, 54, 55, 56, 57, 58
Raupp, M., 45, 49
Ravitch, Diane, 93-94
Readers' theater, *33*
Reading, curriculum modifications for inclusion, *33*
Reading acquisition, delayed, 154-155
Reading Recovery program, 37-38
R.E.A.L. sites
  on cultural diversity, 76
  on diverse language learners, 95
  future perspectives, 166
  on gender issues, 15-16
  on homeless students, 118
  on multiracial and bicultural learners, 134
  for unique learners, 50
Recovering the Gifted Child Academy, 103-106
  attendance and parent involvement, 103-104
  continuing education and, 105-106
  Saturday School, 105
  school as business, 104
  successes and challenges, 105
  "ten secrets to kids' self-esteem," 105, 106
Recovering the Gifted Child Foundation, 103
"Reform Versus Reality" (Hodgkinson), 153
Reiff, Judith C., 63-65
Reiff, K., 64
Reis, S., 45, 49
Religion, in multicultural education, 69, 70
Renzulli, J. S., 44, 45, 46, 49
Research
  on diverse classrooms, 28-29
  on effectiveness of integrated instruction, 86
  in family involvement, 140-141
  field-based observations of inclusion, 29
  into gender identity, 149
  on multicultural education, 61-62
Resource rooms, for gifted minority language students, 46-47
Responsible inclusion. *See* Inclusion
Rhodes, Steve, 91
Rickett, Kemp, 107

Putting it in *Perspectives*
-Review Form-

Your name: _____   Date: _____

Reading title:

Summarize: Provide a one-sentence summary of this reading.

_____

_____

_____

Follow the Thinking: How does the author support the main premise of the reading? Are the facts/opinions appropriately supported by research or available data? Is the author's thinking logical?

_____

_____

_____

_____

_____

_____

_____

Develop a Context (answer one or both questions): How does this reading contrast with or compliment your professor's lecture treatment of the subject matter? How does this reading compare to your textbook's coverage?

_____

_____

_____

_____

_____

_____

Question Authority: Explain why you agree/disagree with the author's main premise.

_____

_____

_____

_____

_____

_____

_____

COPY ME! Copy this form as needed. This form is also available at http://www.courselinks.com Click on: "Putting it in Perspectives."